Appalachian Indian Trails
of the
Chickamauga

Lower Cherokee Settlements

Rickey Butch Walker

Published by:
Bluewater Publications
1812 CR 111
Killen, Alabama 35645
www.BluewaterPublications.com

Bluewater Publications
books by
Rickey Butch Walker

Appalachian Indians of the Warrior Mountains: History and Culture,
ISBN 978-1-934610-72-5, $14.95

Appalachian Indian Trails of the Chickamauga: Lower Cherokee Settlements
ISBN 978-1-934610-91-6, $14.95

Celtic Indian Boy of Appalachia: A Scots Irish Cherokee Childhood,
ISBN 978-1-934610-75-6, $14.95

Chickasaw Chief George Colbert: His Family and His Country,
ISBN 978-1-934610-71-8, $19.95

Doublehead: Last Chickamauga Cherokee Chief,
ISBN 978-1-934610-67-1, $19.95

Warrior Mountains Folklore: American Indian and Celtic History in the Southeast,
ISBN 978-1-934610-65-7, $24.95

Warrior Mountains Indian Heritage-Teacher's Edition,
ISBN 978-1-934610-27-5, $39.95

Warrior Mountains Indian Heritage-Student Edition,
ISBN 978-1-934610-66-4, $24.95

Works in Progress

Hiking Sipsey: A Family's Fight for Eastern Wilderness

Black Folk Tales of Appalachia: Slavery to Survival

When Cotton was King: White Gold of the Muscle Shoals

Soldier's Wife: Cotton Fields to Berlin and Tripoli

Acknowledgements

While putting together an Indian trails book of the Chickamauga faction of North Alabama Lower Cherokees, I sought the assistance of some friends who helped make my job much easier. Lamar Marshall provided many maps and pictures that made the book more interesting. David Walker made some wonderful maps that showed the location of trails and settlements; he also designed the cover. Twila Godwin edited the book and made many corrections to mistakes in punctuation and grammer; she also did the book review. These three people helped make the high quality of the book.

Contents

Introduction

This book is written for the cultural enlightenment of those who are descendants of Indian (Cherokee, Chickasaw, Creek) and Celtic (Irish, Scots, Welsh, and Scots Irish) people. Most of the mixed ancestry people of North Alabama are Celtic and Indian; however, the sad fact is that most of our children have no concept of who they are or of their true roots. The vast majorities of our mixed blood children have never heard the word Celtic nor know what it means, and many do not know the heritage of either culture.

Celtic People

Beginning in the late 1600's, the Celts were the primary traders to Indians; trade decreased after the Turkey Town Treaty of 1816 which took the lands of Morgan, Lawrence, and Franklin Counties from Cherokee and Chickasaw ownership. The Creek Indian lands south of the Tennessee Divide in North Alabama were taken by the Treaty of Fort Jackson in 1814.

The Celtic traders utilized a system of Indian roads, trails, and paths leading from village to village. The following is an excerpt from an article by William Lindsey McDonald (1979) that best describes the first Caucasians who came into this area and made contact with native people.

"The salience of English, Scots, Welsh, Irish, and Scots-Irish family names in North Alabama denotes the prevalence of these first settlers who came in such great numbers to the Muscle Shoals. These people were, as a rule, from two groups of ancient peoples.

In the 5th Century, groups of Germanic people invaded the British Isles. These were the Jutes, Angles and Saxons who settled mostly in Southern England, and, who historically are referred to as the Anglo-Saxons. These are the people who were to become most acquainted with the ways of feudalism, vassals, lords, serfs, and such, that became the way of life in the southern English lowlands. They were also the ones who learned firsthand about the emerging industrial life in the mills located around the larger English cities. The Anglo-Saxons settled along the east coast in the original thirteen colonies and contributed to the cultures of the New England countryside, big cities, sea ports, and the factories and workshops of the industrial East. In Virginia and the other Southern states, the Anglo-Saxons became the leading influence in plantation life with its social structure of slavery, which closely resembled the feudalistic system of

Europe they had known from the 9th to the 15th century.

Not many plantations existed in the Tennessee Valley. Most of the farm life in North Alabama was represented by the less than one-hundred-acre homesteads where the wife and children bore the drudgery of the plow and hoe. It is observed that these hardy subsistence-type farmers were of the Celtic stock. No other race of people on earth was more suited to blaze a trail and populate the wilderness of backwoods America than these Celts. History records no people who were more self-sufficient, independent, or able to withstand extreme hardships than the Celts.

The Celts were people of the European Iron-Age that occupied the British Isles and portions of Europe. They predated the Roman times and were the tribes who resisted, harassed, and refused to be conquered by the legions of the Caesars. They were scattered all the way from Galatia in Asia Minor to Spain and the British Isles in Western Europe. These were the rugged highlander people in Scotland, Wales and Northern Ireland, who resisted conquests of invading armies and the British Crown, and for hundreds of years made their living among the hardest of terrain and weather.

The only system of authority recognized by the ancient Celts was the clan. They did not organize and build towns until a thousand years ago. Unlike the Anglo-Saxons, who recognized only hereditary royalty in the few European ruling families, the Celts held that all members of the clan were descended from the same common ancestor; therefore, they were all of royal lineage. These proud people of the highlands believed in their own self-worth and indestructibility; they became the American pioneers who would survive in the Indian country of the southeastern United States against all the impossibilities. Laying a hand on a Celtic person's body, or meddling in his personal affairs, was considered a high crime. This law of the land still persists among their blood lines in the hills of North Alabama.

The blood-curdling battle cry of the ancient Celtic warrior as he took off his clothes and plunged naked into a kill all or be killed battle became the "rebel yell" of the Confederate soldier during the Civil War. The fierce loyalty to family and clan is still characteristic of the Celtic people of North Alabama. The stubborn inability of those of Celtic blood to think in harmony with those outside his clan can be seen in the prevalence of so many religious denominations in the Bible belt. The legendary stinginess of the Scot is probably the most misunderstood part of his character. His harden work ethic in all that he did was the means of his survival for thousands of years. These were the European people who became the first permanent white settlers of North Alabama; they settled in the Warrior Mountains, Coosa River Valley, and along the Muscle Shoals of the Tennessee River. The Celtic pioneers often intermarried with

Indian people and quickly adopted many of the ways of the Indians for the sake of survival as well as for a better way of life.

Some county seats in North Alabama laid out in a square around the court house are reminders of the Indian villages built around the four principal chief houses of the Cherokees. It has been observed that the small subsistence crossroads community with its store, cotton gin, and a church or two, is about as pure Celtic in character as one can find anywhere. The Anglo-Saxon influence can still be found in a few large farms but even more so in the industrial complex of the larger Tennessee Valley towns. The traditions and cultures of these early people run through the cosmopolitan society of the Shoals in the Twentieth Century. It can be said that the Anglo-Saxon, the Celt, the Chickasaw and the Cherokee left their footprints in the chain of Appalachian foothills that run across the northern part of Alabama" (McDonald, 1979).

Sometime between 2000 and 1200 BC, Celtic people migrated through northern Europe and into the British Isles. Even though the early history of Celtic people was not firsthand, other people who made contact with them recorded incidents of early Celtic culture. In 225 BC, thousands of our Celtic ancestors crossed the Alps from the British Isles and northern Europe to attack the great Roman Empire. During this attack at Telamon, the Romans killed some 40,000 Celtic people whom they referred to as barbarians.

The annihilation of Celts at the Battle of Telamon did not dissuade the Celtic people from their habitation of the British Isles. From northern Europe, the Celtic people had invaded and lived in Ireland, Scotland, Wales, Cornwall, and parts of England. In all of these areas except England, the Celtic lifestyle became the dominant culture. The English are of Anglo-Saxon origin in addition to other ethnic groups; they referred to the Celtic people as barbarians and killed thousands in numerous battles and wars. Eventually, the English dominated the Celts within the British Isles.

Differences in religious beliefs among Catholics and Protestants, domination by the English, and constant warring among Celtic clans contributed to continual unrest among the Celts. The increasing brutality of war and bloodshed prompted many Celtic people to seek freedom in the unfamiliar lands of the New World. During the 1600s, many Celts were able to escape the wrath of war and death in the British Isles by signing on with the English as indentured servants. Numerous Celtic freedom seekers placed their young children aboard ships at the bustling seaport of Cork, Ireland, and as indentured servants, these children of twelve to fifteen years of age were granted passage on ships bound for America; they were to work out their service by 21 years of age.

From the early 1600s through 1700s, more than one million Celtic (Irish, Scots, Scots Irish, Welsh, and Cornish) people migrated to the New World, many in servitude of the English. Since Celtic people did not have strong loyalty to the British, most Celts sought freedom from the English before their period of servitude was completed by moving into Indian lands of the southeastern United States.

In the early years of Celtic occupation in the New World, these Scots Irish servants were a dime a dozen to the English. Black slaves were much more highly valued than the Celtic barbarians. Aristocratic plantation owners would place Celtic people downhill on the river bank while black slaves rolled bales of cotton to them. If a Celt was killed, it was not counted as much of a loss; a black slave was much more highly prized than a Celtic servant or an Indian slave.

Celtic and Indian Contact

Celtic people tried to escape the English and moved as family clans from the colonies into and over the Appalachians. They began to settle in the Indian nations of the Cherokees, Chickasaws, and Creeks from east Tennessee, northwest Georgia, and northern Alabama. Through these contacts, intermarriage became a natural process of blending with the native people.

In the Creek, Chickasaw, and Cherokee societies of North Alabama, interracial marriages of Celtic men and Indian women were commonly acceptable. By 1800, this was evidenced in tribal leadership; all three tribes were controlled by half Scots Irish chiefs. John Watts, Jr, who was half Scots and half Cherokee, was elected chief of the Lower Cherokees after the death of Dragging Canoe. George (Tootemastubbe) Colbert and his brother Levi (Itawamba Mingo) Colbert, chiefs of the Chickasaw Nation, were half Scots and half Chickasaw. Alexander McGillivary, chief of the Creek Nation, was half Scots, one quarter French, and one quarter Creek. Therefore, our North Alabama Indian tribes accepted and many times promoted interracial marriages due to the advantages which were reaped in trade and treaty negotiation.

Many Celtic indentured servants became traders for the English, carrying British goods from Olde Charles Town, South Carolina throughout the area to the Lower Cherokee and Chickasaw towns; the Chickasaw owned by treaty from Huntsville to the upper Chatawatchee (Tombigbee) River. By the early 1700s, the British had an alliance with the Chickasaws and Cherokees. As the Appalachian Mountain portion of the Southeastern United States became inhabited with Celtic people, intermarriage, many times with multiple Indian women, became common instead of the exception. Many Celtic traders were seeking young and beautiful Indian women as wives.

One of the better-known Scots Irish traders was James Logan Colbert, head of a large pack train. Several other pack horsemen rode with Colbert through North Alabama, conducting trade with the Cherokees and Chickasaws. *"James Logan Colbert...sought refuge among the Chickasaws. He eventually became an influential member of the tribe, proving to be a brave leader in their wars...James Colbert married three Chickasaw women. Two of his wives were pure Chickasaw and the third was a half-breed. His first wife gave him a daughter, Mollie. He fathered five sons by his second wife: William, George, Levi, Samuel and Joseph. James Colbert's third wife bore him another son, James, and another daughter, Betsy. His sons became legends among the Chickasaws. Their father had tried to live in the ways of the Indians. The sons attempted to copy the life of the white man. George, Levi, and James lived at various times in Mississippi and Alabama. All the brothers seem to have had more than one wife; their daughters and granddaughters were of such outstanding beauty that they wove interesting chapters of romance along the Natchez Trace...The Colbert brothers were patriots, and at least two of them served in the American Army as scouts, guides and leaders of Indian detachments. William was with General Andrew Jackson in his campaign against the Creeks in South Alabama. One source shows George Colbert participating in the American Revolution under Washington. His military record reveals that he fought under St. Clair in 1791, and under 'Mad' Anthony Wayne in 1794. He led an expedition against the Creeks in March, 1814, and served as a Captain in the U. S. Army under General Andrew Jackson from November 1, 1814 to February 28, 1815.*

Levi, known as 'the Incorruptible,' became the most famous of the Colberts. Itawamba Mingo, as Levi was called by the Indians, was living near his Brother George's ferry in 1805. Later in 1812, he opened his own inn; known as a 'stand,' on the Natchez Trace at Buzzard Roost Creek near the Bear Creek Ford in what would become Colbert County in Alabama. In 1817 he moved to the Monroe County, Mississippi area. This was after he deeded his Buzzard Roost Inn to a daughter. She had greatly pleased her father by marrying Kilpatrick Carter, an early white settler.

In the spring of 1834, Chief Levi Colbert set out for Washington on urgent matters pertaining to the negotiations for removal of the Chickasaw Nation. This would eventually send them to Oklahoma. Along the way he stopped at Buzzard Roost where he became sick and died. It is not known whether they returned his body to his home at Cotton Gin Port, Mississippi, or if they laid the old chief to rest in the red soil of a county that would one day bear his name.

James, the youngest of the Colbert brothers, became a leader of great affluence among his people. His properties included a 500-acre plantation worked by over 100 slaves. He used his wealth to help pay the expenses of 50 Chickasaw families when they were forced to move to the Oklahoma Territory in 1837.

George Colbert, the ferryman, was called "Tootemastubbe" by the Indians. Historians have credited him as being one of two or three who guided the destiny of the Chickasaw during a critical period of their history. He was born in 1744 near the Tennessee River in what would become North Mississippi. In most of the treaties with the white man George served as chief negotiator. History records that he was quite shrewd in this role. He served as Chief of the Chickasaws for about twelve years" (McDonald, 1989).

Not only was Chickasaw society impacted by Celtic intermarriage but also Cherokee lifestyles were rapidly changing because of the influx of Celtic blood. Doublehead's older sister married John Watts who was Scots Irish. From this marriage came two notable mixed ancestry Celtic Cherokee people. As stated earlier, their son John Watts, Jr. became chief of the Cherokee Nation. Also their daughter Wurteh Watts married trader John Benge, who was Scots, and Nathaniel Gist. In 1776, George Gist or Sequoyah was born from the marriage of Wurteh Watts and Nathaniel Gist. Wurteh became the mother of one of the most famous Indian people in the United States — Sequoyah. Doublehead's youngest sister Ocuma married an Irish man by the name of John Melton who lived at Melton's Bluff in present-day Lawrence County, Alabama.

John Benge and Wurteh Watts had three sons —Robert Benge, Talohuskee Benge, and Utana Benge. Robert Benge was known as The Benge, The Bench, Bob Benge, Captain Benge, and Colonel Benge. Bob Benge rode with his great uncle Doublehead and became one of the most feared Cherokee warriors of the Appalachian frontier. Bob Benge was red headed; he was blue-eyed, fair complected, spoke perfect English, and was lethal as a rattlesnake toward his enemies. Talohuskee (Tahlonteskee) Benge signed the 1806 Cotton Gin Treaty with Doublehead and feared assassination that his uncle Doublehead received. In the summer of 1808 Tahlonteskee in agreement with President Thomas Jefferson, agreed to voluntarily move west; in 1809, Talohuskee Benge and some 1130 Cherokee left the area of North Alabama for lands west of the Mississippi. This group of Indians became known as the "Cherokees West" or "Old Settlers." Doublehead was a great Lower or Chickamauga Cherokee leader who lived most of his life along the Muscle Shoals of North Alabama; his first two daughters married Chickasaw Chief George Colbert and his second two daughters married Samuel Riley. Today, descendants of these powerful Celtic Indian families still live in North Alabama.

As already discussed, many North Alabama Indian descendants have mixed ancestry of Scots Irish and Cherokee. Many of our folks do not have the features, which meet the expectations of what an "Indian" looks like. Since our Indian people are of mixed Celtic origin, they are not supposed to look like full bloods; however, we have a unique culture here in North Alabama like no other in the world; therefore, we encourage our kindred mixed bloods to be proud of their heritage no matter what they look like. Probably Mr. John Knox summed up the situation in 1964 as well as anyone. *"A few days ago we were asked, what do you make of all these red-headed, blue-eyed Cherokee Indians you hear about? We gave the usual easy answer: those traders were in the Alabama wilds long before the settlers came. Many became 'Countrymen,' married Indian squaws, joined the tribes. Many — if not most of these — were Scots or kindred Gaels."*

Not all mixed ancestry Indian people had an easy life. Even though intermarriages of our local people basically improved lifestyle, it also created dilemmas and problems in Cherokee society. According to The Dividing Paths by Tom Hatley, *"...it is not surprising that at least some village women chose to enter into sexual liaisons and even marriages with colonial traders....In the Cherokee towns as late as the mid-point of the eighteenth century, indigenous women continued to choose to live with colonial traders. However, a gradual change had taken place in the some villages which had witnessed the first interaction between Cherokees and colonists. The slow learning about Euroamerican society — and vice versa — which had brought a degree of alienation in diplomacy and even in trading was also reflected in the politics of gender relationships. Intimate interaction resulted in a rejection by some indigenous women, not of colonial men as individuals, but of colonial expectations of behavior...The intermarriage of Cherokee women and colonial men posed an immediate challenge to these limits. The paradox posed for Cherokee society at large did not stem from these interactions themselves. Traditional lines of authority and governance, except in the most stressful times, were strong enough to have resisted the potential for disintegration growing from relationships between tribal women and colonial men. The real difficulty faced in the villages was due to the children born to bicultural marriages. The conventional solution was consistent with matriarchal kinship: 'when they part,' Henry Timberlake observed, 'the children go with, and are provided for, by the mother.'*

Some children slipped out of the hold of Cherokee mothers...Male children are retrospectively more visible because at least some seem to have followed their fathers into the leather trade — or their mother's side into warriorhood. The timing of the 1731 Carolina trade statute, which banned tribal or metis participation in colonial commerce, may have reflected the coming of age of a generation of metis youth, and white anxieties about their increasingly high profile in the trade. More direct confirmation of the presence of such children, and their integration into the economic world of their colonial fathers...however, the rules of racial ranking developing in the colonies kept metis individuals on the margin, confined to trading communities far removed from polite towns such as Charlestown, literally middlemen between the world of their mothers and that of their fathers.

Racial gradations prevalent in colonial society, such as 'mustee' and 'mulatto,' either did not exist or were subdued among the Cherokees. The most important and lasting distinction was not whether men or women were white or black, but whether they counted themselves Cherokee or not...Cherokee women, however, continued to keep open the door which, in times of war, the warriors wished to slam shut. At least through most of the century, colonists taken captive often had the chance to become Cherokee....but it was not captives or visitors — outsiders to the tribe — who felt the tension of ethnic identity most directly. Instead it was metis children born within Cherokee villages. As the first generation of these children became adults, the middle ground confidently crossed in the first decades of the century by their parents had become a kind of quicksand.

These abstractions became intensely sharp by the middle decades of the century for young male Cherokee mixed-bloods who had grown up confident in their mothers' lineages....they aspired to full rights in warriorhood but found obstacles in their way. As raiding became more focused on white settlements rather than on other tribes, metis children confronted profound questions of cultural and personal allegiance. For some mixed—blood men, the tensions of proving their Cherokee allegiance were shown in harsh, hostile acts of cultural disavowal.

Under growing white-red confrontation, psychological stress could also push Cherokee metis (and their mothers) toward loyalty to the English. Thus "Indian wenches, half-breeds and others" became a familiar line-up of informants to backcountry officials. Though some mixed-blood males appeared as mediators in times of conflict, women much more often played that role, sometimes acting in concert with "war women." "Half-breeds" caught in the middle were vulnerable, and, like women, were often singled out as victims of violence. Confusion about the victim's ethnic identity was a common excuse given by Cherokee warriors when non-combatants and allies were killed in war" (Hatley, 1995).

Regardless of biracial problems seen during the early 1800s with mixed blood Celtic Indian people, they were able to advance to the highest positions in local Indian societies; however, with passage of the Indian Removal Act in 1830, many of our mixed blood Indian people had to make heartbreaking decisions in order to stay in the land they loved, walk the paths of their ancestors, and seek the freedom from bloodshed, violence, and war.

The primary trade routes traveled by Celtic traders working for the British and later the American government were Indian trails that were also used during Indian removal. These primitive trails meandered across northern Alabama and became major migration routes of the Celtic Indian families as they travelled into the Tennessee Valley, Coosa Valley, and Warrior Mountains of North Alabama. They brought their agrarian lifestyle into the hill country of the southernmost Appalachian Mountains and foothills that was already home to many mixed bloods. In the Warrior Mountains, they continued to intermarry and raise families of mixed ancestry. At last, Celtic people thought they had found among the Indian nations the freedom they had sought over two continents and two thousand years; but, bloodshed would come again and again.

The Celtic Indian families would again be dominated and driven from their homes. Many of the families of mixed ancestry would trudge further west during the Indian removal of the early 1800s, still hoping for their freedom, but many would remain in their southern Appalachian homes refusing to leave. The mixed families who chose to remain were forced into some 150 years of denial of their true heritage, with many claiming to be Black Dutch or Black Irish. They hid in the coves, hollows, and distant creek bottoms of North Alabama and eked out survival in the isolation of the hills as their ancestors had done in the Appalachians and in the highlands of Scotland and Ireland.

Fearing not only for their personal property but also their lives, the remaining mixed Celtic Indian people in North Alabama denied their Indian race, held to white man's ways and religion, and almost lost their Indian and Celtic cultural heritage. As children of mixed ancestry grew older, they were told of their Indian ancestors, but were not allowed to claim their rightful heritage. Since Indian removal, the degree of Indian blood in North Alabama people has steadily diminished and will continue to do so throughout future generations.

With the passage of Sections 2 through 7 of the Civil Rights Act of 1968, it became legal to be Indian and live in Alabama. Many Indian descendants of mixed Celtic ancestry began to seek and reclaim their Indian heritage, but for many it was too late. In 1972, the Indian Education Act passed, allowing tribes across the Southeastern United States to teach their cultural traditions. On March 16, 1980, the Echota Cherokee Tribe was officially organized. During the 1980's, a few North Alabama School systems initiated Indian education programs. Finally we, as mixed ancestry Celtic

Indian people in North Alabama, are still trying to overcome the dual loss of the identity in two ancient societies and assimilate ourselves within a relatively new and unique cultural environment as true American citizens.

Lower Cherokee Chiefs

Dragging Canoe

From 1775 to March 1, 1792, Lower Cherokee Chief Dragging Canoe led the Chickamauga in their fight against white encroachment on their ancestral lands. Dragging Canoe was greatly opposed to the Treaty of Sycamore Shoals in 1775 as evidenced in his speech: *"Whole Indian nations have melted away like snowballs in the sun before the white man's advance. They leave scarcely a name of our people except those wrongly recorded by their destroyers. Where are the Delaware? They have been reduced to a mere shadow of their former greatness. We had hoped that the white men would not be willing to travel beyond the mountains. Now that hope is gone. They have passed the mountains, and have settled upon Tsalagi (Cherokee) land. They wish to have that usurpation sanctioned by treaty. When that is gained, the same encroaching*

spirit will lead them upon other land of the Tsalagi. New cessions will be asked. Finally the whole country, which the Tsalagi and their fathers have so long occupied, will be demanded, and the remnant of the AniYvwiya, the Principal People, once so great and formidable, will be compelled to seek refuge in some distant wilderness. There they will be permitted to stay only a short while, until they again behold the advancing banners of the same greedy host. Not being able to point out any further retreat for the miserable Tsalagi, the extinction of the whole race will be proclaimed. Should we not therefore run all risks, and incur all consequences, rather than to submit to further loss of our country? Such treaties may be all right for men who are too old to hunt or fight. As for me, I have my young warriors about me. We will hold our land."

Dragging Canoe

One of Dragging Canoe's warriors was none other than Doublehead. After the Treaty of Sycamore Shoals, Dragging Canoe told Henderson, *"You have bought a fair land, but there is a black cloud hanging over it. You will find its settlement dark and bloody."* Doublehead followed Dragging Canoe on attacks against white settlers moving in to claim Cherokee lands as their own and he kept the promise Dragging Canoe made to Henderson until 1795. For the rest of his life, Dragging Canoe with the assistance of other tribal factions of the Chickamauga resisted white encroachment and carried out his dark and bloody promise.

Dragging Canoe launched his first attack of the Chickamauga War against the east Tennessee settlements in 1776. The Chickamauga attacks consisted of a series of raids, ambushes, skirmishes, and some full-scale frontier battles with the settlers. The start of the 1775 Chickamauga campaign was a continuation of the struggle against white encroachment into Indian Territory by American frontiersmen from the colonies east of the Appalachian Mountains.

The Chickamauga War actually started in the summer of 1776 between the Chickamauga and frontier settlers along the Watauga, Holston, Nolichucky, and Doe Rivers in east Tennessee. Eventually the war spread into Virginia, North Carolina, South Carolina, and Georgia. By 1780 after the first permanent settlements were made by General James Robertson and his followers on the Cumberland River around the Nashville area, the Chickamauga War spread to those stations established in middle Tennessee, Kentucky, and a few skirmishes in Alabama. Dragging Canoe, Doublehead, and their warriors fought in conjunction with factions of the Chickamauga from a number of other Indian tribes both in the south and in the north.

John Watts, Jr.

Doublehead's nephew, John Watts, Jr. served as chief of the Chickamauga from 1792 through 1795. John Watts' Jr. was elected Chief of the Chickamauga over Doublehead after the death of Chickamauga Chief Dragging Canoe. Chief Watts was wounded at Buchanan's Station near Nashville in September 1792 but recovered and led his army the next year against Cavett's Station near Knoxville, Tennessee.

Chief John Watts was described by Governor Blount as, "unquestionably the leading man in his Nation. He possessed a talent for making friends, red and white." William Martin, son of General Joseph Martin, said of him, "He was one of the finest looking men I ever saw, large of stature, bold and magnanimous, a great friend of my father's." Major G. W. Sevier states, "He was a noble looking Indian, always considered a generous and honorable enemy," and other pioneers paid high tribute to, "his engaging personality" (Brown, 1938).

John Watts, Jr., was born about 1752 and died at Wills Town in 1808; he first lived at Watts Town between present-day Reedy Creek and Town Creek some 25 miles east of the present-day Town of Guntersville in Marshall County, Alabama; later, John Watts, Jr. lived at Wills Town just a few miles north of present-day Lebanon, Alabama and some six miles south of Ft. Payne.

Little Turkey

Little Turkey moved to the position as Principal Chief of the Cherokee Nation in 1795; he was a Lower Cherokee and lived at Little Turkey's Town near the Coosa River just a few miles northeast of present-day Gadsden, Alabama. Little Turkey's Town became known as Turkey Town; the location of the town was on the High Town Path that led east to High Town (Rome, Georgia). The Turkey Town Treaties between the Chickasaws and Cherokees with the United States were negotiated in September 1816.

Little Turkey became a leader of great influence with his Cherokee people. In the Grand Cherokee National Council of 1792, Little Turkey was referred to as the great beloved man of the whole nation. Little Turkey was chief until he died in 1801.

Black Fox

Black Fox was a Lower Cherokee and was elected Chief of the Cherokee Nation after the death of Little Turkey in 1801 and served until his death in 1811. Black Fox lived at Mouse Town at the mouth of Fox's Creek on the northern border of present-day Lawrence and Morgan Counties. The creek was named in honor of Black Fox and still carries that name to this day.

After Black Fox was elected chief in 1801, he had to deal with a lot of differences between the Upper and Lower Cherokees. With the lower towns in the north Alabama area having secured control of the tribal leadership, they were assured favorable distribution of annuity funds. A delegation of Upper Cherokees complained to President Thomas Jefferson that the Lower Cherokees divided all funds from annuities and land sales among those of their own neighborhood. President Jefferson explained that once the funds were turned over to the authorized representatives of the tribe that it was purely a Cherokee affair. Alexander Saunders proposed that the funds be split between the Lower and Upper Cherokees. Both Black Fox and Doublehead had serious conflicts with Major Ridge.

In early 1808, Colonel Return J. Meigs had convinced Black Fox and Taluntuskee to seek the Cherokee council approval for exchanging their lands for territory west of the Mississippi. At the fall council meeting of the Cherokee Nation, Black Fox made the proposal as follows, *"Tell our Great Father, the President (Thomas Jefferson) that our game has disappeared, and we wish to follow it to the West. We are his friends, and we hope he will grant our petition, which is to remove our people towards the setting sun. But we shall give up fine country, fertile in soil, abounding in water-courses, and well adapted for the residence of white people. For all this we must have a good price".*

Major Ridge was very upset and spoke against Black Fox in such an eloquent manner that the tribal council rejected both Fox and his proposal. Black Fox was reinstated at a later council meeting, but felt disgraced for the rest of his life. However, in the summer of 1808, Taluntuskee took the offer from President Thomas Jefferson and in 1809 some 1,131 Cherokees left the Shoal Town area to lands west of the Mississippi River. Taluntuskee told President Thomas Jefferson that his reason for leaving was the fear of assassination as his uncle Doublehead. Jefferson was the first president to strongly advocate Indian removal west of the Mississippi River.

Black Fox, Principal Chief of the Cherokee Nation, died July 22, 1811. Black Fox's death was reported in the *Columbia Centinel*, Boston, Massachusetts on August 31, 1811. His obituary stated, *"In the Cherokee country, Black Fox, a worthy chief of the Cherokee Tribe of Indians, and a great friend of the U.S."*

According to *Chronicles of Oklahoma*, volume 16, number 1, March 1938, by John P. Brown, *"Black Fox died in 1811. He was succeeded by Pathkiller, Nunna-dihi, a very honorable man who was to guide the destinies of the Cherokee through sixteen years."*

Today, Fox's Creek is the name of a small tributary to the Tennessee River that flows into the river at the north border of Morgan and Lawrence Counties at an old Cherokee town site of Mouse Town or Monee Town. Black Fox moved from Mouse Town to Fox's Stand which was near the junctions of three Indian trails-Browns Ferry Road, South River Road, and Black Warriors' Path.

Pathkiller

Pathkiller at one time lived in Lawrence County, Alabama; the creek that flows through the center of the county and drains the area around the county seat of Moulton was initially named Pathkiller's Creek. The name of the creek was changed from Pathkiller to Big Nance's Creek after Doublehead's sister Nancy moved to the mouth of the creek just one quarter mile west of Wheeler Dam.

14

According to Captain Edmund Pendleton Gaines on December 27, 1807, *"we proceeded, same course…6th mile…At 116 [chaines]* (west of Melton's Bluff) *Path Killer's Creek, 3 chains wide from tops of banks"* (Stone, 1971). Pathkiller took over as chief after the death of Black Fox; he as served chief until he died on January 8, 1827. At the time of his death, Pathkiller was living near Turkey Town and is buried at Center, Alabama.

John Ross

John Ross, born on October 3, 1790, was a true Lower Cherokee during the Chickamauga War at Turkey Town; the town was near the present location of Center, Alabama on the Coosa River. John was the son of Daniel Ross and Mollie McDonald; Mollie was the daughter of John McDonald and Ann Shorey who was one half Cherokee. John was elected chief of the Cherokee Nation in 1828 after the death of Pathkiller; he served as chief for 38 years until his death on August 1, 1866.

The grandfather of Cherokee Principal Chief John Ross was Scottish trader John McDonald, for whom John Ross was named. McDonald's primary home in the Cherokee Nation was not in Rossville, but on the waters of Chickamauga Creek, where the Brainerd Mission was later located. It was from this location during the Revolutionary War era that John McDonald supplied the fierce Chickamauga Chief Dragging Canoe with British weapons to make war against the Americans. John McDonald worked for British Superintendent of Indian Affairs John Stuart; Stuart appointed McDonald assistant superintendent or "deputy and commissary" of Indian Affairs for the British. McDonald also worked with British agents Alexander Cameron and Alexander Campbell in providing all the tribes of the Chickamauga Confederacy with arms and ammunition.

John McDonald immigrated to South Carolina from Scotland in the 1760s; by 1770, he had married Ann Shorey, daughter of Ghigooie, a Cherokee of the Bird Clan. Even though Ann's father had been Englishman William Shorey, she had been reared fully as a Cherokee after Shorey died on Lt. Henry Timberlake's journey back to England in 1762. By 1771, John and Ann McDonald settled on Chickamauga Creek near its junction with the Tennessee River. About 1788, John McDonald moved with his family to Turkey Town where John Ross was born, and continued trade with the Chickamauga.

Doublehead

It is very likely that the individual that exerted the most influence on Indian trails in the Muscle Shoals area was the powerful Chickamauga Cherokee Chief Doublehead. His influence dominated North Alabama's historical landscape from 1770 to his death on August 9, 1807. Although he was never officially elected chief, he ruled the Muscle Shoals of the Tennessee River with an iron fist.

Doublehead was born about 1744 and died August 9, 1807; he was also known as Talo Tiske, Dsugweladegi, or Chuqualatague. Doublehead was the son of Great Eagle (Willenawah) and grandson of Moytoy. Among his siblings were Red Bird, Standing Turkey, Sequechee, Nance, WarHatch, Ocuma, Pumpkin Boy, Old Tassel, and Wurteh (grandmother of Sequoyah).

Doublehead was described by Colonel Return Jonathan Meigs in a letter to Benjamin Hawkins on February 13, 1805. *"He is a man of small stature, compact and well formed, very dark skin, small piercing black eyes, the fixture of which when engaged in conversation are as immovable as diamonds set in metal and seem to indicate clearly that he comprehends the subject and in his reply to an address will omit nothing that has been said. He is occasionally guilty of intemperance and then off his guard, and if he considers himself insulted the explosion of his passion resembles that of gunpowder."*

Doublehead moved into the Muscle Shoals area about 1770 and became a powerful Chickamauga Cherokee leader. Doublehead lived at Doublehead's Town at the Brown's Ferry crossing of the Tennessee River at the head of Elk River Shoals in present-day Lawrence County, Alabama until 1802. Doublehead terrorized settlers on the Cumberland River and Appalachian frontier until his 1794 meeting with President George Washington. By the Chickasaw Boundary Treaty on January 10, 1786, most of the extreme northwest Alabama became Chickasaw land; however, Doublehead was permitted to stay because of his daughters' (Tuskiahooto and Saleechie) marriages to Chickasaw Chief George Colbert.

Learning of the wealth in cotton, Doublehead in 1802 petitioned the government for a keelboat, signed the 1805 treaty authorizing Gaines' Trace, and negotiated the 1806 Cotton Gin Treaty. This treaty placed a cotton gin at Melton's Bluff and gave him a 99 year lease renewable for 900 years on Doublehead's Reserve between Elk River and Cypress Creek to him and his heirs. In partnership with John D. Chisholm, they leased this reserve to settlers.

On August 9, 1807, Major Ridge, Alex Saunders, and John Rogers killed Doublehead, either for control of the cotton trade or for his ceding of Indian lands. Some contend that the execution of Doublehead was for his personal gain in making treaties; however, his control of the Muscle Shoals and cotton trade passing along the river was a factor in his assassination. At his death, Doublehead was a very wealthy man and owned some 40 black slaves, approximately 130 head of cattle, 20 head of horses, 150 head of hogs, and other valuable belongings. According to one of Doublehead's slaves, he was buried near his home site on the North River Road at the mouth of Blue Water Creek on the Tennessee River.

The following text from Footsteps of the Cherokees by Vicki Rozeman (1995) lists the villages established in northwest Alabama by the Cherokees and Doublehead:

"Further west, the Cherokees claimed the Chickasaw Old Fields at Ditto's Landing (near present-day Whitesburg, south of Huntsville) and established towns at Moneetown (on Fox Creek in Lawrence County), at Courtland, at Melton's Bluff, on Coldwater Creek (near present-day Tuscumbia), and on Town Creek (near Wheeler Dam).

Chief Doublehead, a Chickamaugan who became a successful businessman, established several different villages in northwest Alabama, including settlements at Bluewater Creek (near Wheeler Dam), on the south bank of Brown's Ferry (below Athens), in Limestone actually Lauderdale County (at the forks of Big Cypress and Little Cypress Creeks), and near Colbert's Ferry (on the Natchez Trace). Doublehead established a land agency called the Doublehead Company; he leased thousands of acres between the Elk River and Cypress Creek to more than fifty white settlers. The land Doublhead leased was in Cherokee territory, and as such, was not supposed to be available for this type of settlement. After Doublehead's death in the summer of 1807, the lease holders ran into legal problems which resulted in their eviction in 1811. Doublehead was also the father-in-law of the prominent Chickasaw chief, George Colbert, who operated the ferry on the Tennessee River at the Natchez Trace. Through land speculation and by controlling transportation routes, Doublehead and his followers controlled the Mussel Shoals (later changed to Muscle Shoals) area for many years. Doublehead's prosperous business interests made him an influential leader in northwest Alabama" (Rozeman, 1995).

It would appear that Chief Doublehead would not change his mind on the construction of roads or relinquishing Indian land; however, when the proverbial carrot of money was waved in front of his eyes, he reversed his stand. Eventually, Doublehead paid with his life for taking handouts to benefit him personally and for his ironclad control of cotton trade down the Tennessee River. Doublehead's executioners used his practice of securing personal gain at the expense of the Cherokee Nation as the prime reason for his planned assassination.

The three men who carried out the execution on August 9, 1807, were Major Ridge, John Rogers, and Alex Saunders. It is ironic that two of the men who assassinated Doublehead were mixed-bloods and one was white. John Rogers was a white man that was married to a Creek woman. Alex Saunders was half Cherokee and Major Ridge was three fourths Cherokee. Members of the Saunders family built Rocky Hill Castle and Saunders Mansion in Lawrence County. John or Samuel Rogers, of the Roger's family, was the namesake of the Town of Rogersville on the north side of the Tennessee River in Lauderdale County, Alabama. In 1839 after they had moved west, Major Ridge and members of his family paid the supreme sacrifice with their lives for the killing of Doublehead and signing the Treaty of New Echota, which gave Cherokee lands east of the Mississippi to the U.S. Government. Doublehead's son, Bird Tail Doublehead along with his kinfolks killed Major Ridge.

Lower Cherokee Settlements

Dragging Canoe, John Watts, Jr., Little Turkey, Black Fox, Path Killer, Doublehead, and other Lower Cherokee leaders helped establish a series of towns across North Alabama during the Chickamauga War which started with the signing of the Treaty of Sycamore Shoals or Henderson Treaty in 1775. The Lower Cherokee or the Chickamauga faction of Cherokees moved south along the Great Bend of the Tennessee River and into the Coosa River Valley. They fought to protect their hunting grounds along the Cumberland River and into Virginia.

Today, very little remains of the Chickamauga Cherokee Indian towns of North Alabama; the physical evidence of these towns is practically nonexistence except for old maps and historical records. Very few historic markers are available to the public identifying these important historic Chickamauga Indian sites; the Chickamauga people consisted of the Lower Cherokee, Chickasaw, Upper Creek, Shawnee, Yuchi, Delaware, and many mixed bloods who fought to save their sacred hunting grounds on the Cumberland River and to prevent white encroachment in their homelands.

Especially in northern Alabama, historical evidence is practically nonexistent; a few historical markers were placed over the last few years identifying the Trail of Tears; the local historical organizations of North Alabama seemed to have neglected some very important cultural and heritage sites of the Lower Cherokee Chickamauga people.

Some of the northern Alabama Chickamauga Indian towns are in vicinity of the present-day cities of Florence-Decatur, Huntsville-Guntersville, Scottsboro-Bridgeport, Gadsden-Centre, and Fort Payne. Some sites of the north Alabama Indian towns include:

Florence-Decatur Area—Colbert's Ferry, Buzzard Roost, Cherokee, Doublehead's Village, Cold Water, Jeffrey's Crossroads, Shoal Town, Roger's ville, Lamb's Ferry, Gourd's Settlement, Cuttyatoy's Village, Doublehead's Reserve, Oakville, Melton's Bluff, Foxes Stand, Doublehead's Town, Mouse Town or Monee Town;

Huntsville-Guntersville Area—George Fields Plantation, Dick Fields Plantation, Flint River Settlements, Gunter's Landing, Brown's Village, Meltonsville, Cherokee Bluff, Corn Silk Village, Creek Path Village, Coosada, Massas, Parches Cove;

Scottsboro-Bridgeport Area—Sawtee Town or North Sauty Town, Crow Town, Lookout Mountain Town, Long Island, Nickajack, Raccoon Town, Running Water;

Gadsden Area—Otali, Duck Springs, Dirty Ankle, Turkey Town, Ball Play, Spring Creek Village, Polecat Town, Little Hogs Town, Hillibulga Village, Chattuga, Wolf Creek Village;

Ft. Payne Area—Bootsville, Broom Town, Watts Town, Wills Town, Joseph Coody Plantation, and Daniel Ross Plantation.

Florence-Decatur Chickamauga Communities

Buzzard Roost

Buzzard Roost was the original settlement of half-blood Scots Irish Chickasaw Chief Levi Colbert and a number of Chickasaw Indians. He lived at Buzzard Roost Spring on the Natchez Trace about two miles west of the Town of Cherokee in Colbert County, Alabama. The large perennial spring is a tributary to Buzzard Roost Creek that runs west toward the Mississippi State Line and empties into Bear Creek where present-day Highway 20 crosses the creek. Buzzard Roost Spring was not only a major water supply for the Chickasaws that inhabited the area, but also for travelers using the Natchez Trace.

Charles Borden and Butch Walker at Buzzard Roost Spring

Major Levi Colbert was known as "Itawamba Mingo" which means Wooden Bench Chief or Wooden Bench King; he was the son of James Logan Colbert and younger brother of George Colbert. Levi was born in 1759 and died June 2, 1834, at Buzzard Roost at 74 years of age. Levi Colbert was possibly the wealthiest and most powerful of the Colbert family.

After moving south from Buzzard Roost, he lived just west of Cotton Gin Port located in Monroe County, Mississippi. Levi owned four thousand cattle, five hundred horses, a large herd of sheep, and several head of swine. At one time, Levi had a part interest in Colbert's Ferry on the Natchez Trace which was said to have been worth $20,000 annually.

Levi Colbert died at the home of his daughter, Phalishta "Pat" Malacha Colbert Carter, at Buzzard Roost Spring in Colbert County, Alabama. Levi originally lived at the Buzzard Roost site and had Kilpatrick Carter to build a new home on the site; however, supposedly during the construction of the home Carter fell in love with Levi's daughter and married her. Levi told Carter if he would build him another house at Cotton Gin Port that he would give his daughter and Kilpatrick Carter the home at Buzzard Roost Spring which was done.

In 1834 after Levi and the Chickasaws negotiated a treaty with John Coffee, they realized that changes should be made before the treaty was ratified; and therefore, a delegation of Chickasaws including Levi Colbert started from Cotton Gin Port to Washington, D.C. Levi became sick and stopped at his daughter's house at Buzzard Roost Spring where he died. He is supposedly buried at the old home site in Colbert County, Alabama.

Colbert's Ferry

James Logan Colbert was of Scots Irish origin and was born in North Carolina about 1721 on Plum Tree Island near the border of Virginia and North Carolina. James Logan Colbert, who was initially a trader to the Indians, was living with the Chickasaws by 1742; he married three Chickasaw women, one of which was a half blood. From his three wives, Colbert had nine children who were William, Sally, Celia, George, Levi, Samuel, Joseph, James, and Susan. The family of James Logan Colbert lived near the Tennessee River close to the mouth of Bear Creek. James Logan Colbert became an important leader of the Chickasaw people and was commissioned as a British Captain; by 1782, James Logan Colbert owned some 150 black slaves.

Three important leaders emerged as friends and cooperated with the British during the Chickamauga War and American Revolution. Their fight against the United States brought these men together: James Logan Colbert with the Chickasaws; Alexander McGillivray with the Upper Creeks; and Doublehead with the Lower Cherokees. James Logan Colbert's oldest son William Colbert and Alexander McGillivray married sisters and were brother-in-laws. Two of Doublehead's daughters married George Colbert, the son of James Logan Colbert. Therefore, a family relationship existed between the leaders of the Chickasaws, Upper Creeks, and Lower Cherokees who were major players in the war with the United States beginning after the signing of the Treaty of Sycamore Shoals in 1775.

Not only did James Logan Colbert become friends and fight conflicts against the American settlers with Creek Chief Alexander McGillivray, but he was also friends and fought with Dragging Canoe and Doublehead in the Chickamauga War. Initially, James Logan Colbert, William Colbert, George Colbert, and other Chickasaws became allied with Doublehead and McGillivray in Chickamauga Confederacy during the war that lasted from 1775 through June 1795. James Logan Colbert carried his sons into battle with him as he rode with the Cherokees and Creeks during the Chickamauga War.

George Colbert

The deterioration of the alliance of the Chickasaws, Upper Creeks, and Lower Cherokees started after the death of James Logan Colbert on January 7, 1784. Some nine years later on February 17, 1793, another blow to the Chickamauga Confederacy came with the death of Alexander McGillivray. By June 1794, Doublehead signed the Treaty of Philadelphia with President George Washington and ended his conflicts with the American colonies in June 1795; on August 9, 1807, the Creeks lost their last Cherokee friend, leader, and supporter with the death of Doublehead.

George Colbert, son of James Logan Colbert, was born about 1744 on the west side of Bear Creek where it empties into the Tennessee River in the present-day northeastern most corner of Mississippi. George was raised and lived all but two years of his life in the original eastern Chickasaw homelands which included northeast Mississippi and northwest Alabama.

George Colbert took two daughters, Tuskiahooto and Saleechie, of Chickamauga Cherokee Chief Doublehead and Creat Priber as his wives; George's wives were said to be among the most beautiful women in the region. Based on tradition, Tuskiahooto was considered one of the most beautiful women in the country and was the favorite wife of George Colbert. She was George's principal wife and lived at the Colbert's Ferry home until she died around 1817. In the treaty of 1834, George made sure to include his wife's burial site at Colbert's Ferry in the reserve that was set aside for his personal use.

George Colbert begin running a ferry across the Tennessee River in 1798 as a means for travelers to cross the otherwise impassable river. In December 1801, George Colbert agreed to move his ferry to the Natchez Trace crossing of the Tennessee River as part of his agreement with General James Wilkinson. The United States Government agreed to build cabins for travelers, a store, stables, a large two storied dwelling house, a new ferry boat, and

other facilities for George Colbert's family to operate a ferry where the Natchez Trace crosses the Tennessee River in present-day Colbert County, Alabama.

George Colbert's home at the ferry was built after the Chickasaw Treaty of 1801, with some claiming it was completed by 1808 and possibly much earlier. George's home was the site of a significant conference between the Cherokees, Creeks, Choctaws, Chickasaws, and the United States Government in September 1816 and was designated for this meeting as the "Chickasaw Council House." At the conference representing the government were Andrew Jackson, David Meriwether, and Jesse Franklin. The Chickasaws ceded their land north of the Tennessee River in present-day Lauderdale County, Alabama, as well as some territory south of the river with certain tracts being reserved for George Colbert, including his ferry.

George had virtually a monopoly for the river crossing, and he charged fifty cents per passenger and one dollar per horse and rider. Later reports suggest that Colbert once charged Andrew Jackson $75,000 to ferry his army across the river, but Jackson's own records indicate the amount was only a few hundred dollars that was actually paid.

George Colbert's Home on Natchez Trace

George Colbert, Tootemastubbe or The Ferryman, was the most well-known son of James Logan Colbert. He was tall, slender, and handsome with long straight black hair that came down to his shoulders. His features were Indian, but his skin was lighter than other members of the Chickasaw tribe. He dressed neat and clean like white men of his day; some say he was illiterate, but had great influence among both Indians and white people. He was described as speaking common English, very shrewd, extremely talented, very wicked, genius, but is an artful designing man. Indian agent Colonel Return J. Meigs described him as, *"Extremely mercenary miscalculates his importance, and when not awed by the presence of the officers of the government takes upon himself great airs."*

Since his beautiful wife Tuskiahooto died in 1817, and the United States mail route was officially changed to follow Jackson's Military Road through Florence in 1817, George was ready to leave his ferry operations on the Tennessee River. Therefore, because of the death of his principal wife Tuskiahooto, the loss of the government mail route, and the opening of the Gaines Trace, George Colbert closed the ferry on the Natchez Trace, moved to Tupelo, Mississippi, in 1817, and began his very successful farming operations on his plantation.

Cherokee

This was a Cherokee village in present-day Colbert County, Alabama near the junction of the Natchez Trace and South River Road. According to some sources, four Chickamauga Cherokee Indian villages were located west of Cane Creek in Colbert County, Alabama, on predominately Chickasaw land; it is thought that the Town of Cherokee is so named because of a Cherokee village in the vicinity.

The land at the Town of Cherokee belonged to the Chickasaw Nation by treaty with the United States and the town was actually established in Chickasaw territory. Chickasaw Chief George Colbert said he give his father-in-law Doublehead and the Cherokees permission to live on Chickasaw land; George married two of Doublehead's daughters, Saleechie and Tuskiahooto.

Doublehead's Village

Doublehead's Village was established in the early 1770's and was located on the Tennessee River in present-day Colbert County, Alabama. The village was near the Community of Mhoon Town and some five miles north of the present-day Town of Cherokee. Doublehead's Village was upriver and east of Chickasaw Chief George Colbert's Ferry at the Natchez Trace crossing of the Tennessee River. Also near the village was a large source of freshwater that was called Doublehead's Spring; another spring by the same name was located at Shoal Town some 35 miles upstream from Doublehead's Village just one fourth mile west of the mouth of Blue Water Creek.

Cold Water or Tuscumbia Landing

Cold Water was a Chickamauga Indian town established as a French trading site in the early 1700's. By the 1770's, the Cherokees had established a settlement which was located near the junction of Spring Creek with the Tennessee River; today, the site is known as Tuscumbia Landing in Colbert County, Alabama.

Opothleyaholo (Laughing Fox)
1778-3/22/1863

In March 1780, Colonel John Donelson led a party of white settlers down the Tennessee River by the Indian village of Cold Water from Knoxville in route to settle the Cumberland River Valley; the area was claimed by the Lower Cherokees and other Chickamauga tribes. Donelson's group was attacked by the hostile Chickamauga Indians at both ends of the Muscle Shoals, but only five of their group suffered wounds while passing the shoals of the Tennessee River.

On June 13, 1787, some of Doublehead's warriors killed Mark Robertson, the younger brother of Colonel James Robertson near Nashville, Tennessee. Without waiting for permission from the Governor, Robertson with a force of 130 men began to pursue the enemy to the mouth of Blue Water Creek and then down the Tennessee River to Cold Water Village. Robertson's men were following a 100 mile Indian trail south that became Doublehead's Trace from Franklin, Tennessee to the mouth of Blue Water Creek in present-day Lauderdale County, Alabama.

When Robertson's forces reached Cold Water, the Chickamauga Indians were taken completely by surprise and made a run for their canoes. Robertson's men opened fire killing some fourteen Lower Cherokees and six Upper Creeks along with some French traders who were instigating the raids in the Cumberland River Valley. Robertson's forces burned the town and returned to Nashville, Tennessee. Robertson with the assistance of Cumberland Valley settlers defeated the Chickamauga at the French trading post at Cold Water in present-day Tuscumbia, Alabama; however, Robertson's campaign at Cold Water failed to diminish raids on the Nashville, Tennessee area. Chickamauga warriors under Doublehead's command would continue their war against the Cumberland settlements into June 1795.

The Coosa Path or Muscle Shoals Path was a major Indian trail from the east that ended at the landing near Cold Water Village. The old Indian route from northeast Alabama to Cold Water Village was called the Coosa Path by Captain Edmund Pendelton Gaines on the rainy day of December 29, 1807, when he was surveying the

Gaines Trace from Melton's Bluff in North Alabama to Cotton Gin Port in northeast Mississippi. The same trail was also called the Muscle Shoals Path by Cherokee Chief Path Killer in October 1813.

From Oakville, the Coosa Path became a removal route for 511 Creek Indians led by Creek Chief Opothle-Yaholo in December 1835; on February 8, 1825, Opothle-Yaholo said, *"Leave us what little we have. We sell no more. Let us die where our fathers died. Let us sleep where our kindred sleep."* In September 1836, some 2,000 Creek Indians followed Black Warriors' Path north to Oakville where they hit the Coosa Path to the west. The Creeks were placed on boats at Tuscumbia Landing and transported down river. As many as nine contigents of Creek Indians were removed west by water from Tuscumbia Landing.

Later during Indian Removal in the late 1830's, many Cherokees were moved from Decatur around the Muscle Shoals to Tuscumbia Landing by the Decatur to Tuscumbia Railroad. Most all these Cherokee Indians were transported down river from Tuscumbia Landing by boats to Waterloo where they were placed on steamers headed west.

Jeffrey's Crossroads

The first mixed settlement in the area of present-day Town of Leighton in Colbert County, Alabama, was established by Celtic-Lower Cherokee Indian people; the village became known as Jeffrey's Crossroads in honor of the Jeffreys Family. By 1770, the area of the Indian village was controlled by Chickamauga Chief Doublehead's faction of the Lower Cherokees and his warriors. Prior to 1808, many of the Jeffreys Family, mixed blood Celtic Indian people of Scots Irish and Cherokee ancestry, made this one of the oldest mixed Indian-white settled towns in North Alabama. Today, many of the Jeffreys

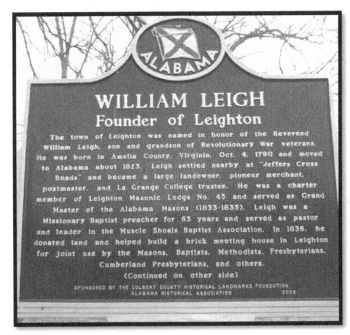

descendants are state recognized Indians and belong to the Echota Cherokee Tribe of Alabama.

The territory around Jeffreys Crossroads was actually recognized by the United States government as Chickasaw land by the Chickasaw Boundary Treaty of January 10, 1786. The town remained Indian land until the Turkey Town Treaty of 1816; white settlers began buying up the land during the 1818 federal lands sales. Today, the Indian Town of Jeffreys Crossroad is known as Leighton, Alabama. Originally, the east half of Leighton was in Lawrence County and the west half was in Franklin County from 1816 until 1867; on February 6, 1867, the west half of the town became Colbert County. In 1895, the east half of the town was annexed into Colbert County; the county was named in honor of the Chickasaw Colbert family.

The first railroad west of the Appalachians came through the Town of Leighton and was known as the Decatur to Tuscumbia Railroad. During the 1830's, many Cherokee Indian people that were being removed west rode the railroad from Decatur through Leighton to Tuscumbia Landing on the Tennessee River; the rail line was a route around the Elk River Shoals, Big Muscle Shoals, and Little Muscle Shoals which were barriers to navigation along the Tennessee River from Decatur to Tuscumbia. The navigational water barriers along the Tennessee River at the shoals were created by vast layers of resistant chert (flint) rock; therefore, the railroad was used to circumvent these natural obstacles to water travel through the Muscle Shoals.

Shoal Town

In the 1809 Cherokee census by Return Jonathan Meigs, there were 110 Cherokee males, 104 Cherokee females, and 9 whites living in Shoal Town. Prior to the death of Doublehead on August 9, 1807, there were probably many more Indian residents as indicated in the book *Two Hundred Years at Muscle Shoals* by Nina Leftwich in 1935; she described a very large Cherokee town. *"Both the French and the English contended for the Indian trade along the western waters; the French planted a post at Muscle Shoals before 1715. Because of the increasing importance of trade with the whites the Cherokees planted villages near the Muscle Shoals area in the last quarter of the eighteenth century. There was Doublehead's village on the Tennessee and a large settlement* (Shoal Town) *at the mouth of Town Creek, extending a mile along the river and far up the creek"* (Leftwich, 1935).

Shoal Town was in Lawrence, Colbert, and Lauderdale Counties of North Alabama; the village was located between Blue Water Creek, Big Nance Creek, and Town Creek on the Big Muscle Shoals of the Tennessee River. Shoal Town was located some six miles from the eastern end of Big Muscle Shoals at the junction of Doublehead's Trace and the South River Road; these roads connected the Indian town to other Cherokee villages.

During Captain Edmund Pendleton Gaines survey on December 28, 1807, he notes the following, *"8ᵗʰ mile… at 119 chs. Cross the path* (South River Road) *which leads from Shoal-Town, eastwardly, to the Goards Settlement* (Courtland)*, about 3 miles distance"* (Stone, 1971).

Shoal Town was considered one of the largest Cherokee Indian villages in the Big Bend of the Tennessee River. At the location, the Blue Water Ferry crossed the river from the eastern side of the mouth of Blue Water Creek to the western side of the mouth of Path Killer's (Big Nance) Creek.

Shoal Town was the home of Talohuskee Benge, the half brother to Sequoyah. Later, Talohuskee's great uncle Doublehead moved to the Shoal Town area about 1802. Talohuskee Benge, son of Doublehead's niece, Wurteh Watts and trader John Benge, lived at Shoal Town with Doublehead and probably operated the ferry, a common practice at large Cherokee River Towns.

Shoal Town-1817 Peel and Sannoner Map

While living at Shoal Town, Doublehead requested help from the U.S. Government; however, he was no stranger to the government when asking for help, money, or handouts. This particular incident is recorded in Henry T. Malone's (1956) book *Cherokees of the Old South*:

"A scarcity of corn caused by a drought in the Cherokee Nation during the year 1804 was a crisis which Meigs faced in his typical fashion. The first request for food came from Doublehead and other Cherokees in the Muscle Shoals area on the Lower Tennessee River. The Agent immediately sent them three hundred bushels of corn, for

which the Indians paid $110. Meigs, however, requested and received permission from the War Department to return the money; he thought it his duty 'to give the necessary relief — believing that humanity and interest combine to make it proper especially when interesting negotiations with them are now soon to be opened.' Meigs' policy pleased his government. Henry Dearborn sent him the President's congratulations, urging Meigs to continue helping needy Indians: 'You will embrace so favorable an opportunity for impressing the minds of the Cherokees with the fatherly concern and attention of the President to the distresses of his red children.'"

Today, Doublehead's Resort is located in Lawrence County, Alabama, at the site of the Lower Cherokee settlement of Shoal Town. The resort is a modern facility catering to thousands of people each year and is located on the east bank of Town Creek near where it empties into the Tennessee River.

The resort area extends up the river toward Big Nance Creek and has become a popular tourist site. Along the bank of Town Creek are numerous two-story cabins which can accommodate entire families. Each cabin has a water-front dock which provides boating facilities for resort visitors. The resort also boasts a lodge, swimming facilities, horseback riding, and many other accommodations that make for a pleasurable stay. If Doublehead were alive today, he would have to be proud of the facility at his old homesite that bears his name; therefore, the legends of Doublehead live on at this beautiful recreational facility in the county his descendants still call home.

Roger's ville

Roger's ville was a Cherokee Indian village that was located at the junction of the North River Road and the Sipsie Trail; the Indian town was some four miles north of the Tennessee River where Cherokee John Lamb operated a ferry. During the 1809 census of the Cherokee Indians by Return Jonathan Meigs, there were 20 Cherokee males, ten Cherokee females, and six white settlers living in Roger's ville. The Sipsie Trail that passes through the present-day Town of Rogersville became known as the Lamb's Ferry Road that ran from the river to Pulaski, Tennessee.

Lamb's Ferry

The Sipsie Trail crossed the Tennessee River at Lamb's Ferry some four miles south of the present-day Town of Rogersville in Lauderdale County, Alabama. The Sipsie Trail was an Indian route that was used by Doublehead's Chickamauga warriors during their attacks on the Cumberland settlements around present-day Nashville, Tennessee. According to microcopy 208, roll 7, and number 3533, John Lamb was a Cherokee Indian; he signed a letter dated August 15, 1816, with The Gourd, Charles Melton, and other Cherokees. These Cherokees along the Muscle Shoals requested by letter the return of Negro Fox to be tried by Cherokee law. Negro Fox had left the area with James Burleson and other white men who had killed two Cherokees at Mouse Town.

John Lamb had established his ferry that crossed the Tennessee River along the old Sipsie Trail before 1809; the trail had been widened to a wagon road by a mixed-blood Celtic Indian man by the name of McCutcheon in 1783. McCutcheon, who was a Scots Irish Cherokee, opened the Sipsie Trail during the same period of time that Doublehead controlled the area of the Muscle Shoals. From his stronghold along the Muscle Shoals of the Tennessee River, Doublehead and his Chickamauga warriors used the Sipsie Trail to wage a bloody war against the Cumberland settlers around the Big Lick, present-day Nashville, Tennessee, until June 1795. McCutcheon's Trail led from present-day Spring Hill, Tennessee, to Pulaski, and to the Tennessee River south of present-day Rogersville.

At the end of the Chickamauga War, Lamb decided that he would open and operate a ferry for people coming south from middle Tennessee; travelers could ride a ferry across the Tennessee River instead of fording the river on horseback. When John Lamb started operating the ferry, the old Sipsie Trail to the north of the Tennessee River became known as the Lamb's Ferry Road. The Lamb's Ferry Road intersected an east to West Indian trail known as the North River Road in present-day Rogersville. The Sipsie Trail became known as the Cheatham Road from Tuscaloosa to Moulton, Alabama; it was known as the Lamb's Ferry Road from the ferry crossing of the Tennessee River to Rogersville, to Minor Hill, Pulaski, and then to Nashville, Tennessee.

John Lamb's Ferry became a thriving enterprise and was used by many travelers heading south of the Tennessee River; the crossing was in the area between Elk River Shoals which was upstream and Big Muscle Shoals which was on the downstream side of the ferry. Lamb's Ferry was located on the Tennessee River some six miles upstream from Shoal Town and downstream some five miles from the mouth of Elk River. The river crossing was operated as a Cherokee Indian ferry until the area was taken by the Turkey Town Treaty of 1816; by 1818, a large number of white settlers flooded the Lamb's Ferry area during the federal land sales.

Lamb's Ferry was an important site during the Civil War. According to Civil War journals, on May 4, 1862, Union General John Adams and his cavalry troops were at Lamb's Ferry when they received orders to move down the Tennessee River to Bainbridge Ferry. From May 10 through the 14, 1862, skirmishes between the Union and Confederate troops occurred around Lamb's Ferry; the area remained occupied by Union soldiers until May 14, 1862. On April 28, 1863, after trying to cover up Streight's Raid through North Alabama, General Grenville M. Dodge moved his Union troops toward Corinth, Mississippi. As the Union forces were retreating, Dodge's men burned Lamb's Ferry, the Town Creek railroad trestle, and LaGrange College. After the Civil War, a cotton gin and warehouses were built at Lamb's Ferry; the ferry stayed in operation until the early 1900's.

Goard's (Gourd's) Settlement

The fifth downstream Indian town was a Cherokee village called Goard's Settlement which was at the present-day town of Courtland. On December 28, 1807, Captain Edmund Pendleton Gaines made this note on his survey from Melton's Bluff to Cotton Gin Port: *"8th mile…. At 119 chs. Cross the path which leads from the Shoal Town, eastwardly, to the Goard's Settlement, about 3 miles distance"* (Stone, James H., 1971). Based on Gaines measurements of some 8.7 miles westerly from Melton's Bluff, then easterly for three miles, Gourd's settlement was in the center of present-day Courtland, Alabama. Eventually, three Indian roads intersected at Gourd's Settlement: the Gaines' Trace, the South River Road, and the Sipsie Trail, which later became the Cheatham Road or portions of present-day Highway 33.

Gourd's Settlement was obviously named after a Cherokee Indian man called Gourd. According to *Letters from Alabama 1817-1822* written by Anne Royall on January 12, 1818, page 131, is the following: *"Guide says Gourd was very kind; he knew him for fifteen years. He helped subdue the Creeks, and made an excellent soldier."* Anne Royall described Gourd's log house as being on the west side of Town Creek, ten years after Gaines' account; however, she wrote her letter after the fact and might have been wrong on the exact location; furthermore, Gaines was a surveyor and made precise measurements and locations.

Gourd's Town was at the junction of the South River Road and the Sipsie Trail, an early Indian route from Tuscaloosa to the French Lick (Nashville, Tennessee). Also a prehistoric village containing an Indian mound was located at the site on the banks of Path Killer Creek which later became known as Big Nance. According to Captain Edmund Pendleton Gaines on December 27, 1807, *"we proceeded, same course…6th mile…At 116 [chaines] (west of Melton's Bluff) Path Killer's Creek, 3 chains wide from*
32

tops of banks" (Stone, 1971). In 1807 when Captain Gaines identified Path Killer Creek (named after Cherokee Chief Path Killer), he was traveling portions of the South River Road but was intent on surveying a line from Melton's Bluff on the Tennessee River to Cotton Gin Port on the Tombigbee River; therefore, he basically followed the Old Chickasaw Trail to the heart of the Chickasaw Nation.

According to a February, 1829 Lawrence County court record, *"a road from Gourd Landing on the Tennessee River to intersect the road from Courtland to Lamb's Ferry at or near Gordon's fence the nearist and best way... Order, 1829, Jury of Review of a road from Courtland to Gourds."* This road either crossed or followed portions of both the Sipsie Trail and Gaines Trace.

Cuttyatoy's Village

Another Indian town located near the end of the Elk River Shoals and connected to other settlements by the South River Road was Cuttyatoy's Village. The village was actually on Gilchrist Island in the mouth of Spring Creek in Lawrence County, Alabama, at the western end of Elk River Shoals near the south bank of the Tennessee River.

According to the <u>American Whig Review</u>, Volume 15, Issue 87, March 1852, page 247: *"Colonel (Joseph) Brown...a participant in the battle of Talledega (November 9, 1813)...met Charles Butler... and learned from him that...Chief Cuttyatoy, was still alive...he was then living on an island in the Tennessee River, near the mouth of Elle (Elk) River, and that he had with him several Negroes ... taken by him at Nickajack on the 9th of May, 1788... with ten picked men, Brown proceeded to the island, went to the head man's (Cuttyatoy) lodge and exhibited to him General (Andrew) Jackson's order, and demanded that Cutty-a-toy's Negroes be immediately sent over to Fort Hampton...In crossing the river, Colonel Brown and his men took up the Negroes, and Cutty-a-toy's wife behind them, to carry them over the water while the Indian men crossed on a raft (Brown's Ferry) higher up (stream)."* Cuttyatoy and his men utilized the South River Road to reach Brown's Ferry. Colonel Joseph Brown and his men reached Fort Hampton that morning while Cuttyatoy and his men arrived in the afternoon.

Today, Cuttyatoy's Village is under the backwaters created by Wheeler Dam. The old Indian town site lies buried below the surface of Wheeler Lake, as are most of the river villages that were located on islands of Elk River Shoals. Between the mouth of Spring Creek on the south side and Elk River on the north side of the Tennessee River, the islands of Elk River Shoals are under some twenty feet or more of water. It was between these islands of the Elk River Shoals that General Joe Wheeler's cavalry crossed the Tennessee River on October 9, 1863.

Doublehead's Reserve

Doublehead's Reserve was in present-day Lauderdale County, Alabama, between the Chuwalee (Elk River) and Tekeetanoeh (Cypress Creek). The reserve was the home of Doublehead and consisted of thousands of acres of land that extended some ten miles from the north side of Tennessee River. According to the Cotton Gin Treaty of January 7, 1806, Doublehead was given a 99 year lease on the reserve which was renewable for 900 years to him and his heirs; however, the treaty with the Cherokees concluded on July 18, 1817, relinquished all of Doublehead's claims to the land he was given by the Cotton Gin Treaty.

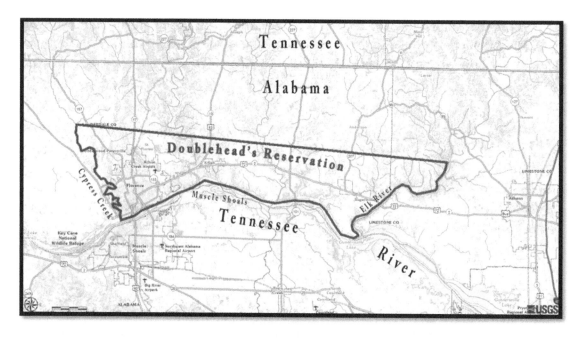

Doublehead, Kategishee, and other Cherokees who live on Doublehead's Reserve at Muscle Shoals of the Tennessee River wanted a road from Cumberland River to pass by the shoals. Eventually, Doublehead built a road from Franklin County, Tennessee, to the shoals and tried to get the government to connect it with the main road to the Tombigbee settlements. This road became known as Doublehead's Trace and was laid out on portions of the Old Buffalo Trail that ran from the French Lick (Nashville, Tennessee) on the Cumberland River.

Oakville

Oakville is located in Lawrence County, Alabama, approximately one half mile east of the West Fork of Flint Creek and some five miles north of the base of the Warrior Mountains in the flat plain of the Moulton Valley. The site is about one mile north of present-day Highway 157; today, the area is still known as the present-day Community of Oakville.

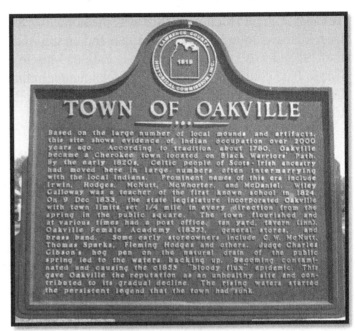

At one time, Oakville was a large prehistoric Woodland and Mississippian Indian village that was centered near a huge spring that flowed some 500 yards west before disappearing into a large limestone crevasse. The Indian town contained five mounds with a ceremonial mound that is the second largest earthen Indian structure in the State of Alabama. Eventually, all but two of the mounds were destroyed during farming operations, but today the two remaining mounds along with some 120 acres are protected as part of the Oakville Indian Mounds Educational Center.

According to local historians and old settlers, Oakville was an Indian trading town that prospered during the

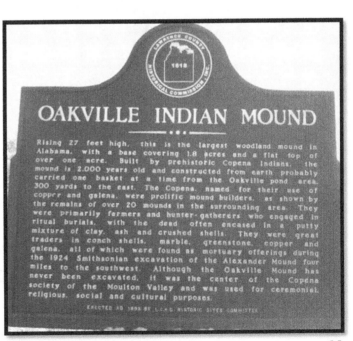

time that Chickamauga Cherokee Chief Doublehead controlled the area. Two very important Indian trails that were used extensively crossed at Oakville just some 200 yards south of the ceremonial Indian mound. The Black Warriors' Path came from the south and traversed north from Oakville some 15 miles to Melton's Bluff on the Tennessee River; Melton's Bluff was the home of Doublehead's sister Ocuma and her Irish husband John Melton. The other Indian trail that ran through Oakville came from the east and was known as the Coosa Path or Muscle Shoals Path. From Oakville, the Coosa Path continued west to the Chickamauga Indian village of Cold Water which later became Tuscumbia Landing on the Tennessee River in present-day Colbert County, Alabama.

Melton's Bluff Plantation

Melton's Bluff was a Lower Cherokee Indian village and cotton plantation approximately seven miles west of Brown's Ferry on the Tennessee River in present-day Lawrence County, Alabama. The site was also a prehistoric Indian town located on the west side of Jack's Slough, at Tennessee River mile 288.5. The site contains a large

ceremonial Indian mound covering over one acre and stands some fifteen to twenty feet high. In addition approximately one hundred feet from the Tennessee River, a small snail mound is located between the large mound and the present river bank.

During historic occupation by the Lower Cherokee Indians, the site west of the mounds for about one mile became known as Melton's Bluff, named after an Irishman, John Melton who married Doublehead's sister Ocuma. Melton's Bluff Plantation was a historic Cherokee town that was purchased by General Andrew Jackson from half-blood Cherokee David Melton on November 22, 1816. At Melton's Bluff Plantation located

36

between Tennessee River miles 287 and 288.5, the South River Road continued west while Black Warriors' Path turned north, crossed the river, and passed Ft. Hampton, Bridgewater, Elkton, and on to the French Lick.

In Letters from Alabama 1817-1822 by Anne Newport Royall is a description of a route to Melton's Bluff from Florence as follows: *"Melton's Bluff, January 8th, 1818... I was three days on the road to this place. Melton's Bluff is at the head of Mussel Shoals...I went direct to the foot of the Shoals, 70 miles from Huntsville, crossed the river, and come upon the south side of Tennessee River...three miles in width! The largest body of water that I ever saw. It was at this time very high and muddy; and the noise produced by the water washing over the rocks was tremendous... we saw a boat hung on a rock, about the middle of the stream...I took a guide, one of the pilots, and crossed the river next morning, in a ferry boat...upon leaving the ferry... I was to pass by several Indian farms... About ten o'clock we came in sight of the first Indian farm... you cross Town Creek in a canoe and swim your horses; this will cost you one dollar...I, with my horses, were safely on the other side... Rhea (my guide's name) said I had two more creeks to pass... however, these were easily forded...Rhea... had piloted boats through the Muscle Shoals, fifteen years; sometimes four at a time, at ten dollars each. He sails down one day, and walks back to the next... this land is so clear of undergrowth that you may drive a wagon any where through the woods...we passed many Indian houses in the day, and some beautiful springs. Melton's Bluff is a town, and takes its name from...John Melton...Irishman by birth...attached himself to the Cherokee Indians... Melton's Bluff... a very large plantation of cotton and maize, worked by about sixty slaves and owned by General Jackson, who bought the interest of old Melton."*

This firsthand account in January 1818 of Ms. Royall confirms the existence of a road, which still had Indian houses standing, along the south bank of the Tennessee River. The Cherokee and Chickasaw Indians had given up the land in September 1816 which was approximately fifteen months prior to Ms. Royall's visit to Melton's Bluff. The route of the South River Road was clearly established and had been in existence for some time.

The following portion of a story on Melton's Bluff by Rayford Hyatt (1993) gives details on the Indian village:

"The place was named for a white man, Melton, who settled there probably as a trader, married a Cherokee woman, thereby becoming a member of the Cherokee Nation. James Saunders in 'Early Settlers' says his name was James Melton. Anne Royall in 'Letters from Alabama' says he was John. A Cherokee Treaty of 1806 ceding

lands north of the Tennessee River exempted a tract 2 by 3 miles to Moses Melton and Charles Hicks in equal shares. Oliver D. Street in a paper on 'The Indians of Marshall County' says that Meltonsville of Marshall County was named for Charles Melton, an old man of Herculean frame who once lived at Meltons Bluff. Whichever he was, the others were probably his sons.

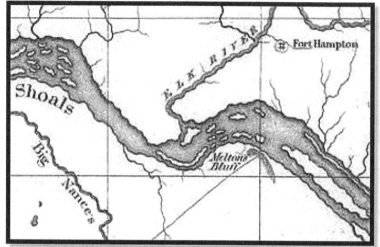

Melton's Bluff-1817 peel and Sannoner map

Meltons Bluff was located at the head of the Muscle Shoals in the SE 1/4 - SE 1/4 Sec 25 T3S R7W. Most of the buildings were in a line on top of the bluff. Anne Royall in 'Letters from Alabama' who stayed at the Bluff for a long period in 1818-19 says Melton got started by robbing flat boats coming down the river. It is more likely that Indians did the robbing and he traded for the slaves and goods. He also for many years furnished river pilots to boats through the Muscle Shoals for a fee with the pilots walking back to the Bluff from Florence.

In 1774 a settlement party of 15 whites and 21 slaves from South Carolina led by William Scott, were descending the Tennessee by flat boat to Natchez when they were attacked at the head of Muscle Shoals by a number of Cherokees under The Bowle. All of the white people were killed, and the slaves and goods taken. The Cherokee tribe disavowed the act of The Bowle and his followers who, fearing capture and punishment, fled to the west and located on the Arkansas River and with subsequent additions to their settlement they remained there many years.

In later years, Melton seemed to operate in a profitable legal manner. Besides houses of entertainment and boating activities at the Bluff, he owned large cotton and corn plantations on both sides of the river. There were numerous travelers down the river. Goods came down by flatboat from the Watauga settlement bound for New Orleans. Settlers from Virginia and Carolina crossed the mountains and descended by boat, some bound for the lower Mississippi and others for the lower Tombigbee. Those bound for the latter stopped at the bluff, travelled by horseback to Cotton Gin Port, built more boats and descended. Those going on downstream sometimes had to lay over a long time at the Bluff waiting for a rise in the river to get over the Shoals.

In 'Letters from Alabama', Anne Royall states that Melton had removed across the river in present Limestone County and died there about 1815 of old age. General Andrew Jackson leased his Melton Bluff plantation, it consisted of cotton lands, about 60 slaves and an overseer who lived in Melton's old log house of two stories, located a short distance from the village. General Jackson had trouble with his overseers and fugitive slaves, and was an anxious absentee landlord.

In 1818 the village stretched along the top of the bluff, consisted of two large houses of entertainment, several doctors, one hatters shop, one warehouse, and several mechanics. Living there were ten permanent families. There were a lot of travelers there at this time looking at lands and waiting for the coming land sales.

Melton's Bluff village died out soon after the land sales in the fall of 1818. All lands in present Lawrence County became the property of the United States and had to be purchased from it. The first event that then occurred at Melton's Bluff was a failed attempt to set up the city of Marathon, apparently by General Andrew Jackson, General John Coffey, and other speculators. The town which was surveyed into blocks and lots by Coffey, who was then surveyor general, and was almost a mile square and located at and west of Melton's bluff. A few of the 556 lots were sold with a down payment, but all were relinquished, and there is no evidence any buildings went up.

A block in the center of Marathon was set aside as a public square, so there may have been hope that it would be selected as county seat. Moulton was selected, and it and Courtland built quickly into towns, and this may have caused the downfall of Marathon. The former site of Melton's Bluff is now TVA property, and Marathon is a part of the Wheeler Plantation."

John Melton moved to present-day Limestone County, Alabama on the north side of the Tennessee River where he died on June 7, 1815, as confirmed in a letter from his wife Ocuma. Shortly after his death, John Melton's wife wrote a letter to Colonel Return J. Meigs voicing her concerns about her husband's brother getting all the property they had accumulated as found in microcopy 208, roll 7, and number 3229, and dated June 30, 1815. Mrs. Ocuma (Obema) Melton's letter to Colonel Meigs is as follows:

"My husband John Melton died at his residence below Ft. Hampton 7 instant. He became a resident of Cherokee Nation 35 years ago and married me not long *afterward according to established custom of my nation. He died of considerable property which I am told me and my children will be deprived of by his brother, a citizen of the United States who resides on Duck River in Tennessee.*

Please advise me what to do."

Fox's Stand

Fox's Stand was the namesake of Black Fox (Inali, Enoli, or Eunolee), who was the Principal Chief of the Cherokee Nation from 1801 to his death in 1811. Fox's Creek, also named after Black Fox, is a small tributary to the Tennessee River; the creek flows into the river at the north border of Morgan and Lawrence Counties at the Chickamauga Cherokee Indian site of Mouse Town or Monee Town. For a while, Black Fox lived in Mouse Town near the mouth of Fox's Creek on the Tennessee River; the Indian town was some five miles upstream from Doublehead's Town at Brown's Ferry in present-day Lawrence County, Alabama. Later, Black Fox moved some three miles west of Doublehead's Town; he ran the stand/store on the old Brown's Ferry Road that ran from Gourd's Settlement which is present-day Courtland, Alabama, to present-day Huntsville, Alabama.

General John Coffee
6/2/1772-7/7/1833

Black Fox's Stand or trading post was located on the south side of the Tennessee River between the drainages of Fox and Mallard Creeks; the stand was west of the Browns Ferry crossing of the Tennessee River. Fox's Stand was some five miles east of Gourd's Settlement and some six miles southeast of Melton's Bluff; Melton's Bluff was the home of Doublehead's sister, Ocuma and her husband John Melton. Fox's Stand was near the junctions of three Indian trails-Browns Ferry Road, South River Road, and Black Warriors' Path.

After Cherokee Chief Black Fox's death, his son, who is identified as Black Fox II, ran the stand. During the time that General John Coffee was surveying the Indian boundary lines for the Turkey Town Treaty, Black Fox II operated the trading post in Lawrence County, Alabama; his name appears on documents after the death of his father in 1811. General John Coffee put the following note in his diary, *"26ᵗʰ July, 1816. Borrowed Capt. Hammond's large tent- left my old one – breakfasted with the Captain. Started on and got to Wilders where I dined, Bought corn to carry with me – bill $1.50. Went to the river – crossed at Brown's Ferry – paid ferriage & c $1.25. Hired young Wilder to go on to Col. Barnett & c. This night went to **Black Foxe's** and lay all night; bought _ bushels of corn to carry with me. Hired ____ Lancaster to carry six bushels to Major Russell's, for which I am to pay three and half dollars –bought some salt from **Fox**, hired him and McClure to carry the corn to the wagon road about two miles – paid bill at **Fox's** $6.75."* Coffee continued on to Major William Russell's settlement to survey the Indian boundary lines; Russell's home was the present-day City of Russellville, Alabama.

Coffee's notes continue, *"1ˢᵗ August 1816. This morning we start in towards Madison County – lay all night at the Path Killer's creek near Jones'. **2d August.** This morning we hired Vanpelt to carry letters to Col. Brown inviting him to meet us at Campbell's Ferry on the 12ᵗʰ. Come to the **Black Foxe's** – bought 2 1/2 bushels corn – paid the bill $1.75 –Same day came on – crossed the Tennessee River at Brown's Ferry and came to Wilders where we lay all night."* After the Turkey Town Treaty of September 1816 took the Cherokee lands in Franklin, Lawrence, and Morgan Counties of North Alabama, the young Black Fox II moved into the northeastern part of Alabama; he lived in this portion of the state that remained in the Cherokee Nation until 1838.

Doublehead's Town

Doublehead's Town was located at Brown's Ferry near the head of Elk River Shoals. *"Yet, Doublehead was without influence or position until about the year 1790, when he established a town on the Tennessee River at the head of the Muscle Shoals. An early map of the Cherokee Country shows this village at a site near the south bank of Brown's Ferry below Athens. He later in 1802 moved it to the north bank of the river near the mouth of Blue Water Creek in Lauderdale County, Alabama... Inhabitants of Doublehead's Town, originally about 40 in number, were mostly cast-offs from other Cherokee and Creek villages. This motley bunch became infamous in Tennessee history as The Ravagers of the Cumberlands"* (McDonald, 1989).

Historical records indicate that Doublehead lived in his Cherokee Indian town at Brown's Ferry from 1770 through December 1801. According to <u>History of Alabama</u> by Albert James Pickett (1851), *"Dec. 1801: Emigrants flocked to the Mississippi Territory...constructing flat-boats at Knoxville, they floated down the river to the head*

41

of the Muscle Shoals, where they disembarked at the house of Double-Head, a Cherokee Chief...placing their effects upon the horses, which had been brought down by land from Knoxville, they departed on foot for the Bigby settlements." Based on this historical note, Doublehead was still living at Brown's Ferry until 1802. The route immigrants utilized for bringing their horses to Brown's Ferry was no doubt portions of the South River Road.

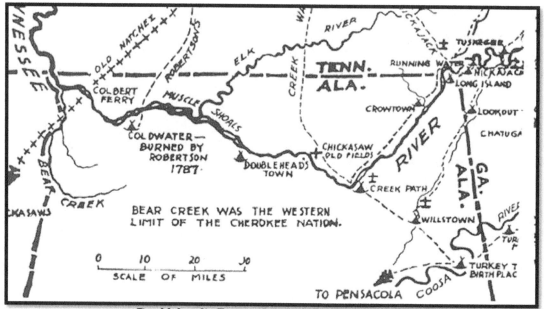

Doublehead's Town at head of Elk River Shoals

In 1803, Patrick Wilson traveled along the southern side of the Tennessee River and followed the same route as the South River Road. The following excerpt describes the route along the South River Road:

"The expedition continued on the Natchez Trace to present day Alabama, here Wilson observed land controlled by the Chickamauga Cherokee, who...were highly resistant to territorial encroachment in the Tennessee Valley... At the Muscle Shoals... the expedition left the Natchez Trace to follow the south bank of the Tennessee River. Here the party rested in a Chickamauga Cherokee town (Doublehead's Village at Brown's Ferry) administered by Tal Tsuska (Doublehead), a controversial and historically significant chief who controlled transportation routes... continuing in Cherokee territory, Wilson's party traveled north, passing through "Watts or Wills Town"... Wilson's narrative ends in Hiwasee, a Cherokee town no longer in existence" (Hathorn and Sabino, 2001). By the time of Wilson's expedition in 1803, Doublehead

had already moved from Brown's Ferry to the Shoal Town area on the north side of the river near Blue Water Creek.

Doublehead's Town at Brown's Ferry was also known for a brief period as Cox's Ferry. A man by the name of Cox, who was supposedly the son of Zecharaiah Cox, had apparently married Betsy the stepdaughter of Captain John Brown who eventually moved with his family to Otali; for a brief period the crossing was called Cox's Ferry. Some two miles west of the Indian village, the Brown's Ferry Road intersected Black Warriors' Path and the South River Road.

Doublehead's Town was on the south bank of the Tennessee River at river miles 293 and 294. The town site lies between present-day Mallard Creek Campground and the old Brown's Ferry Road. Doublehead's home was thought to be on a point just downstream from the ferry location but within sight of the old river crossing. Doublehead ran a house of entertainment that catered to all kind of needs of travelers. It is said that he was very generous to allow two older ladies, both of whom had a bunch of girls, to live in his house. Many have speculated that Doublehead's entertainment probably included many types of mischief. Doublehead had learned very rapidly about making money from his mixed-blood friends. One such business partner was Captain John D. Chisolm; he died in 1828, and is buried north of Florence on Chisholm Road.

Today, you can walk over the fields along the old river bank and find plenty of evidence of a large, extensive, and historic dwelling site. Old nails are in abundance along with pieces of glassware, historic pottery, slave made bricks, and even a large area of garlic, buttercups, and other plants that indicate historic occupation. In particular, the garlic grows on a small knoll just a few hundred yards from the ferry site. We refer to this knoll as Doublehead's homesite and the plants as Doublehead's garlic. His garlic has been transplanted to the Oakville Indian Mounds Park. Remains of chert projectile points indicate prehistoric Indian occupation as early as the Archaic Period; therefore, Doublehead's Town site was used for thousands of years by native people.

Mouse Town or Moneetown

Some three miles easterly, from the head of Elk River Shoals at the junction of Fox's Creek and Tennessee River was the Cherokee Indian town of Moneetown or Mousetown. This was the first Cherokee town beginning on the east edge of present-day Lawrence County and was our county's most upstream Cherokee town on the south side of the Tennessee River. The Indian village was located between Courtland and Decatur on Fox's Creek on the north side of Trinity Mountain.

According to a letter from Waco, Texas, May 9, 1882, and printed in The Moulton Advertiser on May 25, 1882, page 2, column 4, *"Lawrence was the banner County in Alabama in furnishing soldiers in the Texas struggle. Had not Dr. Shackleford and the Red Rovers been captured near Goliad, just after the fall of the Alamo, there would, doubtless, be many a veteran of that gallant band now living...Lawrence County still has her representatives in that band of patriots. I noticed...Aaron Burleson. The latter will be remembered by the old people who lived between Courtland and Decatur in the year 1817. If any such are now living. He was a brother of Gen. Ed Burleson of Texas Revolutionary fame. He was engaged in the killing of some Indians at Mousetown on Foxe's Creek, east of Courtland in 1817, for which he fled the country, went to Missouri, thence to Texas. He has made many greasers as well as red skin bite the dust...He now lives in Bastrop, Bastrop County."*

In another account, the Indian village is called Moneetown. *"James Burleson settled with his family on the north side of the mountain on Fox Creek. Here near an Indian village called Moneetown, the family became involved in a feud following an altercation between a son-in-law, Martin, and the Cherokees. After three of the Indians were slain, James Burleson and his son, Edward, fled to Missouri"* (Gentry, 1962).

In personal communication on December 18, 2003, Mr. Paul Ausbon and Mr. Bill Sams, whose ancestors lived on the river at Brown's Ferry, reported that Mousetown was located at the junction of Fox's Creek and the Tennessee River. Mr. Ausbon told me that he was born in 1925 and had known all his life of the Indian town that was called Mousetown by his grandparent and parents. Both men told that the Mousetown area was a favorite fishing location of their families. For years, the story of Mousetown was passed down to Mr. Paul Ausbon. According to his grandparents, an Indian fight occurred at the old town site. They said the town was on the present-day Lawrence and Morgan County line, north of Trinity Mountain some two miles from Highway 20.

Rayford Hyatt (1993) gives the best description of the altercation between Burleson and the Cherokees as follows:

"The last Indian and white battle in present Lawrence County, of which we have found any record, occurred near Meltons Bluff (Mousetown) in 1816. This indicates that some whites had already come into the area and were leasing farms from the Cherokee Indians.

James Saunders, in 'Early Settlers,' writing many years later from oral tradition, says the fight occurred on Foxes Creek near a village called Moneetown when James Burleson and family killed three Cherokees and fled to Missouri. The 1820 census shows Burleson still in Lawrence County. This is the related Burlesons of later Texas fame.

In the 'National Intelligenser,' Washington, D.C., September 5, 1816, is given editorially the substance of a letter, dated August 13, 1816, to Col. Winston from James Burleson. It states in effect 'that he, Burleson, and others who had settled near Meltons Bluff (Mousetown), on the south side of the Tennessee River to the number of eight men were attacked by a party of Cherokees armed with guns and warclubs, the number not known, on the night of the 11th inst. The whites resisted and three Indians were killed and one wounded. The fear of the Indians caused consternation among the settlers, and many moved away leaving promising crops.'

The 'Intelligenser' of September 10, 1816, from information at Huntsville dated August 17, 1816, enters further into details concerning the disturbance. "'It seems that a Mr. Taylor had rented a field from some Cherokees. In his absence they offered some insult to Mrs. Taylor, who escaped to the home of her father, James Burleson. Burleson, Taylor and others went to the Indian settlement, where they found a number collected. They demanded an explanation. The Indians raised a yell and said fight. An attempt was made by the whites to cut them off from their arms. This produced a conflict.'"

Huntsville-Guntersville Area Chickamauga Settlements

George Fields Plantation

In 1809 census of Cherokee Indians as reported by Return Jonathan Meigs, there were eight Cherokee males and three Cherokee females living on George Fields Plantation. Pictured below are George Fields and his third wife Sarah Coody. George Fields (born 1774), Turtle Fields (born 1776), and Richard Fields (born 1778) were brothers; they were the sons of Susannah Emory and white man by the name of Richard Fields. Susannah Emory was the granddaughter of Scotsman Ludovic Grant and his Cherokee wife. Susannah's parents were Englishman William Emory and Ludovic Grant's half blood daughter; therefore, the Field brothers were one quarter Cherokee.

George Fields Plantation was located in Morgan County, Alabama, just north of present-day Lacey Springs Community; he was born in 1774 and died April 14, 1849, in Indian Territory west of the Mississippi River. George was married three times. His first marriage was to Mary about 1792 and she was born about 1776; his second marriage was to Jennie Brown about 1796, and she was born about 1780, the daughter of Robert Brown, and died after 1836; his third marriage was to Sarah Coody about 1806, the daughter of Joseph Coody and Elis Tassel, and born about 1783 and died after 1860.

George Fields

Sarah Coody

George Fields was a captain of a group of Cherokees under General Andrew Jackson's army in the Creek War of 1814; he served from October 7, 1813, until April 11, 1814. On November 9, 1813, George Fields was wounded at the Battle of Talladega fighting with General Andrew Jackson during the Creek Indian War. George Fields moved from Alabama to Indian Territory between 1836 and 1837.

Dick Fields Plantation

Richard (Dick) Fields

Richard (Dick) Fields was born about 1778; he was the brother of George Fields and also had a plantation in North Alabama. According to the 1809 census by Meigs, Dick Fields Plantation had five Cherokee males, five Cherokee females, and eight white people living on the farm. Richard also fought with General Andrew Jackson during the Creek Indian War. Richard Fields moved to Texas about 1820 and became a chief of the

Texas Cherokees along with the Cherokee Chief Bowle; he was killed in a political dispute by his people in 1827.

Flint River Settlements

These Chickamauga Indian settlements were along the Flint River east of the present-day City of Huntsville, Alabama. Two of Doublehead's daughters had reservations on Flint River near the Hurricane Fork in Madison County, Alabama: Peggy Doublehead that married William Wilson and Alcy Doublehead that married Giles McNulty settled on reservations that were adjacent to the original Madison County line.

Peggy Doublehead was born about 1800 and died around 1834. On April 3, 1824, Peggy married William Wilson in Madison County, Alabama. William Wilson was born in 1796; he and Peggy had four children. William and Peggy had a land grant in Madison County, Alabama that was reservation number 128. Their reserve was on the Flint River adjoining the Madison County line and surveyed on December 11, 1820, with Giles McAnulty and Aaron Armstrong being the chain carriers. Giles became Peggy's brother-in law after he married Alcy Doublehead.

Doublehead married the fifth time to Kateeyeah Wilson about 1797. Kateeyah's father was thought to be George Wilson (half Cherokee and half Scots-Irish) and her mother was Ruth Springston (half Cherokee and half Scots). Ruth Springston was the daughter of William Springston and Nancy Augusta Hop; therefore, Kateeyah was a niece to Nannie Drumgoole, since Nannie and Kateeyah's mother, Ruth, were half-sisters. Kateeyah was a sister to Thomas Wilson and William Wilson. She was born around 1760, and her step-daughter, sister-in-law, or cousin Peggy married her brother, William Wilson. Kateeyeah and Doublehead had four children, who were three quarters Cherokee and one quarter Scots-Irish: Tassel, Alcy, William, and Susannah.

Alcy Doublehead was born about 1800 and died after 1838; she married Giles McAnulty/McNulty who helped survey her half-sister Peggy's reservation. Giles McAnulty was on a list of persons entitled to a reservation for life under the treaty with the Cherokees of February 27, 1819. Alcy and Giles also had reservation number 132 on the Hurricane Fork of the Flint River adjoining Thomas Wilson.

Thomas Wilson's Plantation

According to the 1809 Cherokee census taken by Return Jonathan Meigs, there were eight Cherokee males and nine Cherokee females living on Thomas Wilson's

Plantation in present-day Madison County, Alabama. Thomas' place was very close to Peggy Doublehead and William Wilson's reserve. William was the brother of Thomas Wilson who had reservation number 131 that was located on the north side of the Tennessee River near the old Cherokee boundary line and the Hurricane Fork of the Flint River.

Browns Village

Near the present-day Community of Red Hill on the west bank of Browns Creek was a Lower Cherokee town; the village was occupied by the Cherokee Indians by 1790. Browns Village was named for the head man of the town Colonel Richard Brown, who was the son of Captain John Brown that lived at Otali (end of mountain) which is the present-day Town of Attalla. Colonel Richard Brown, the brother-in-law of Captain John D. Chisholm who married Patsy Brown, fought with General Andrew Jackson at the Battle of Talladega and the Battle of Horseshoe Bend; his people received Jackson's praise for their military aid during the Creek Indian War.

Browns Village was situated on two important Indian trails: The Black Warrior Road leading from Ditto's Landing south of present-day Huntsville, Alabama to Black Warrior Town at the fork of the Sipsey and Mulberry Rivers in Cullman County, Alabama near the Community of Sipsey; and the High Town Path leading from Old Charles Town, South Carolina, to present-day Rome, Georgia (High Town), then to Turkey Town, through Browns Village, then to Chickasaw Bluffs at present-day Memphis, Tennessee.

Cherokee Bluff or Beards Bluff

In the mid 1700's, the Lower Cherokees established an outpost on Beards Bluff overlooking the south side of the Tennessee River near Guntersville, Alabama. The site became known as Cherokee Bluff after the area was vacated by the Shawnee Indians who had a major village at the site between 1650 and the early 1700's. Cherokee Bluff was the scene of a battle between the Cherokees and the Creeks in the latter part of the eighteenth century.

Corn Silk Village

Corn Silk Village was one and one-half miles southeast of Warrenton on the Corn Silk farm of the Street plantation. This Cherokee town was a small Indian village on the banks of Corn Silk Pond; the village was named for the head man who was known as Corn Silk.

Creek Path Village

Cherokees settled along the Creek Path and the Tennessee River as early as 1784 inhabiting the Guntersville area. Creek Path Town or Kusanunnahi was located on the east bank of Brown Creek some six miles southeast of Guntersville; this Cherokee village got its name from being situated on the Creek Path which extended from Talladega Creek to the Tombigbee River. The town was a very important having about four or five hundred inhabitants and was one of the larger Cherokee villages in Alabama at that time. The Creek Path was part of the route that was used by General Andrew Jackson during his war against the Creeks in 1813-14.

In 1820, Creek Path Mission School was one of the earliest mission schools established for the Cherokees. Catherine Brown was the daughter of half blood Cherokee Captain John Brown Sr., a famous Cherokee Indian; Catherine and her sister Anna established the Creek Path Mission School just six miles south of present-day Guntersville, Alabama. Catherine died on July 18, 1823, of tuberculosis at Trianna in Limestone County, Alabama; she was buried at Creek Path Mission. Prior to establishing the Creek Path Mission, Catherine, a three-quarter blood Cherokee, attended Brainerd Mission and at age seventeen was the first convert; she was baptized and joined the church at Brainerd in January 1818. The Brainerd Mission had been organized by Reverend Gideon Blackburn east of Chattanooga, Tennessee.

Originally Brainerd Mission had sixty pupils, among them several members of the powerful Cherokee Lowrey family. At age sixteen, Lydia Lowrey, a daughter of Major George Lowrey who was later the assistant chief of the Cherokee Nation, joined the church and was baptized January 31, 1818. Lydia soon after married Milo Hoyt, son of Doctor Hoyt; she died in the Indian Territory July 10, 1862.

Coosada

Coosada Island Town was located in the middle of the Tennessee River approximately 10 miles above the present-day City of Guntersville; the village was an old Indian town established in the early 1700s. In 1714, a battle between the Creeks and Cherokees was fought on Coosada Island.

Four major Indian trails from the east converged at the Coosada Island where three crossed the Tennessee River at the Indian village site and the South River Road ran the southeast bank of the river; this ford in the river was called the Upper Creek Crossing and was located at the shoals on the upstream or the north end of the island. An early site at the upstream end of Coosada Island was called the Larkin Landing where flatboats and keel boats would stop for supplies as they were moving up and down the Tennessee River; it is believed that Sauty was a shortened version of Coosada. Coosada Island later became known as Pine Island and is now under the backwaters of Guntersville Lake.

Gunter's Landing

Another Cherokee Indian town in Marshall County, Alabama was Gunter's Village; the town derived its name from the head man John Gunter. Gunter's was one of the largest Indian towns in the area. According to the 1809 census of the Cherokees by Return Jonathan Meigs, Gunter's Landing had 554 inhabitants; 252 were Cherokee males, 257 were Cherokee females, and 45 white folks.

Gunter's settlement was on the old Creek Path that extended from the Coosa Old Town at the mouth of Talladega Creek, to Ten Islands on the Coosa River, thence toward the mouth of Big Wills Creek at present-day Attala. The Path followed Line Creek through Sheffield Gap to the top of Sand Mountain through modern Boaz and Albertville, and crossed the Tennessee River downstream from Gunter's Landing at the mouth of Brown's Creek.

John Gunter was a Celtic trader of Welch or Scots Irish lineage; most historians agree that John Gunter was Welsh. He was born in North Carolina, went to South Carolina as a child and migrated into north Alabama around 1785 at the conclusion of the Revolutionary War. John Gunter was one of the first white persons to settle in what is now Marshall County, Alabama; the City of Guntersville got its name from this early white settler. Gunter came to the great bend of the Tennessee River where he was fortunate to find a salt deposit. He decided to settle near the river and trade with the Indians, the majority of which were Cherokees. Gunter opened a trading post on Creek Path (kusanunnahi), where it intersected the Tennessee River. Beginning in 1814, Gunter operated a powder mill in Chickamauga country; about 1820, Gunter began operating a ferry across the Tennessee River known as Gunter's Landing.

John Gunter married a Cherokee woman named Ghigoneli Bushyhead who had been brought to the area by her father Bushyhead in order to trade for salt; Bushyhead and Gunter signed a treaty stating *"as long as the grass grows and the waters flow the Indians can have salt."* John Gunter called his young fifteen year old Indian wife Katherine; they had seven Celtic and Cherokee mixed blood children. Their three sons

50

were Samuel, Edward, and John Gunter, Jr; their four daughters were Aky, Catherine, Elizabeth, and Martha. John Gunter owned some forty black slaves that he willed at his death to his wife and children. The Gunter home was located at the foot of the hill just west of the present-day George Houston Bridge; the large "L" shaped two story house had a "dog trot" hall between the two main sides with a large smokehouse located at the end of the "L" portion of the house.

John Gunter and his family were living at Gunter's landing in October 1813 when General Andrew Jackson and his army came through on their way to fight the Creeks. Jackson's Army crossed the Tennessee River at Ditto's Landing near present-day Whitesburg Bridge, marched across Brindley Mountain to Brown's Valley and camped for two days near present-day Warrenton. Lower Cherokees from Gunter's Village gave General Jackson important military aid during the Creek Indian War.

John Gunter later rose to a leadership position with the Lower Cherokees; he was adopted into the tribe that was the major member of the Chickamauga Confederacy.

In the 1830's during the Indian removal, many Creeks and Cherokees passed by Gunter's Landing on the way west to Indian Territory. Doctor Billy Morgan was the doctor assigned by the government to take care of the Creek Indian people arriving at Gunter's Village. Today, Billy Morgan's house on present-day highway 227 is in bad disrepair and should be restored as an important historic site since the house is

Butch Walker at Billy Morgan's Home

actually on the John Benge Detachment removal route.

Meltonsville

Charles Melton's village was at the site of the present old village ford on Town Creek prior to running into the Tennessee River in Marshall County, Alabama. Charles Melton was the head man of the town and was originally from Melton's Bluff in Lawrence County, Alabama; he operated a store at Melton's Bluff in Lawrence County and sold goods to John Coffee while he was doing the surveys for the Turkey Town Treaty in February and March of 1816.

The following excerpt identifies Charles Melton one of John Melton's sons. According to *General John Coffee's Diary -1816* is the following: "***21st Feb'y 1816.*** *This morning Maj. Hutchings left us to go to meet Gen. Jackson – Mr. Bright surveys and we pass on down the river. When at Huntsville I did not pay my bill – neither did I pay it at Mr. Austin's – I paid Mrs. Austin for buiskit, candles and washing $2.00 – paid Charles Melton 3 bushels corn $1.50 – fodder, $1.00 – whiskey 75¢. Paid to Charles for Reed $2.00. Encamped all night on Big Nance Creek."*

From Big Nance Creek, John Coffee continues down the Tennessee River to the mouth of Caney Creek in present-day Colbert County, Alabama and run a boundary line up Caney Creek and crossed Gaines Trace. Coffee continued the line to Cotton Gin Port before starting back to Melton's Bluff on March 2, 1816. The line Coffee was surveying became the Chickasaw boundary in the Turkey Town Treaty of September 1816.

Coffee's diary continues, "***6th March, 1816.*** *This day we reached Melton's Bluff about one o'clock. Bought sundry supplies &c Viz; whiskey $1.00-whiskey, $1.371/2- 3 dinners, 75¢ - 20 lbs. Bacon 9¢ $2.50 Paid for corn and fodder to Charley Melton $5.00"*

Charles was the son of Irishman John Melton and Doublehead's youngest sister Ocuma; after the Turkey Town Treaty of September 1816, he moved east and established Meltonsville in Marshall County, Alabama. Meltonsville was a Lower Cherokee town that was founded after the Turkey Town Treaty of 1816 took all the land from the Cherokees in Lawrence, Morgan and Franklin Counties.

Massas

In Brown Valley, near the present line between Blount and Marshall Counties, there was a Creek and Cherokee village situated on two trails. Both led to Ditto's Landing on the Tennessee River, one through Brown's Valley and the other in a course opening further to west. The name of the town was Massas, near Rock Landing on the Tennessee River.

Parches Cove

In the early 1800's, Parched Corn or Parched Corn Flour, a Lower Cherokee Indian, established under his leadership a Cherokee settlement in a cove on the south side of the Tennessee River in the beautiful rich bottomland that teemed with wildlife; therefore, the cove which is just west of present-day Guntersville Dam and southeast of Huntsville became known as Parches Cove. In a letter dated August 9, 1805, Doublehead requested the cooperation of Principal Chief Black Fox and others including Parched Corn Flour in order to get more provisions from the U.S. Government. The Lower Cherokee Indian village at Parches Cove was at the confluence of the Tennessee River and Pigeon Roost Creek.

George Wilson, the grandson of Doublehead, was the son of Peggy Doublehead and William Wilson; he was born about 1832 and was named after his grandfather George Wilson that married Ruth Springston, a half sister of Nannie Drumgoole who was a wife of Doublehead. George settled in the cove a short distance below present day Guntersville Dam; his mother and father had a land grant in Madison County, Alabama, with reservation number 128 near Hurricane Fork of the Flint River just east of present day Huntsville, Alabama. Some of George Wilson's family hid out in Parches Cove and avoided removal to the west; some of his descendants still call north Alabama home.

Tali

The old Indian village of Tali was visited by Desoto's expedition on July 10, 1540; the town was located on McKee's Island which was about three fourths of a mile long and in the Tennessee River near the present-day Town of Guntersville. There is not any evidence that the island became a major town of the Lower Cherokee during the period of the Chickamauga War or prior to Indian removal of the 1830s.

Scottsboro-Bridgeport Area Chickamauga Settlements

Sawtee Town or North Sauty Town

The mouth of North Sauty Creek is at Tennessee River mile 377; just three miles from the mouth of the creek is the Saltpeter Cave that was inhabited by the Lower Cherokee and known as Sawtee Town. The Cherokee town was at one time the county seat of Jackson County, Alabama. During the Civil War, the big cave at Sawtee Town was mined by the Confederates for saltpeter which was used in making gun powder.

In the 1809 Cherokee Indian census, Return J. Meigs reported 110 Cherokee males and 123 Cherokee females Indians living in Sawtee Town. The town was located on the North River Road on North Sauty Creek just southwest of the present-day City of Scottsboro in Jackson County, Alabama. On October 3, 1806, Doublehead wrote to Colonel Return Jonathan Meigs about a Cherokee council meeting called at Sautey or Sawtee Town near the Tennessee River. Doublehead stated that the Rogers Party which was headed by a white man by the name of John Rogers was stirring up trouble for the Cherokee.

Buck's Pocket

The mouth of South Sauty Creek is at Tennessee River mile 373; some eight miles from the Tennessee River up South Sauty Creek is a canyon some 800 feet deep known as Buck's Pocket. The overhanging cliffs provided rock shelters for the Indians that lived in the beautiful canyon for thousands of years. Springs and underground caves were scattered across the canyon floor; water from South Sauty Creek would run underground during very dry seasons of the year.

Buck's Pocket was located on South Sauty Creek at the corners of Dekalb, and Marshall Counties and across the river from Jackson County of North Alabama. Also known as Morgan's Cove, South Sauty Creek runs through Buck's Pocket; today, the area now the 2,000 acre Buck's Pocket State Park.

The most famous resident of this Cherokee community was Granny Dollar; she was born in 1827 as Nancy Callahan and died at 104 years of age on January 28, 1931. Nancy

Granny Dollar and Buster

was the daughter of a Cherokee man by the name of William Callahan and a mixed blood mother who was half Cherokee and half Irish. When she was just a child, her father moved his second wife into their home; eventually the Cherokee family had 26 children. During Indian removal, Granny Dollar remembers her family hiding out in a cave; according to local folklore, her family hid in the Saltpeter Cave on North Sauty Creek at the old Cherokee village of Sawtee. At age 79, Nancy (Granny Dollar) Callahan married Nelson Dollar whom she lived with until he died 20 years later; she died on Lookout Mountain and is buried in the Lookout Mountain Cemetery.

Lookout Mountain Town or Stecoe

This Indian town was one of the five lower towns of Chickamauga Chief Dragging Canoe. The village was located at the present-day Town of Trenton in Dade County, Georgia about 15 miles south of Running Water Town. The town had about 80 homes; according to the 1809 census of the Cherokees by Return Jonathan Meigs, Lookout Mountain Town had 83 Cherokee males, 83 Cherokee females, and two whites. The village was adjacent to Lookout Mountain Creek in a valley that was some three miles wide; the town was on the east side of Lookout Mountain that runs from Chattanooga, Tennessee to Gadsden, Alabama.

Long Island Town or Anisgayayi

Long Island Town was one of the five lower towns of Chickamauga War Chief Dragging Canoe. The settlement was located on an island in the middle of the Tennessee River just east of the present-day City of Bridgeport in Jackson County, Alabama. About a dozen houses were located on the south end of the island; the town was about five miles down the Tennessee River from Nickajack. An old Indian trail followed the corridor of Highway 117 from the Cherokee villages of Long Island and Crow Town across the Tennessee River and then across Sand Mountain to Valley Head, Alabama.

Crow Town or Kokeai

Crow Town was a Chickamauga Cherokee Indian village that was named after The Crow; a sub-chief of the one of the five lower towns of the Great Lower Cherokee War Chief Dragging Canoe. It was on an Indian trail known as the South River Road that followed the south side of the Tennessee River across northern Alabama. The town was on the east side of the Tennessee River across from the mouth of Crow Creek and southeast of the present-day City of Stevenson in Jackson County, Alabama; Crow Creek flows off Crow Mountain which lies west of the Tennessee River.

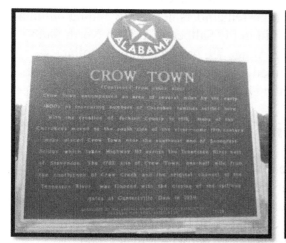
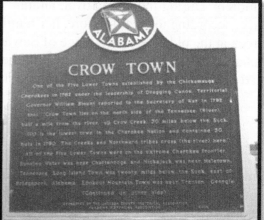

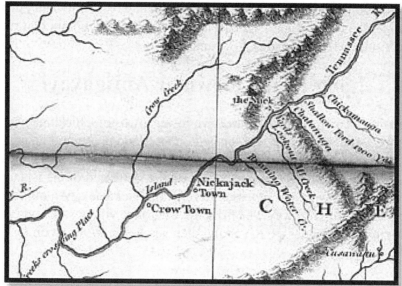

Crow Town-1802 Arrowsmith map

Crow Town consisted of some 30 houses with several inhabitants; in the 1809 census of the Cherokees by Return Jonathan Meigs, Crow Town had 35 Cherokee males and 40 Cherokee females. John Norton, an early traveler through the Chickamauga country in 1816, wrote in his diary about going to a ball play game at Crow Town. Some say that Crow Town was on the north side of the river near the mouth of Crow

Creek; however, four old maps dating 1796, 1802, 1810, and 1817 show Crow Town on the southeast side of the Tennessee River.

Raccoon Town

The Raccoon Town census in 1809 included 120 Cherokee males and 142 Cherokee females; the census was taken by Return Jonathan Meigs who was the United States government Indian agent. The 1809 census of Raccoon Town probably included the Cherokee individuals that occupied the area on east side of the Tennessee River near the mouth of Raccoon Creek; the town was just upstream and across the river from the mouth of Mud Creek.

Nickajack

In the 1809 census of the Cherokee Indians taken by Return Jonathan Meigs, the Chickamauga town of Nickajack contained 14 Cherokee males, 17 Cherokee females, and 17 white folks. The Indian village was no doubt much smaller during 1809 than it was when Dragging Canoe was waging his war against white encroachment on Cherokee lands.

Nickajack was Chickamauga Cherokee Chief Dragging Canoe's stronghold and the major village of his five lower towns. The settlement had some 40 Chickamauga houses and a huge cave that were used by Indian people for thousands of years. The cave was called "Nigger Jack's Cave" by the Chickamaugans that lived in the community. Nickajack was located in Marion County, Tennessee.

Nickajack Cave

On November 4, 1780, a free black man by the name of Jack Cavil was captured in Clover Bottom east of Fort Nashboro by the Chickamauga. Some 200 Chickamauga warriors killed nine men who were working in the area and took the black man captive. Jack Cavil was carried to the town of Dragging Canoe and held prisoner in the cave; he eventually became a member of the Chickamauga and lived in the town that became known as Nigger Jack's Town or Nickajack.

Today, only the top of Nickajack Cave is visible above the backwaters of Nickajack Dam which is just a few miles downstream from the cave's entrance; the floor and living area of this huge cavern that was used by Dragging Canoe and the Chickamauga is several feet beneath the surface of the water. Note in the photo a bass fisherman in his boat sits at the entrance of the cave fishing; the boat is 18 to 20 feet in length and provides one an idea of the large size of the cave opening.

Running Water or Amogayunyi

Running Water was located on the southeast side of the Tennessee River about four miles up river from Nickajack Town; it was one of the villages of the five lower towns of Dragging Canoe. This Chickamauga town was near the mouth of Running Water Creek and the Tennessee River near the Tennessee River Gorge just west of present-day City of Chattanooga, Tennessee. The Indian town was considered one of Dragging Canoe's five lower towns. After his death at Stecoyee on March 1, 1792, Dragging Canoe was buried in Running Water Town.

Robert Benge lived at Running Water Town; at this site, Robert (Bob) Benge announced that he was going to start a raiding campaign against white settlers in southwestern Virginia. Running Water consisted of some 100 homes and was a common crossing place for the Chickamauga Indians. The South River Road and McIntosh's Road or Georgia Road was two major Indian trails that ran a concurrent route past Running Water Town.

Gadsden Area Chickamauga Villages

Otali

Otali, a Cherokee word that means mountain, was a Chickamauga Cherokee Indian town located at the southwestern end of Lookout Mountain between Wills Creek and the Coosa River. This Lower Cherokee Indian village was originally called Atale a corruption of the Cherokee word for mountain Otali. The Indian town is now known as the present-day site of Attalla, in Etowah County, Alabama. Etowah was a Cherokee word that meant edible tree; evidently named from fruit producing trees in the area.

A major Indian trail known as the High Town Path passed through Otali; the old Indian route came from Chickasaw Bluffs at the junction of the Wolf River and the Mississippi River at the present-day site of Memphis, Tennessee. The High Town Path passed through the Indian village of Flat Rock at present-day Haleyville, Alabama, and followed the Tennessee Divide through Winston, Franklin, Lawrence, and Cullman Counties prior to dropping off the mountain and passing through the Chickamauga Indian town of Browns Village at the Red Hill Community near present-day Guntersville. From Guntersville, the path went around the end of Lookout Mountain at Otali. From Otali, the High Town Path went to Turkey Town, then to High Town (present-day Rome), and then to Olde Charles Town which is present-day Charleston, South Carolina.

Otali became the home of Captain John Brown; his father was also known as John Brown, a white trader to the Chickasaws during the mid 1750's. The older John Brown married a full blood Cherokee woman; he traded with the Chickasaws along with James Adair. John Brown was a pack horseman for the Cherokee traders, and later a Chickasaw trader and partner of Jerome Courtonne in the Chickasaw Breed Camp on the Coosa River; Chickasaw warriors would meet the pack trains coming from Charleston, and escort them to the Chickasaw towns to the west. His sister married Oconostota, a famous Cherokee Indian known as the Beloved Warrior of Great Tellico.

Captain John Brown was half Cherokee Indian and was also known as Yonaguska which translates to "Drowning Bear." Captain John Brown was thought to have migrated to Otali after the Turkey Town Treaty of September 1816; he was the ferry operator at the famous Brown's Ferry crossing of the Tennessee River in present day Lawrence County, Alabama. Captain John Brown's step daughter Betsey married a Cox and they operated Brown's Ferry which became known as Cox's Ferry for a short period of time; Betsey eventually relocated to Arkansas. While at Browns Ferry in Lawrence County, another of John Brown's daughters Patsy Brown, sister of Cherokee Colonel Richard Brown, married Captain John D. Chisholm. Patsy later divorced Chisholm who was the legal advisor of Doublehead; Doubleheads Town was located at the Browns Ferry site on the south bank of the Tennessee River in present-day Lawrence County, Alabama.

The half blood Cherokee Captain John Brown was born about 1756 and died in 1827; it is documented that he had three wives. His first wife was unknown but he had two children Richard and Patsy Brown. Patsy married John D. Chisholm. Another of the wives of Captain John Brown was a half blood Cherokee woman named Sarah Webber who had Betsey that first married a Cox and Walter Webber; John and Sarah also had David, John, Jr., and Catherine.

His third wife was Betsey or Wattee; they had Polly who married Alexander Gilbreath, Alexander, Edmund, and Susannah or Susan. Not only did the half blood Captain John Brown have a son named John Brown, but it should be noted that Richard and David both had sons that were also named John Brown; therefore, possibly many of the descendants of the white John Brown and his full blood Cherokee wife were named John Brown which can cause a lot of confusion in genealogy.

Captain John Brown's daughter Catherine established the Creek Path Mission School in 1820, six miles south of Guntersville. It was in Attalla that David Brown, the half blood Cherokee Indian son of John Brown, assisted by the Reverend D. S. Butterick, prepared the "Cherokee Spelling Book;" the book was printed in Knoxville, Tennessee, and was ready to use in the schools by January 1820. David Brown died on September 15, 1829. Colonel Richard Brown had a son who was called Chief John Brown; Chief John Brown died October 24, 1861, in Sallisaw, Oklahoma, Indian Territory.

Duck Springs

Duck Springs was an Indian village a couple of miles north of present-day Reese City near Highway 11 in Etowah County, Alabama. In 1820, Duck Springs School was an Indian school started by Methodists missionaries that served Cherokee children in the area. The village was named after The Duck or Chief Duck.

Jesse Beener Horton fought in Creek War with General Andrew Jackson and lived at Duck Springs from 1818 and died in 1839 in Etowah, County at the location of the Indian town. Jesse Horton actually lived in Cherokee territory and was probably related to the Cherokee by marriage. Since many who fought with Jackson at Horseshoe Bend were Indian or mixed bloods and the area was not open to white settlement, Horton had some sort of marital connections with the Cherokee Indian people around Duck Springs.

Dirty Ankle or Black Ankle

This Lower Cherokee Indian village was known for its horse racing track; during the occupation of the town by the Lower Cherokees, Indian people would gather from miles around to watch and bet on the outcome of horse races. The Chickamauga settlement was several miles north of the Cherokee Indian village of Otali (Attala, Alabama) and a few miles north of Duck Springs. The old Indian community was located in Little Wills Valley on Highway 11 near the site of present-day Town of Kenner in Etowah County, Alabama.

Turkey Town or Tahnoovayah

Turkey Town was a Chickamauga Indian village named for Cherokee Chief Little Turkey; the town was on the High Town Path that led from Otali (present-day Attalla), to Turkey Town, and then to High Town which is present-day Rome, Georgia. Turkey Town was just northeast of Gadsden on present-day highway 411 between Gadsden and Centre, Alabama near the Coosa River. Little Turkey became the Principal Chief of the Cherokee Nation after the death of Hanging Maw in 1795 and resided in his village that became known as Turkey Town until his death in 1801.

John McDonald

The British were supplying the Chickamauga Confederacy with arms, ammunitions, and powder to help the English defeat the American colonies; even though the Americans had officially declared the Revolutionary War over on April 11, 1783, the Chickamauga fought on with John McDonald supplying war materials from Running Water Town, a Chickamauga town situated at a Creek Indian crossing of the Tennessee River just west of Lookout Mountain.

John McDonald had been appointed as the assistant Superintendent of Indian Affairs by the British under the command of Superintendent John Stuart. At Running Water, British agent Alexander Cameron and McDonald were being provided supplies, goods, and ammunition from Savannah or Pensacola; however, pressure from the American forces pushed the British arms suppliers farther south to Turkey Town. The British were using Turkey Town and other Chickamauga villages as their base of operations in the Southwest; they were stockpiling food and military supplies for all tribes of the Chickamauga hostile to the American government.

About 1788, the Scots Irish John McDonald, who had married half blood Cherokee Anne Shorey daughter of Englishman William Shorey and a Cherokee mother, moved from Running Water Town together with his family including his daughter Mollie and her husband Daniel Ross to Turkey Town. Initially, McDonald had been supplying the Chickamauga from his stores some 15 miles south of the Tennessee River on Chickamauga Creek near present-day Chattanooga, Tennessee. At the time he moved to Turkey Town, McDonald was corresponding with William Panton of Panton, Leslie, & Co., a British supplier of trade goods that had become allied with the Spanish interests; William Panton of Pensacola and Creek Chief Alexander McGillivray were the best of friends.

John Ross

Turkey Town was also much closer to the old abandoned French Fort Toulouse that was possibly being re-garrisoned by the Spanish; or that a new fort would be garrisoned north of Turkey Town near present-day Ft. Payne, Alabama. With the help of British agents, McDonald continued to supply arms, ammunition, and powder to the Chickamauga from Turkey Town; it was at Turkey Town where John McDonald's grandson John Ross was born on October 3, 1790, to McDonald's daughter Mollie and Daniel Ross. John Ross was born a true Chickamauga Cherokee at Turkey Town and was destine to become the longest serving chief of the Cherokee Nation.

Creek Indian War

During the Creek Indian War, Cherokee Colonel Richard Brown raised a group of some 25 local Indians to meet John Strother at Turkey Town; a route led south from Turkey Town to Hickory Ground, and then to old French Fort Toulouse. Within some 15 miles south from Turkey Town, a large mixed force of Cherokees and Tennessee Volunteers under Jackson's command attacked the Red Stick Creeks at Tallasahatchee; David Crockett participated in this first major campaign of the Creek Indian War at the Battle of Tallasahatchee.

Turkey Town Treaty of 1816

After the Chickamauga War and Creek Indian War, Turkey Town remained an Indian town of great importance; the Turkey Town Treaty of September 1816 was negotiated at Turkey Town. The treaty of gave up Cherokee and Chickasaw lands in the North Alabama portion of the Warrior Mountains; both tribes had legitimate claims by previous treaties to the Indian lands in the present-day counties of Franklin, Colbert, Lawrence, and Morgan Counties. According to the terms of the Turkey Town Treaty, the last Indian lands of the Warrior Mountains were bought from the Cherokees and Chickasaws on September 14 and 18, 1816, respectively. The Chickasaws were paid

$125,000.00 with the Cherokees being paid $60,000.00 for land that now makes up Colbert, Franklin, Lawrence, and Morgan Counties.

The Chickasaws and Cherokees had overlapping land claims with the Cherokees claiming land west to Natchez Trace some 10 to 15 miles west of Caney Creek in Colbert County. The Chickasaws claimed land east to the old official Chickasaw boundary, which runs from the Chickasaw Old Fields (Hobbs Island) south to the High Town Path then west along the High Town Path to Flat Rock in present day Franklin County. From Hobbs Island, the boundary ran northwest diagonally across Madison County.

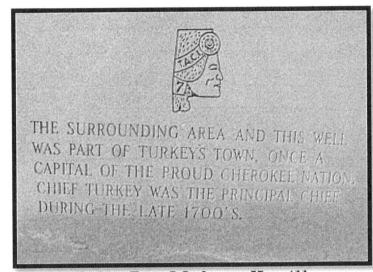

Turkey Town Marker on Hwy 411

The Chickamauga Chief Doublehead and the Cherokees farmed and controlled the Tennessee Valley to Natchez Trace by agreement with Chickasaw Chief George Colbert. The Turkey Town Treaty signed by the Cherokees on September 14, 1816, ceded Colbert, Franklin, Lawrence, and Morgan Counties; however, the U.S. Government established the Chickasaw's new eastern boundary from Franklin County's Flat Rock Corner on Little Bear Creek to Caney Creek in Colbert County until 1832.

The High Town Path was recognized as the southern boundary of the cessions for both the Chickasaw and Cherokee, until the Turkey Town Treaty of 1816; the treaty identified the new cession boundary as a straight line drawn from Flat Rock on Little Bear Creek in Franklin County to Ten Islands on the Coosa River. Previous treaties recognized the Continental Divide along which ran the High Town or Ridge Path.

Turkey Town Conclusion

In the 1835 census, the Turkey Town area had only 43 families with 254 individuals with the majority of the people being mixed Indian and white; only five of the families owned black slaves. In June of 1838, the remaining Indian families of

Turkey Town were rounded up and herded into stockades by United States Army soldiers for removal to the west which started in earnest during the fall of 1838. After the removal, white settler families moved in and claimed the former Indian lands of the Chickamauga Cherokee of Turkey Town; remnants of the Indian settlement fell in ruin. Old Alabama Highway 151 was an Indian trail that led from Brainerd, Tennessee to Turkey Town, Alabama.

When I recently visited the site of Turkey Town, a large marble monument marking the location of the prominent portion of the Cherokee settlement and an old well dating around 1810 was all the aboriginal evidence that remained of this once thriving Chickamauga town. I was disappointed that very little historical structures and information about Turkey Town were available at the site of such an important Indian village; it is sad that we in Alabama preserve very little of our ancestral and cultural landscape.

Ball Play or Aletowah

Ball Play Town was the Cherokee village where Ball Play Creek ran into the Coosa River. It was located on the southeast side of the Coosa River east of Turkey Town. Ball Play was named after the major sport of the Cherokee which was stick ball.

The village was northeast of the Community of Hokes Bluff in Etowah County, Alabama. The Ball Play Landing is where a lot of people coming down the Coosa River got off the boats in Etowah County; a ferry transported people across the Coosa River from Etowah County to Cherokee County.

Spring Creek Village

Some 200 Lower Cherokee Indian people lived in this town which was located on Spring Creek in Cherokee County, Alabama.

Polecat Town

This Chickamauga Cherokee Indian village of some 60 Indian residents was located on Terrapin Creek in Cherokee County, Alabama near the present-day Centre, Alabama.

Little Hogs Town

This Chickamauga village was located on Terrapin Creek in Cherokee County, Alabama and had a population of some 60 Indian villagers.

Hillibulga Village

This Chickamauga town was on the Coosa River in Cherokee County, Alabama and contained a population of some 500 Chickamauga Indian people.

Chattuga

This Chickamauga village had a population of some 40 Indian people and was in Cherokee County, Alabama.

Wolf Creek Village

This Chickamauga village was on Lookout Mountain in Cherokee County, Alabama and contained some 200 Indians.

Sleeping Rabbit's Town

Sleeping Rabbit's Town was probably north of present-day Town of Anniston; in Meigs 1809 census of Indians, the town had 43 Cherokee males and 36 Cherokee females.

Ft. Payne Area Chickamauga Villages

Bootsville

Bootsville was established by a local Cherokee Indian called "The Boot;" two different Cherokee men were known by the name of "The Boot." According to local folklore, these two Cherokee Indian men in the area of Bootsville were known as Big Boot and Little Boot; these two Indians were probably father and son. One Cherokee known as The Boot, which was probably Big Boot, was listed as being killed at the Battle of Horseshoe Bend on March 17, 1814; he was a member of Captain Jonathan McLemore's Company. The Boot that was killed at Horseshoe Bend was known locally as Big Boot; he was more than likely the father of Little Boot or John Fletcher who was also known as "The Boot or Chutcoe."

John Fletcher was born about 1796; he was a mixed blood Cherokee of Scots Irish ancestry; Fletcher is a Scots Irish name. Most names in the southeastern United States that end with "er" or start with "Mc" are very likely of Scots Irish lineage. The family name ending in "er" usually indicates the occupation of the Scots Irish family; for example, baker is one who bakes, miller is one that operates a mill, walker is one who walks horses; carpenter is one who builds, fletcher is one who fletches arrow shafts, and many other "er" type people.

John Fletcher, Little Boot or The Boot, lived in the Indian town that took his name; the Cherokee village was west of Big Wills Creek at the eastern edge of Sand Mountain. In the late 1800's, the land was bought by the Horton family who settled in the previous Indian community. According to family history, when Griffin Ruben Horton moved to Bootsville in the late 1800's, he lived in the old log cabin that was originally the home of The Boot. According to the accounts of these first white settlers, there were several Cherokee log cabins still standing that were the homes of the Indian inhabitants of the Town of Bootsville.

John Fletcher's home was on a hill overlooking a beautiful flat valley between Sand Mountain and Pine Ridge; the large spring of water was known as Bootsville Spring and flowed into Jack Creek and then into Big Wills Creek. The main branch was to the east of The Boot's home place and was fed by the big spring within a hundred yards of his house. Probably many of John Fletcher's family members are buried in unmarked graves in the Bootsville Cemetery just less than one half mile west of his original home and spring.

In September 1816, "The Boot" or John Fletcher signed the Turkey Town Treaty with Cherokee Chief Pathkiller and Cherokee Colonel Richard Brown; Turkey Town, some 25 miles south of Bootsville, was the Cherokee town where the treaty was signed. The Turkey Town Treaty gave up Cherokee and Chickasaw lands in Franklin, Colbert, Lawrence, and Morgan Counties in northwest Alabama.

In 1824 the Methodist missions to the Cherokees were under the direction of Richard Neely and Thomas D. Scales; a Methodist church school was started in 1825 at Oothcaloga under the direction of Asbury Owen. After urging of Bishop William McKendree, some Cherokees became active in preaching for the Methodist Church; in 1826, Turtle Fields was appointed as the first Cherokee itinerant preacher in the Methodist Church. Other Methodist preachers to follow were John Fletcher (The Boot),

Edward Gunter, and Joseph Blackbird; Cherokee Chief John Ross became the most famous Methodist convert.

John Fletcher (The Boot) was converted to Christianity in 1825; he was licensed to preach and became a Methodist Cherokee minister in 1827. Fletcher was ordained a deacon in the Methodist Episcopal Church in Nashville, Tennessee; he later received ordination as elder in Lebanon and preached effectively in the Cherokee language to his people in Wills Valley. By 1830, some 1,028 Cherokee people were members of the Methodist Church as a result of personal evangelizing and camp meetings during the 1820s.

In 1826, John Fletcher was a Methodist preacher who spoke in his native Cherokee language; Edward Gunter, the son of John Gunter, interpreted some of the sermons of The Boot into English. John Fletcher would speak at revival meetings; Turtle Fields, the first ordained Cherokee Methodist preacher, would complete the camp meeting. According to Henry T. Malone's 1956 book, _Cherokees of the Old South_, "At a special conference ceremony in Tennessee celebrating the sixth anniversary of Methodist missions to the Cherokees, John Fletcher spoke in his native language on the subject of the Indian missions. Edward Gunter then translated Fletcher's message, and added a speech of his own. Turtle Fields completed the program with an oration also in English." Cherokee Chief John Ross was converted to Christianity at a meeting in the Chickamauga area south of present-day Chattanooga, Tennessee during a Methodist revival meeting and became an active Methodist.

A trail passing through Bootsville Gap came from Coosada (an Indian village on an island in the Tennessee River just upstream from Guntersville), leading east through Bootsville, then Fort Payne, then to Broom Town in Cherokee County, Alabama, and then to High Town (present-day Rome, Georgia) where it joined the High Town Path that led to Charleston, South Carolina. The third county seat of Dekalb County, Alabama, was at Bootsville; the county seat at Bootsville was from 1839 to 1841. Dekalb County became a county in Alabama in 1836.

From Bootsville, John Fletcher migrated west during the 1838 removal to Indian Territory and continued to be a Methodist Christian missionary among his Cherokee people for many years. On September 6, 1839, John Fletcher (The Boot) signed the Constitution of the Cherokee Nation with the reunited Western and Eastern Cherokees at their National Council Convention which met at Tahlequah, Oklahoma in the Cherokee Nation west. The Boot signed the new constitution document along with several other Cherokees from his Alabama home near Bootsville including John Benge, George Guess, Edward Gunter, George W. Gunter, Jesse Bushyhead, Lewis Melton, and several other Cherokees. John Fletcher, The Boot, died August 8, 1853, while preaching in the Canadian District of Indian Territory.

The Community of Bootsville is in present-day Dekalb County, Alabama, on highway 458 that runs off highway 35 at the Community of Pine Ridge on the eastern base of Sand Mountain and west of Fort Payne, Alabama. Bootsville is some five miles north of Lebanon, Alabama, which was the approximate location of Wills Town on Big Wills Creek in Dekalb County.

Broom Town

Broom Town was the home of a Cherokee man known as "The Broom." The Indian town was approximately 14 miles east to southeast of Fort Payne, Alabama. The village was located on the northeastern border of present-day Alabama, where the Lower Cherokee had moved under pressure from settlers to the north and east. The village was eventually abandoned by the Cherokee during the 1838 Indian removal in the area.

The Cherokee where forced west of the Mississippi River by the United States Army and were gathered at nearby Fort Payne. The Cherokees from Broom Town and the surrounding Fort Payne area were led west on the Trail of Tears to Indian Territory under the supervision of Wagon Master John Benge. Chief Broom's daughter Nancy, a member of the Wolf clan married a white man by the name of Nathan Hicks; they were the parents of Charles, William, and Elizabeth Hicks.

Charles Hicks became a Cherokee chief who actually run much of the Cherokee affairs under Chief Pathkiller. Charles Hicks had equal shares to land west of Melton's Bluff in present-day Lawrence County, Alabama, with Moses Melton. According to microcopy 208, roll 7, and number 3740, Captain Charles Hicks sends a letter dated January 15, 1817, *"About reserve made to me and Moses Melton on Spring Creek near the mouth of Elk River by the Treaty of General Jackson with the Chickasaws. To whom I pay taxes and get deed."* In microcopy 208, roll 7, number 3800, Charles Hicks identifies people still on the reserves in Lawrence County, Alabama, *"Muscle Shoals Reservation-yourself and Bird, Doublehead's son, and his daughter Elcey are all in this country except the heirs of Moses Melton."* In microcopy 208, roll 7, number 3675, Hicks realizes that the reserve is to be sold to Andrew Jackson, *"I am informed that John D. Chisholm has gone to Nashville to sell to General Andrew Jackson reserves at Muscle Shoals. Request you stop it."*

On September 11, 1808, the Cherokee Council in Broom's Town passed an act forbidding the blood law: *"Be it known, that this day, the various clans or tribes which compose the Cherokee Nation, have unanimously passed an act of oblivion for all lives for which they may have been indebted, one to the other, and have mutually agreed that after this evening the aforesaid act shall become binding upon every clan or tribe, and the aforesaid clans or tribes, have also agreed that if, in future, any life should be lost without malice intended, the innocent aggressor shall not be accounted guilty. Be it known, also, That should it happen that a brother, forgetting his natural affections, should raise his hands in anger and kill his brother, he shall be accounted guilty of murder and suffer accordingly, and if a man has a horse stolen, and overtakes the thief, and should his anger be so great as to cause him to kill him let his blood remain on his own conscience, but no satisfaction shall be demanded for his life from his relatives or the clan he may belong to."* The law was approved by Enola or Blackfox as Principal Chief and Pathkiller as Second Chief; it bears the signature of Charles Hicks as secretary to the Council.

The Broom was killed at the Battle of Horseshoe Bend in March 1814. He served with General Andrew Jackson under the command of Captain John Speirs (Spears) Company. Today the area of Broom Town is known as Barry Spring.

Watts Town (Titsohhellengh)

On the 1817 Mississippi Territory maps, Watts Town was originally located just east of the Creek Path and on an old Indian trail leading from Turkey Town to Coosada. Watts Town was between present-day Reedy Creek and Town Creek some 25 miles east of the present-day Town of Guntersville, Alabama. Watts Town Creek run into the Tennessee River at the Indian village of Meltonsville in the present-day Guntersville State Park.

The creek was originally known as Watts Town Creek, but today it is just called Town Creek; Watts Town was located between the fork of Town Creek and Reedy Creek. The town was named in honor of Lower Cherokee John Watts, Jr., who was elected the second chief of the Chickamauga Cherokees. Evidently the Watts name was dropped from the creek and it became known as Town Creek; Watts Town was located near the present-day Community of Viewpoint in Dekalb County, Alabama.

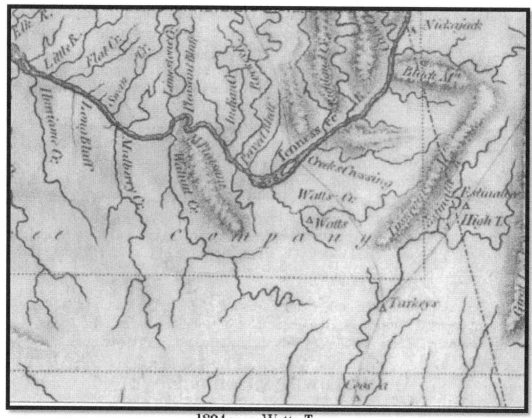
1804 map-Watts Town

Will's Town or Ahhesahtaskee

In the 1809 census of the Cherokee by Return Jonathan Meigs, there were 129 Cherokee males, 141 Cherokee females, and 34 whites living in Wills Town. Wills Town was located on Big Wills Creek a few miles north of present-day Community of Lebanon in Dekalb County, Alabama.

During the American Revolution, John Stuart sent British agent Alexander Campbell to Wills Town to provide support to the Indians during the Chickamauga War against the southern colonies. By 1777, Campbell had his headquarters at Wills Town which was a large Lower Cherokee Indian village located on Big Wills Creek near the present-day Community of Lebanon which is some seven miles south of Fort Payne. Some ten years later in 1788, Campbell was joined by British Agents Alexander Cameron and John McDonald who set up their operations in Wills Valley at Turkey Town some 20 miles south of Wills Town. These British agents were successful in providing arms, ammunition, powder, supplies, and food to the various Indian tribes

70

throughout Wills Valley that were collectively called the Chickamauga. The Chickamauga in Wills Valley included the Lower Cherokee, Upper Creek, and Shawnee; they were given provisions in exchange for the scalps of white settlers who were intruding onto Indian lands.

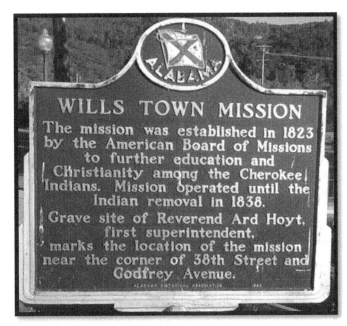

Half blood Cherokee Will Webber was the namesake for Wills Valley, Big Wills Creek, and Little Wills Creek. The creeks meander along Wills Valley between Lookout Mountain and Sand Mountain, through the Town of Collinsville, and to present-day Attala, Alabama where Wills Creek run into the Coosa River. William Webber was also called Redheaded Will; he was the son of a Cherokee woman and a British officer named Webber. Will Webber came to Wills Valley from Nequassee, North Carolina.

Wills Town was the home of the second Chickamauga Chief John Watts, Jr.; he was born at Wills Town about 1752 and died in Wills Town in 1808. John was the brother of Wurteh Watts and uncle of George Guess. It is highly probable that Chief John Watts Jr. lived on the west bank of Big Wills Creek near an old ford of a road crossing coming from Wills Town Mission. A beautiful two story log cabin that had hand split chinking boards between the huge hand hewed chestnut logs still stands near the site, but the Cherokee log home is in the process of rotting down.

In November 1792, Captain Samuel Handley was attacked and taken prisoner near the Crab Orchard on the Avery Trace or Cumberland Road. He was taken to Wills Town in the heart of Chickamauga country where he met British agents John McDonald and Alexander Campbell. Samuel Handley was interrogated after he was released and you can read the debriefing by Governor William Blount on pages 115 and 116 of the book *Doublehead: Last Chickamauga Cherokee Chief.* Samuel Handley wrote a letter from Wills Town on December, 10, 1792, telling of being a captive in the town. Handley also later tells that the Chickamauga had three companies of mounted cavalry commanded by John Taylor and Will Shorey; Will was the half-blood Cherokee brother-in-law of John McDonald. Captain Handley did not know the name of the third commander of the Indian cavalry; Handley also tells of 150 Upper Creeks being at Wills Town.

George Guess (Sequoyah) was the son of Colonel Nathaniel Guess (Gist) and his Indian wife, Wurteh Watts, who was a niece of Old Tassel and Doublehead. When he was a young Celtic Indian boy, Sequoyah migrated with his mother Wurteh Watts and settled at Wills Town in Wills Valley. Wurteh Watts was the daughter of Scots Irish trader John Watts and Wurteh, who was the daughter of Great Eagle and granddaughter of Moytoy. Wurteh Watts was married to four different men: Robert Due, Bloody Fellow, John Benge, and Nathanial Guess (Gist); all her husbands were Scots Irish except Bloody Fellow with whom she had no children.

George Guess (Sequoyah) was a blacksmith, silversmith, and an all-round mechanic; he made metal implements such as hoes, axes, tomahawks, and such other farming tools needed by the Cherokees in Wills Valley. George was an uneducated genius who invented an alphabet for his Cherokee people so they could read and write in their own language. Congress voted George Guess an annuity of $500 per year, and had his picture painted and placed in the government archives at Washington, DC. Sequoyah voluntarily migrated west of the Mississippi River on more than one occasion to visit his people and settled with the "Old Settlers" about 1823. Sequoyah's half-brother Tahlonteeskee (Talohuskee Benge) of Shoal Town was the leader of the "Cherokees West" that left the Big Muscle Shoals of North Alabama in 1809.

Robert Benge lived at Wills Town and was a quarter-blood, red-headed Chickamauga Warrior; he was the son of the white Scots Irish Trader John Benge and Wurteh Watts. Bob Benge was born about 1766, and took 45 white scalps; he was ambushed and killed April 9, 1794. Benge was also known as "The Bench;" he was the half-brother of Sequoyah and father of Wagon Master John Benge (1788-1854).

Mixed blood John Benge was the son of the most feared Scots Irish Chickamauga Cherokee Robert (The Bench) Benge. John Benge was one of the detachment conductors appointed by then Cherokee Principal Chief John Ross. He served in Morgan's Cherokee Regiment during the War of 1812. At the Battle of Horseshoe Bend, Andrew Jackson and a militia of more than 600 Cherokee warriors surrounded about 1,000 Creek warriors; John Benge, Thomas Benge, The Boot, The Broom, George Guess (Sequoyah), and many others from Wills Valley fought in the Battle of Horseshoe Bend for the American forces. John Benge voted against removal and served as a wagon-master of a detachment of Cherokees from the Wills Valley area on the Trail of Tears; his removal contingent followed old Indian roads and trails that became known as the Benge Route.

By 1822, a Cherokee Methodist minister by the name of Turtle Fields was a resident of Wills Town. Turtle Fields was a descendant of Ludovic Grant, and a brother to George Fields and Richard Fields; he was born about 1776 and died about September 1844. Turtle Fields married three times. He married his first wife about 1804; she was unknown and born about 1788. His second marriage was Ollie Timberlake about 1816; she was born about 1770. His third wife was Sarah Timberlake in 1837 and she was born about 1815. Turtle Fields served with the Cherokee allies of the American forces in the Creek Indian War and fought at Horseshoe Bend in John McLemore's Company in March 1814.

Today, in Will's Valley, very few remnants of the Chickamauga Cherokee are visible such as the Will's Town Mission Cemetery, a sandstone chimney at the site of Fort Payne cabin where the Cherokees were incarcerated until removal, the home of Andrew Ross-the brother of Cherokee Chief John Ross, Trail of Tears markers that indicate the route of the Benge Detachment led by wagon master John Benge, a few historic markers, and a marble monument at the Turkey Town site. It is sad that practically little physical evidence exists of our colorful and wonderful historic aboriginal Indian ancestors that ruled North Alabama for thousands of years before the coming of white settlers.

Joseph Coody Plantation

According to the 1809 census of the Cherokees taken by Return Jonathan Meigs, there were two Cherokees males, two Cherokee females, and two whites living on the Coody Plantation. The plantation was located in Wills Valley near Lookout Mountain.

Joseph Coody was born on Feburary 19, 1779, in Virginia, and died on October 11, 1859. He married Jennie Ross who was the daughter of Daniel Ross and Mollie

McDonald; Jennie was born on June 11, 1787, and died on September 12, 1844. Jennie was a sister to John Ross who became principal chief of the Cherokee Nation. Joseph and Jennie (Jane) lived near Lookout Mountain with her father, Daniel Ross; Daniel Ross lived at present-day Ft. Payne, just a short walk north of the Wills Town Cemetery. In the 1820's, the family of Joseph and Jennie Ross Coody moved to Rossville where her brother John Ross lived; at Rossville, they operated a tanyard.

Daniel Ross Plantation

Daniel Ross lived at present-day Ft. Payne, Alabama; he and his Cherokee family lived in a log house called Cherokee. Daniel married Mollie McDonald the daughter of John McDonald and Anne Shorey. The original two-story log house built by Daniel Ross is the center of a home just north of Ft. Payne that is still standing. According to the 1809 census by Return J. Meigs, three Cherokee males, five Cherokee females, and one white was living on the Daniel Ross Plantation.

Daniel Ross Home north of Wills Town Cemetery, Ft. Payne

Pre-Indian Removal Forts

Camp Bradley

Camp Bradley was located on the north side of Canoe Creek on the Coosa Path that led from the Tennessee River at Ditto's Landing south of Huntsville to Ten Islands on the Coosa River; the camp was between Camp Wills and Fort Strother and was used during the Creek Indian War. The camp was probably named after Colonel Edward Bradley who served in the First Regiment of the Tennessee Volunteer Infantry. Bradley's unit was part of General William Hall's Brigade and fought at the Battle of Talladega on November 9, 1813, during the Creek Indian War.

Camp Coffee

Camp Coffee was located on the south side of the Tennessee River about a mile east of Whitesburg Bridge south of present-day Huntsville, Alabama. Camp Coffee was located near four major Indian trails which were the Coosa Path, South River Road, Black Warrior Road, and the Creek Path. Notice on the map that Camp Coffee was just south of Chickasaw Island, Chickasaw Oldfields, or later Hobbs Island which is in the middle of the Tennessee River.

Camp Coffee was an important Creek War outpost of General Andrew Jackson; the camp was named for General John Coffee. General John Coffee was stationed at Camp Coffee during the Creek Indian War; Coffee was ordered by Jackson to destroy Black Warrior Town while stationed at Camp Coffee.

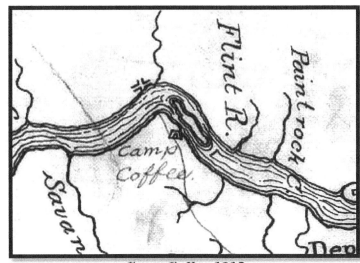

Camp Coffee-1815

Camp Wills

In September 1813 at the Cherokee Indian town of Otali (present-day Attalla,

Alabama), General Andrew Jackson established a supply depot that was known as Camp Wills on the bank of Big Wills Creek. Camp Wills was located near three important historic Indian trails. The east to west Indian trail known as the High Town Path passed around the south end of Lookout Mountain at Otali. The Creek Path was a north to south route from Gunter's Landing on the Tennessee River toward Ten Islands on the Coosa River. The Coosa Path led from Ditto's Landing on the Tennessee River south of Huntsville, Alabama to Ten Islands on the Coosa River.

Around Otali which was located at the south end of Lookout Mountain, the

Cherokee Indian familes of the Browns, Fields, Ratliffs, and many other native families provided Jackson a company of soldiers during the Creek War. Many of these Indian soldiers were mixed Scots Irish and Cherokee.

It was at Camp Wills that General Andrew Jackson directed the first campaign of the Creek Indian War after promoting John Coffee to Brigadier General. General Coffee was sent to Tallasahatchee to destroy the Red Stick Creek Indian village. Camp Wills was strategically located between Camp Coffee at Ditto's Landing on the Tennessee River south of Huntsville and Fort Strother at Ten Islands on the Coosa River.

Fort Armstrong

Fort Armstrong was an outpost of General Andrew Jackson during the Creek Indian War; it was located on the Coosa River in Cherokee County, Alabama near Cedar Bluff. The fort was garrisoned by mostly mixed blood Lower Cherokees who lived in the nearby area and fought the Red Stick Creek Indians. Colonel Gideon Morgan was stationed at Fort Armstrong during the Creek War. Morgan wrote to Return Jonathan Meigs on February 4, 1814, from Fort Armstrong; he states that many Lower Cherokees were assembled at the fort and fighting the Creeks.

Fort Deposit

During the Creek Indian War, Fort Deposit was built by General Andrew Jackson forces in October 1813 on the south bank of the Tennessee River near the mouth of Thompson's Creek; it was a major supply base for fighting the hostile Red Stick Creek Indians. General Andrew Jackson's armed troops had met up with the militia of John Coffee and Davey Crockett near Dittos Landing. At Fort Deposit, Jackson recruited some 200 Lower Cherokees to help them fight the Red Sticks.

Fort Deposit was on the east bank of Thompson's Creek at Tennessee River mile 352.6; the fort had only two log buildings and was about eight miles northwest of the present-day Town of Guntersville, Alabama. Fort Deposit was used for storing military supplies and equipment. The ferry at Fort Deposit was used for the transportation of Jackson's troops and supplies across the Tennessee River. A series of nearby caves was used for storing of ammunition and powder; the largest storage cave was on the north side of the river and had to be reached by ferry.

Fort Hampton

Fort Hampton was located east of Elk River and some five miles north of the Tennessee River in present-day Limestone County, Alabama. It was the only American fort that was built to remove white settlers and squatters off of Indian lands. The fort was named in honor of General Wade Hampton who fought in the Revolutionary War. The log fort housed two companies of soldiers.

In June 1810, Fort Hampton was built to remove white pioneers from Chickasaw lands, since the Chickasaw Indians had not given up their claims to the property. White families that leased land from Doublehead had built homes, established fences for their livestock, and planted crops. In June 1810 and again in June 1811, soldiers were sent to the area around Fort Hampton to force the settlers back across the Tennessee state line by destroying their crops and burning their fences, houses, and out buildings. The North River Road and Black Warriors' Path (Mitchell Trace) were two early Indian trails that passed in close proximity of the fort. Black Warriors' Path forded the Tennessee River near Melton's Bluff and the North River Road ran parallel to the north bank of the Tennessee River. The Browns Ferry Road from Huntsville to Courtland passed east of the fort and crossed the river at Browns Ferry.

On November 9, 1813, after the Battle of Talladega of the Creek Indian War, Colonel Joseph Brown with ten of Andrew Jackson's best men went to Cuttyatoy's

Village on an island near the mouth of Spring Creek in the Tennessee River of present-day Lawrence County, Alabama; Brown secured the black slaves that had been taken by the Chickamauga on May 9, 1788. Brown's father and two brothers had been killed during a raid on their boat and the slaves had been taken by Cuttyatoy.

The next morning, Brown and his men forded the Tennessee River to the east side of Elk River in present-day Limestone County, Alabama; they took the black slaves and Cuttyatoy's wife to Fort Hampton. Cuttyatoy and his men went upstream to Browns Ferry where they crossed the Tennessee River on a large raft and arrived at Fort Hampton in the late afternoon. Brown immediately called upon the commandant of the fort, Colonel Williams, who told Brown to take his slaves home with him.

In 1817, Fort Hampton became the county seat of Elk County which included the present-day Lauderdale and Limestone Counties. After the area around Fort Hampton was given up by the Indians in the Chickasaw Treaty of 1816, the fort was abandoned and not used after 1821. After the post was no longer used, Fort Hampton fell into disrepair; eventually the log fort rotted down.

Fort Payne

Fort Payne was located in Dekalb County, Alabama; it was built near Wills Town Mission as a removal era stockade for the collection of Cherokee Indians for the

1838 removal that became known as the Trail of Tears. The fort was named after Captain John G. Payne who selected the site of the Indian removal post. The fort was built in April 1838 near the Lower Cherokee village known as Wills Town which contained a significant number of Indian people. The site selected for the fort also had a large spring which could provide enough water to meet the needs of all the Indians rounded up and held in the internment camp until removal. After the lower Cherokees were removed from the area in the fall of 1838, the fort was abandoned and

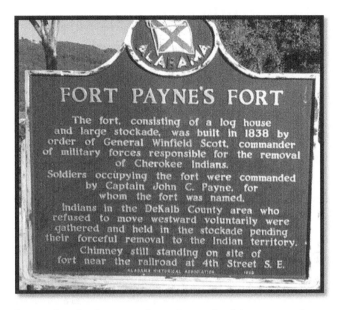

fell into disrepair; all that is left of the fort today is the remains of a rock chimney and scattered stone ruins.

Fort Likens

Fort Likens was located at Barry Springs in Cherokee County, Alabama; the springs were probably named after Richard Barry who lived at the site. The fort was in Broom Town Valley and used as collection point during the 1838 removal of Lower Cherokee Indians in northeast Alabama. Fort Likens was a log stockade that was made in a circular pattern.

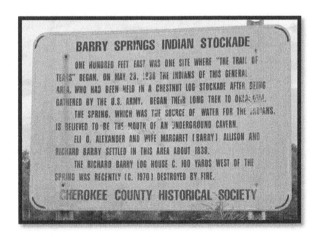

Fort Lovell

Fort Lovell was a removal era post of the collection of Lower Cherokees in the area around Turkey Town northeast of present-day Gadsden, Alabama. The fort was a log stockade and outpost used for gathering local Lower Cherokee Indian people in preparation for Indian Removal of 1838 that became kown as the Trail of Tears.

Fort Strother

Ft. Strother-1818 Melish Map

Fort Strother was a fort that was built by General Andrew Jackson during the Creek Indian War in November 1813. The fort which was located in present-day St. Clair County, Alabama, on the Coosa River near Ten Islands served as a base of operations for military actions against the Red Stick Creeks.

General Jackson and his army used the Fort Strother to make attacks at Tallashatchee on November 3, 1813, and at Talladega on November 9, 1813. After General John Coffee defeated the Red Sticks at Tallashatchee, he returned to Ft. Strother. From the fort, they launched another attack on the Red Stick Creeks at Talladega which they defeated. It was also from Fort Strother that Jackson moved to attack the Creeks at the Battle of Horseshoe Bend in March 1814.

North Alabama Removal Routes

The tragic stage for the decimation of our North Alabama Indian people was finally set after some 275 years of fighting diseases and wars brought about by the lust and greed of the European invaders. Finally, our native people began to crumble from the European onslaught and pressure.

The native lands of the North Alabama were threatened by many treaties such as the Cotton Gin Treaty of January 1806, the Treaty of Fort Jackson in March 1814, the Turkey Town Treaty of September 1816, the Indian Removal Act of May 1830, and the Treaty of New Echota of December 1835. The following years of forced removal

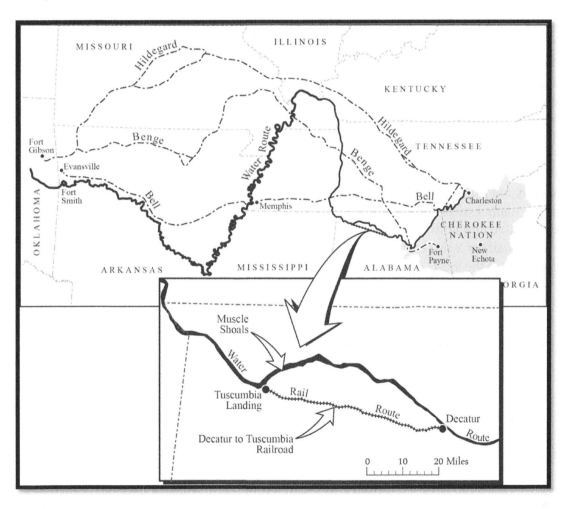

decimated our local native people who had lived for thousands of years in harmony with the land of the Muscle Shoals, Tennessee River, Warrior Mountains, and Coosa River.

The Cherokee, Creek, and Chickasaw Indians became a conquered people. This was not done quickly, easily, or by a single method; they were conquered militarily, but through treaties which were legally and legislatively favoring the whites, our aboriginal lands were taken by the United States Government. Many Indian people were removed from their homelands and forced to emigrate west of the Mississippi River, but many mixed bloods were able to assimilate into the general population and avoid removal by hiding out. The Indian removal represents one of the harshest, most opportunistic acts in American history.

There were several important sites across North Alabama that played major roles during the Indian removal process. Six of these locations included Fort Payne, Gunters Landing, Melton's Bluff, Decatur, Tuscumbia Landing, and Waterloo. In 1838, many Lower Cherokee Indian people were placed in an internment camp at Fort Payne in preparation for removal to the west. Gunters Landing was not only a ferry crossing of the Tennessee River for the Wagon Master John Benge Detachment from Fort Payne, but it was also used to load Indians on flatboats to be transported to Decatur. At Decatur, many Lower Cherokees were placed on railcars and transported by railroad around the shoals to Tuscumbia Landing; this was the only railroad used for removal of Cherokee people during the Trail of Tears. During the first years of removal shortly after the death of Doublehead in 1807 and after the Turkey Town Treaty of 1816, many Lower Cherokees along the Muscle Shoals left Melton's Bluff for the west or to move into northeast Alabama. Near Melton's Bluff, boats carrying Indian people would wait for a rise in the river so they could safely pass through the Muscle Shoals for lands in the west. At Tuscumbia Landing, Indian people were off loaded from the railcars and placed on keelboats; they were transported by water from Tuscumbia Landing to Waterloo where the boarded steamers headed to the west.

1809 Cherokee Removal

In January 1806, Cherokee Chief Doublehead, his great nephew Tahlonteskee, and other Cherokees signed the Cotton Gin Treaty which gave up Cherokee claims to land north of the Tennessee River except for Doublehead's Reserve. The reserve lay between Elk River (Chuwalee) and Cypress Creek (TeKeetanoeh) in present day Lauderdale County.

The signing of the Cotton Gin Treaty brought the wrath of other Cherokee leaders upon the individuals who signed the treaty giving up Cherokee Lands. Major

Ridge, a powerful Cherokee leader, made known that Doublehead and others would pay with their lives for relinquishing Cherokee lands. At a meeting of Cherokee headmen in Tennessee, Doublehead paid with his life at the hand of Ridge, Alex Saunders, John Rogers, and their accomplices. Alex Saunders and John Rogers had ties to Lawrence County and probably profited from the assassination of Doublehead.

After the assassination of Chief Doublehead by his own people, due to the circumstances of the Cotton Gin Treaty of 1806, several Lower Cherokees living in the North Alabama area and related to Doublehead moved west to avoid the same fate. The following is from "The Cherokees" by Grace Steele Woodard published in 1963 and found on page 131:

"However, in 1808, the Compact 1802 was not needed to effect the removal of some 1,130 Chickamaugans to lands west of the Mississippi (today Dardanelle, Arkansas, in Pope County). Jefferson had merely to suggest to Tahlonteskee and other Chickamaugans that if they did not care to remain in the same country with their enemy countrymen, they could remove to Dardanelle Rock. Thus, in the spring of 1808, Tahlontuskee fearing assassination notified President Jefferson that his people were ready to migrate. Following their migration, Tahlonteskee's band of Cherokees called themselves "Cherokees West" or "Old Settlers."

Since Tahlonteskee signed the 1806 Cotton Gin Treaty, he feared the same punishment that Doublehead received for giving up land north of the Tennessee River; therefore, he and his Cherokee followers agreed to move from the Shoal Town area around the Big Muscle Shoals of the Tennessee River to the west during the summer of 1809. It is believed by some that Sequoyah, George Guess, went west after the 1816 Turkey Town Treaty in search of his half brother, Tahlonteskee.

1816 Cherokee Removal

Even though some Cherokees in the North Alabama area left with Tahlonteskee's group in 1809, many Cherokee people still lived in the Tennessee Valley along the Muscle Shoals from the river to the High Town Path. Within the great valley of the Tennessee, cotton became the agricultural "king" for making money. With the new government cotton gin at Melton's Bluff and black slaves for farm labor, both the Chickasaws and Cherokees, who shared ownership of the river valley, became wealthy; however, the government and settlers wanted the cotton wealth of the Tennessee Valley which was controlled by the Indians.

In September 1816, with several more years of pressure, the Chickasaws and Cherokees finally relinquished their claim to Franklin, Lawrence, and Morgan Counties. Therefore, due to the circumstances of the Turkey Town Treaty of September 16 and 18, 1816, another contingent of Lower Cherokees moved west, from North Alabama. Shortly after the Turkey Town Treaty forced the removal of Lower Cherokees occupying the land of Morgan, Lawrence, and Franklin Counties, some 30 to 40 slave holding plantation familes from North Carolina and Virginia moved to the area; these wealthy planters took the Indian cotton grounds during the 1818 federal land sales of previous Indian territory ceded in September 1816. These eastern cotton barons brought their families in a large wagon train into the ancestral lands of the Chickasaw and Cherokee along with some 6,000 black slaves; many of the cotton plantation owners acquired thousands of acres of land and became extremely wealthy. Today, there are still large tracts of land in the Tennessee Valley that belong to these plantation families.

The first documented removal from Melton's Bluff in Lawrence County is found in the following excerpt given in the 1969 printing of *Letters from Alabama 1817-1822* by Anne Royall on pages 134 and 135 with the Letter XXIV dated January 14, 1818:

"Melton's Bluff is a town, and takes its name person by the name of John Melton, a white ceased two years since, at an advanced age ...You recollect Rhea whom I have mentioned: he married one of Melton's daughters-a most amiable woman, and very lame. When the Cherokee Indians abandoned this territory last fall, some of them went up the river to the Cherokee nation, there to remain till boats were provided for their removal to the west, by the government; others went directly down the river to Arkansas-of whom Rhea's wife was one.

The order for their departure was sudden and unexpected. Rhea, at that time was absent from home, but returned on the same day and learning what had happened, was almost frantic jumped into a canoe, and soon overtook the boats. He flew to his wife, and clasped her in his arms. Neither spoke a word, but both wept bitterly. In a few moments-he resumed his canoe and returned to the Bluff, and she went on. They had no children. Whether Rhea was prohibited by the treaty from accompanying his wife, or whether he was under a prior engagement, none here are able to inform me-but certain it is, he is now married to a white woman."

Rhea had moved to Melton's Bluff about 1803 and had married one of John Melton's half-blood Cherokee daughters. According to Royall, he had guided as many as four boats at a time, ten dollars each, through the Elk River Shoals, Big Mussel

Shoals, and Little Mussel Shoals for some 15 years. Also, at this time, James Melton, Rhea's half-blood Cherokee brother-in-law, was a river boat guide that piloted boats through the Shoals for Malcolm Gilchrist, one of the early settlers of the Courtland area.

Shortly after the Turkey Town Treaty was signed, several Cherokees left Melton's Bluff in Lawrence County for lands in the west during the fall of 1816. In addition, Andrew Jackson did not wait until the dust of the 1816 removal had settled to begin staking his claims to Indian lands and property in Lawrence County.

Just after the Turkey Town Treaty of 1816, Melton's Bluff came under the ownership of General Andrew Jackson. David Melton was the half-blood Cherokee son of Irishman John Melton. According to Anne Royall's letter on January 14, 1818, John Melton died two years prior; according to his wife Ocuma, John died on June 7, 1815. After the death of John Melton, Andrew Jackson pressured Melton's son into selling the plantation. The following is an excerpt from *Melton's Bluff* by William L. McDonald:

"General Andrew Jackson in partnership with his wife's nephew, Colonel John Hutchings, purchased Melton's Bluff from a David Melton in 1816. It is believed that David was a son of the old pirate, John Melton. This deed, signed November 22, 1816, described the property as follows:

"I David Melton of the Cherokee Nation do by these presents bargain and sell ... unto General Andrew Jackson and Captain John Hutchings all my right title and interest to the tract of land where I now live, and agree to give them possession of all the improvements laying north and east of the spring, including said spring, on said tract where I live and adjoining where I live, and the houses and ... land southeast of the spring. Possession to be given of as many Negro houses as will house the Negroes of the said Andrew and the said John ... and possession of the other houses on or before the first day of February... For which I acknowledge to have received the consideration of sixty dollars in cash and in full of the above sale."

Just prior to the fall removal in 1816, Melton's family along with other Cherokees went to the west or Cherokee lands to the east; Andrew Jackson acquired not only the land that belonged to the Melton family, but also about sixty slaves and other possessions. The Indian fighter had now gone full circle by enlisting Cherokees to fight the Creeks, then beating the Cherokees out of their land and possessions; but, Jackson had much worse in store with the Indian Removal Act of 1830.

1818 Cherokee Removal

After Jackson had acquired Melton's Bluff which he named Marathon, another group Cherokee's was facing removal. On January 20, 1818, while at Melton's Bluff, Anne Royall observed some 300 Cherokees camped just two miles east of the Bluff in Lawrence County. These Cherokees were in the process of moving west of the Mississippi River. The following writing was found in Letter XXX dated January 20, 1818 and on pages 154 and 155 of the book *Letters from Alabama 1817-1822*:

"Hearing eleven boats had arrived about two miles from hence, and had halted up the river; we set off, as I said before, in a little canoe, to see the Indians, which are on their way to their destination beyond the Mississippi. Government, agreeably to their contract, having completed the boats, the news of the arrival of the Indians had been received with much interest; but being unable to proceed by water, we quit the canoe, and proceeded by land in our wet shoes and hose.

We arrived at the Indian camps about eleven o'clock. There were several encampments at the distance of three hundred yards from each other, containing three hundred Indians. The camps were nothing, but some forks of wood driven into the ground, and a stick lay across them, on which hung a pot in which they were boiling meat; I took it to be venison. Around these fires were seated, some on the ground, some on logs, and some on chairs, females of all ages; and all employed, except the old women. There were some very old gray-haired women, and several children at each camp. The children were very pretty; but the grown females were not."

The group of Cherokees observed by Royall was probably waiting for a rise in the river in order to pass through the Elk River Shoals safely. Keelboats and flatboats waited at the head of Brown's Island until the water conditions permitted safe passage. At Brown's Island, the river channel divided as it passed around either side. Before the channels rejoined on the island's downstream end, rapids on both sides of the island created dangerous situations for boats. At the upstream end of Brown's Island was Brown's Ferry which Ms. Royall said was visible eight miles upstream from Melton's Bluff. It was near Brown's Ferry at the head of the shoals where Doublehead had lived until about 1802.

1832-1834 Water Route

By 1830, Andrew Jackson had successfully gotten the Indian Removal Act passed by Congress. The intent of the act was to remove all Indian people from the

Eastern United States to areas west of the Mississippi River. Many Indian removals had already been completed but Jackson wanted all native people removed from the East. One of the major routes of Cherokee removal was down the Tennessee River through Muscle Shoals toward the west.

During 1831, work began on the construction of a canal around Big Mussel Shoals to aid in the navigation of the Tennessee River. The government had released 400,000 acres to be sold for funds to complete the canal. The following was found in Nina Leftwich's book *Two Hundred Years at Muscle Shoals*, *"A land office was established at Courtland in 1829 to dispose of the lands given to the state for the purpose of building the canal around the Shoals. Dr. Jack Shackleford was made receiver for the Courtland office and the lands were soon disposed of and the office was closed."*

Some $644,000.00 was used in the construction which was completed in 1836; however, during low water, Elk River Shoals prevented downstream traffic and Little Muscle Shoals prevented upstream traffic. The old canal was eventually abandoned in 1838 and soon filled with sediment.

In addition to the contingents of Cherokees who lived in and were removed west from Lawrence County, other groups of Cherokee were removed west through the Elk River Shoals, Big Mussel Shoals, and Little Mussel Shoals of the Tennessee River, while the canal was being built. During high-water seasons, keel boats and flatboats could pass over the hazards of the Shoals if extreme caution was observed.

During the first voluntary removals, many Cherokees traveled through the rapids of Elk River Shoals, Big Mussel Shoals, and Little Mussel Shoals to areas west of the Mississippi. The well-known water removals of Cherokees down the Tennessee through the Muscle Shoals included the Currey removal contingent of Cherokees who passed by Melton's Bluff and through the Muscle Shoals on flatboats in 1832. The following is from *Indian Removal* by Grant Foreman:

Currey was ready by April 1832 to depart with the little band collected by him. The Cherokees he said "dread the length of time necessarily consumed in passing on board of flat-bottomed boats to the mouth of White River, as they are not accustomed to long voyages, would be liable to contract disease". Instead of the thousand emigrants promised him, he had but 380 persons, 108 blacks, forty whites, and the remainder mixed, with a few full-bloods. Twenty-one were from Tennessee and the remainder from Georgia.

They left the Cherokee agency at Calhoun on April 10 in nine flatboats, and passing down the Tennessee river through the rapids at Muscle Shoals, arrived a week later at Waterloo. They were transferred to the steamboat Thomas Yeatman which departed about the twentieth and passed out of the mouth of the Tennessee River three days later. They proceeded down the Ohio and Mississippi and up the Arkansas river, reaching Little Rock on the thirtieth, part of them were disembarked at the Cherokee Agency just above Fort Smith, on the left bank of the Arkansas River, and the remainder were taken farther up to the mouth of the Illinois."

Again in 1834, Benjamin F. Currey's contingent of Cherokees passed through the Muscle Shoals. Curry, who was superintendent of removal, utilized Lieutenant Joseph W. Harris of New Hampshire, a West Point graduate of the class of 1825, to conduct the Cherokee emigrants to their western home. The flatboats were set for departure on March 13, 1834. The following by Foreman's Indian Removal gives the detail:

Waiting for dilatory arrivals two weeks after the time set for departure, on March 13, 1834, the boats dropped down to the landing and the next afternoon when the John Cox and Sliger had taken on board seventy-two emigrants they cast off. This party was in charge of Harris's assistant, a white man named John Miller who was married to a Cherokee woman; he was under orders to collect the stragglers and those living along the banks of the Hiwassee and Tennessee Rivers who were ready to depart and would be awaiting the boats; and then to wait at Muscle Shoals for the remainder of the party.

Harris delayed the departure of the main body of emigrants until the arrival of a company of seventy mountain Indians known- as the Valley Town, who brought their belongings in three heavy six-horse wagons...

Doctor Edington of Calhoun accompanied the emigrants as far as Tuscumbia where he would be relieved by another. After ten days rations had been issued, the next day at eleven o'clock the Blue Buck with 125 emigrants on board cast off an hour later "after some trouble in which persuasion, threats and force were alternately resorted to, the remainder of the party were embarked and the Rainbow, the Squeezer and the Moll Thompson unmoored and dropped into the current.

At midnight the party overtook the Blue Buck moored snugly to the bank with all on board asleep. Her skipper was ordered to cast off and an hour later the boats passed out of the Hiwassee River into the Tennessee. At eight o'clock, twenty-five miles below, Harris overtook Miller's contingent at Brown's Ferry and by noon had joined the remainder of the fleet. Before night the boats successfully negotiated the shoals and rapids in the Tennessee River known as the "Suck," the "Boiling Pot," the "Frying Pan," and the "Skillet." After safely passing through the Muscle Shoals, they arrived at Waterloo, Alabama, on the nineteenth, having made 267 miles in six days of water travel. The voyage had been uneventful thus far, though considerable trouble had been caused by the introduction of whisky among the Indians whenever stops were made near white settlements, and numerous cases of measles had developed in the party.

It should be noted that both of the parties safely passed through the Muscle Shoals during March and April. During the spring of the year, water levels on the Tennessee were high enough to provide for uneventful passage of the dangerous Muscle Shoals. Future removal contingents were transported around the shoals probably because of the extreme danger of destroying boats and losing lives.

1837-1838 Railroad Removal Route

The first railroad west of the Alleghenies was built to carry goods and products around the Muscle Shoals. The railroad had stops at Hillsboro, Courtland, and Town Creek in Lawrence County to take on materials, water, and fuel. The following is a description of the rail line through Lawrence County as given on page 252 in the book *The Tennessee* by Donald Davidson in 1946.

"They built a railroad. It was a "dinky" railroad, by modem standard, but it was a railroad-the first one west of the Appalachians. In 1832, they ran a line over the short distance between Tuscumbia and the river. In 1834, they carried it east to Decatur, a distance of forty miles. This, the Tuscumbia, Courtland, and Decatur Railroad, was a very primitive affair, built of "string pieces of wood scantlings on which flat bars of iron, a half an inch by two and a half inches, were laid." But it served a great need, since it provided an easy portage around Muscle Shoals, and it predicted more railroads and better railroads to come."

Since the rails were so thin, they had a tendency to roll up on the end. The turned up ends were called snake heads. A crew aboard the train would jump out and hammer down the snake heads.

The great mussel shoals was a barrier to transportation and was the major reason for constructing a rail line to Decatur from Tuscumbia. Even though the primary purpose was for the transport of goods around the Muscle Shoals, the railroad became a mechanism for Cherokee Removal during the forced removal of 1837 and 1838.

1830's Fulton Train Engine

The picture of the Fulton train engine is like the one used in the railroad from Decatur to Tuscumbia.

After completion of the railroad, most of the Cherokee contingents removed west were transported by the railroad from Decatur to Tuscumbia. These Cherokees passed through Hillsboro, Courtland, and Town Creek in Lawrence County on their way to the Tuscumbia Landing. At the landing, they would board boats for removal westward.

The following excerpt from page 224 and 225 of *Indian Removal* describes a March 3, 1837, Cherokee contingent moved by railroad through present-day Morgan, Lawrence, and Colbert Counties:

"The boats reached Gunter's Landing on the *sixth and were tied up to the island to prevent* the *Indians from going ashore and getting drunk... The steamer Knoxville was waiting for them here, and when the eleven flatboats were made fast to her, the flotilla set off at nine o'clock on the seventh...*

On their arrival at Decatur, *the Indians were placed on board open cars and compelled to sit in the cold from three-o'clock until dark awaiting the engine that did not arrive. The bewildered Indians who had never before seen a railroad train were left to find a place to sleep; "The train of cars from the west was momentarily expected, and the Indians were afraid to lie down for fear of being run over. No lights were furnished them, and they were grouping in the dark, in a pitiful manner;" but their humane physician succeeded in having a warehouse opened for them in which they made their beds on the floor for the night. In the morning the emigrants were again placed on the cars that delivered them in Tuscumbia by night. Here they camped awaiting the arrival of the boats that were to take them down the river. While in camp it rained hard and long, the weather was cold and windy, and the Indians were wet, cold, and miserable.*

About ten o'clock on the thirteenth the steamboat Newark and two keel-boats arrived and "moored to the landing near which the Indians encamped; immediately the whole posse of them were in motion bringing their effects to the boats..."

It appears that the rail trip from Decatur to Tuscumbia took all day; therefore, the train probably stopped at each station and had several snake heads to nail down.

Again another excerpt from the book *Indian Removal* pages 292 and 293 describe the train route on June 8, 1838:

"The boats succeeded without incident in passing through the remainder of the rapids and into smooth water by noon the next day. They ran all that day and night; passed Gunter's Landing at nine o'clock, stopped once "to wood" and at night landed six miles above Decatur, "and such of the people as choose have gone ashore to sleep and cook." Starting early on the morning of the ninth they reached Decatur at six o'clock to take the train to Tuscumbia but were compelled to remain until the next day. Then "the Indians and their baggage were transferred from the boats to the Rail Road car. About 32 cars were necessary to transport the Party, and two Locomotive Engines."

"As the Indians were much crowded on the train the twenty-three soldiers were discharged. The first detachment reached Tuscumbia at three o'clock and boarded the steamboat Smelter which "immediately set off for Waterloo at the foot of the rapids without waiting for the 2nd train of cars with the remainder of the party." When the

second party reached Tuscumbia they went into camp awhile awaiting transportation by water. As the guard had been discharged, whisky was introduced among them, much drunkenness resulting, and over one hundred of the emigrants escaped. The remainder was carried by water aboard a keel boat and a small steamer about thirty miles to Waterloo."

A third railroad contingent of removal Cherokees to be transported through Lawrence County around the Muscle Shoals occurred on June 21, 1838, as given on pages 294 and 295 of *Indian Removal.*

"On June 13 the second party of 875 captive Cherokee Indians departed from Chattanooga in charge of Lieut. R. H. K. Whiteley, with five assistant conductors, two physicians, three interpreters, and a hospital attendant. After the preceding day had been spent in organizing the party and reuniting separated families as far as possible, they were placed on six flatboats and dropped down the Tennessee river to Brown's Ferry where more prisoners joined them. For two days they remained there while clothing was purchased and offered to the Indians who refused to receive it "neither would they be mustered, as all attempts to obtain their names were without success."

When they left there the flotilla was increased to eight flatboats; tied together in pairs these safely negotiated the dangerous rapids and arrived at Kelly's Ferry in the evening. On the morning of the eighteenth with four flatboats moored on each side, the steamboat George Guess continued the descent of the river.

On the twentieth they arrived at Decatur and the next morning departed on two trains, arriving at the boat landing below Tuscumbia in the evening. One old woman died at Decatur and a man was killed by the cars when he attempted to rescue his hat. Before reaching Decatur twenty-five Indians had escaped from the party. The emigrants were required to remain at Tuscumbia several days before boats could be secured to carry them over Colbert Shoals, and during their stay two children died. They passed the shoals on the twenty-eighth and encamped opposite Waterloo, Alabama, while awaiting the arrival of the steamboat Smelter. During the stay here, three children died, there was one birth, and 118 Indians escaped."

Even though most of the Cherokees had been forced from the area of the Warrior Mountains by 1817, many had to pass through their former homelands after Jackson negotiated the Indian Removal Act of 1830. Since many Cherokees of mixed ancestry had already hid out in the Warrior Mountains area by the 1830's, escapees of the emigrating Cherokees found refuge with friends and relatives located in the Lawrence County area.

Several events preceded the Cherokee Removal. On December 20, 1828, the Georgia legislature passed an act which declared that in any controversy arising between white people and Indians, the latter should be disqualified as witnesses. The Georgia law gave the whites absolute dominance over the Indians; leaders removed themselves and their families to Red Clay, Tennessee where tribal council meetings could be held.

The Indian Removal Act of May 28, 1830, provided for the consolidation of Indian lands. The Treaty of New Echota was signed by General William Caroll and John Schermerhorn representing the U.S. government on December 29, 1835, at New Echota, Georgia. Signing for the Cherokee were Major Ridge, James Tau - yeske, Archilla Smith, Andrew Rogers, John Gunter, John A. Bell, Charles Foreman, William Rogers, George Adair, Elais Boudinot, James Starr, and Jessie Half-breed (Previous Cherokee law dictated that it was illegal for anyone to sign away Cherokee land rights).

The Treaty provided for the enrollment of the Cherokee for removal and for the appraisal of their property. The first party to be conducted westward by the government under the terms' of the New Echota Treaty consisted of 466 Cherokees, half of whom were children. This group assembled at Ross Landing (near the present-day city of Chattanooga, Tennessee) on March 1, 1837, to begin their journey. The group embarked in a fleet of eleven flatboats divided into three groups. On March 6, 1837, the boats reached Gunter's Landing and the next morning the flatboats were tied to the steamer Knoxville in order to proceed down the Tennessee River. Upon arriving in Decatur, the Indians were placed in railroad cars and delivered to Tuscumbia. From Tuscumbia, the group traveled on keel boats which were attached to the steamboat Newark; they were then taken to Little Rock and from there to Fort Coffee.

The second emigrating party set out from the Cherokee Agency at Calhoun, Tennessee on October 14, 1837, traveling overland through Kentucky, Illinois, and Missouri. The group was comprised of 357 Cherokees. Because of deprivation and hardship, fifteen deaths occurred on the march.

Forced Indian removal began in May of 1838. General Winfield Scott distributed his troops throughout the Cherokee country where stockade forts were erected for gathering in and holding the Indians preparatory to removal. Squads of troops were sent out from the forts to search for and detain any Indians hidden away in the caves and mountains.

Seventeen thousand Cherokees were collected into various stockades. Cherokees numbering around 5,000 were moved to Ross Landing and Gunter's Landing and were transported to the west bank of the Mississippi River, where the journey continued by land. The next twenty-eight hundred Cherokees were divided into three detachments, the first of which left Ross Landing on June 6, 1838. This group traversed a series of dangerous rapids called the Suck, the Boiling-pot, the Skillet, and the Frying pan on the Tennessee River. They traveled to Gunter's Landing and Decatur by boat.

From Decatur, the Indians were transported by train to Tuscumbia. Because there was so little room on the train, guards were dismissed and many escaped. Many of these Indian people remained in the area between Decatur and Tuscumbia, hid in the forest regions, and later married white persons or were able to identify them with white ancestry. From Tuscumbia, the remaining captives traveled by water to Waterloo, Paducah, Memphis and on to Little Rock and Fort Coffee. Many more expeditions were needed to move the Cherokees to their new western homes. In October 1838, about 13,000 Cherokees began a long over land journey to the West, which ended in the spring of 1839. This particular march was noted in history as the "Trail of Tears." It is asserted that over 4,000 Cherokees died as a direct result of the removal. Many Cherokee mixed-bloods and their descendants assimilated into the general population and avoided removal; today, their descendants remain in North Alabama.

1838 Benge Route

Wagon master John Benge was the son of Robert (Bob, Bench, Colonel, Captain) Benge who was born about 1766 probably at the Cherokee village of Toquo, on the Little Tennessee River in Monroe County, Tennessee. Some historians say that Robert Benge married Black Fox's daughter, and some say he married Jennie Lowery. Robert's son, Chief John (Wagon Master) Benge, was born about 1787, and he married Run

After (Ganelugi) McLemore and Quatie Conrad. John Benge led the "Benge Detachment" during removal to the west.

On or about September 28, 1838, John Benge led some 1,100 Cherokees with 60 wagons and 600 horses from Wills Valley at Fort Payne west to Indian Territory. The Benge Detachment left Ft. Payne and traveled south toward Lebanon, Alabama; then, the detachment turned west toward Meltonsville at the mouth of Town Creek on the Tennessee River.

From Meltonsville, the group continued south along the river to Gunter's Landing where they crossed the Tennessee River. The group traveled along the north side of the Tennessee River to Flint River where they turned north along the east bank of the stream. Benge's detachment crossed Flint River prior to reaching the Tennessee state line; they exited Alabama near Ardmore and headed to Pulaski, Tennessee.

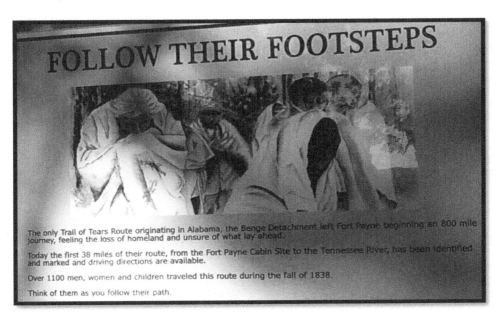

FOLLOW THEIR FOOTSTEPS

The only Trail of Tears Route originating in Alabama, the Benge Detachment left Fort Payne beginning an 800 mile journey, feeling the loss of homeland and unsure of what lay ahead.

Today the first 38 miles of their route, from the Fort Payne Cabin Site to the Tennessee River, has been identified and marked and driving directions are available.

Over 1100 men, women and children traveled this route during the fall of 1838.

Think of them as you follow their path.

Now, we come to the trails and paths that led two great societies together -- Indian and Celtic.

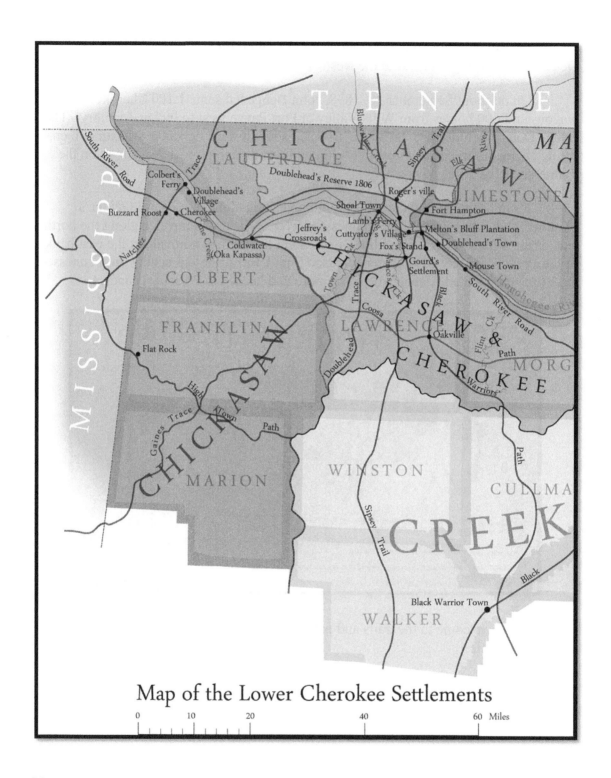

Map of the Lower Cherokee Settlements

0   10   20   40   60 Miles

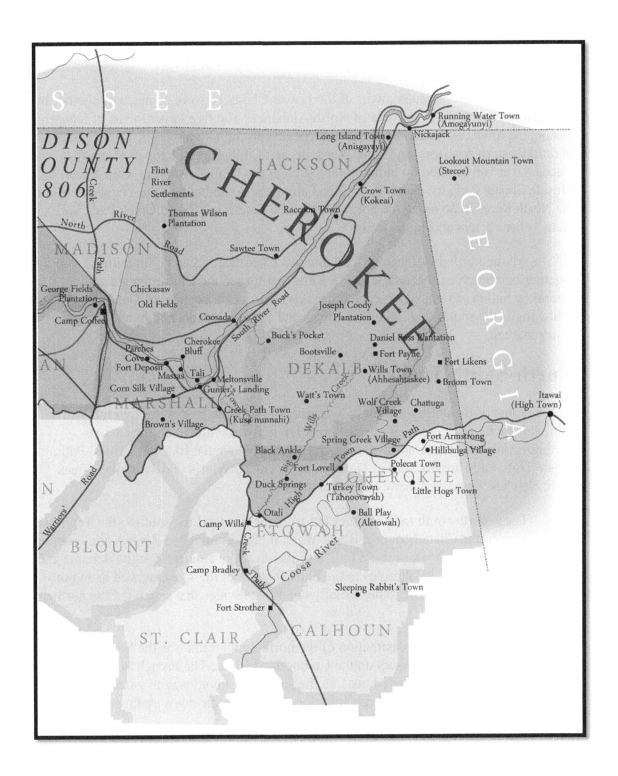

S   S   E   E

DISON
OUNTY
806

MADISON

North

River

Road

Path

Creek

George Fields
Plantation

Camp Coffee

Chickasaw
Old Fields

Flint
River
Settlements

Thomas Wilson
Plantation

Sawtee Town

Coosada

Parches
Cove

Cherokee
Bluff

Fort Deposit

Masas

Tali

Corn Silk Village

Meltonsville

Gunter's Landing

MARSHALL

Creek Path Town
(Kusa-nunnahi)

Brown's Village

Black Ankle

Fort Lovell

Duck Springs

Otali

Camp Wills

BLOUNT

Warriors'

Road

Camp Bradley

Fort Strother

ST. CLAIR

CHEROKEE

JACKSON

Long Island Town
(Anisgayayi)

Raccoon Town

Crow Town
(Kokeai)

South River Road

Buck's Pocket

Bootsville

Joseph Coody
Plantation

Daniel Ross Plantation

Fort Payne

DEKALB

Watt's Town

Wills Town
(Ahhesahtaskee)

Wolf Creek
Village

Chattuga

Wills

Creek

Town

Big

High

Spring Creek Village

Fort Armstrong

Hillibulga Village

Polecat Town

CHEROKEE

Turkey Town
(Tahnoovayah)

Ball Play
(Aletowah)

ETOWAH

Creek

Path

Coosa River

Sleeping Rabbit's Town

CALHOUN

Running Water Town
(Amogayunyi)

Nickajack

Lookout Mountain Town
(Stecoe)

GEORGIA

Fort Likens

Broom Town

Itawai
(High Town)

Little Hogs Town

97

Primary Indian Trails

All the Chickamauga towns of the Lower Cherokee were connected together by Indian trails and paths in the area of North Alabama. The five lower towns of Dragging Canoe, the towns of Black Fox and Doublehead's stronghold along the Muscle Shoals in northwestern Alabama, and John Watts, Jr. and Little Turkey's towns along the Coosa River were linked by Indian routes such as the High Town Path, Coosa Path or Muscle Shoals Path, the South River Road along the south bank of the Tennessee River, the North River Road along the north bank of the Tennessee River, Creek Path, and many other ancient aboriginal trails.

All the northern Alabama Chickamauga Cherokee Indian communities were tied together by numerous secondary Indian paths that forged the Chickamauga and Cherokee Indian settlements to each other across the north portion of Alabama. The following is the routes that linked the towns and villages established by the Chickamauga.

North-South Trails

Some of the north to south Indian trails in Alabama passes through the Warrior Mountains with most crossing the east-west High Town Path which runs across northern Alabama. These north-south Indian trails include the Black Warriors' Path, Sipsie Trail, Old Buffalo Trail or Doublehead's Trace, Byler's Old Turnpike, Creek Path, Natchez Trace, and many other minor trails.

These north-south Indian routes led from the French Lick south to the Tennessee Valley, then to the Chattahoochee, Black Warrior, and Tombigbee River Valleys south of Bankhead Forest. Most of these Indian trails ran major ridges through Alabama and were probably used as local routes to the bluff shelters of the forest as well as major routes south and north. The routes usually lay along divides that separated the northern Alabama drainages.

The major northern destination of the north-south trails was the French Lick or Big Lick (Nashville, Tennessee) on the Cumberland River. The French Lick became a hub for Indian trails that radiated out like the spokes of an old wagon wheel. The following list of trails from the French Lick connection indicates a trading system that spanned the middle of the United States.

French Lick, Big Lick, or Fort Nashboro

The French Lick (Nashville) Connection

- **Natchez Trace** ran south from Nashville to Natchez by way of Colbert's Ferry near Cherokee, Colbert County, Alabama.

- **Doublehead's Trace (Old Buffalo Trail)** ran north from Tuscaloosa to Haleyville, Town Creek, Shoal Town (Wheeler Dam area) on Tennessee River; to Loretta, Tennessee, to Duck River, Franklin, and then to French Lick.

- **Sipsie Trail** ran north from Tuscaloosa through Double Springs, Moulton, Courtland, Minor Hill, Pulaski, along Richland Creek, and then to the French Lick.

- **Black Warriors' Path** ran from St. Augustine, north to Ft. Mitchell near the Chattahoochee River, to Elyton (Birmingham), to Melton's Bluff on Tennessee River, to Fort Hampton, to Bridgewater at the bend of Elk River, to Elkton, to Columbia, and then to the French Lick.

- **The Great South Trail** or **Old Huntsville Road** ran from the French Lick south into Alabama to Chickasaw Island (Huntsville, Alabama), then to Tuscaloosa, Alabama. It was known in settler days as the Great Tennessee Trail or Huntsville Road.

- **The Cisca and St. Augustine Trail** ran from the French Lick leading south through Chattanooga, Tennessee.

- **The Black Fox Trail** ran from the French Lick southeast to Little Echota in northeast Georgia.

- **The Lower Harpeth and West Tennessee Trail** ran from the French Lick southwest toward Chickasaw Bluffs (Memphis, Tennessee) where it joined the High Town Path.

- **The Wilderness or Kentucky Road** ran from the French Lick northeasterly through the Cumberland Gap, Kentucky.

- **The Cumberland and Great Lakes Trail** ran from the French Lick north through Lexington, Kentucky.

- **The Cumberland and Ohio Falls Trail** ran north from the French Lick to Louisville, Kentucky.

- **The Nashville-Saline River Trail** ran from the French Lick northwest across Kentucky to Berry's Ferry, Salt Lick, and Sawneetown, Missouri.

East-West Trails

Some major Indian roads ran east to west through North Alabama and include the High Town Path, Coosa Path or Muscle Shoals Path, Old Chickasaw Trail, Gaines' Trace, Brown's Ferry Road, South River Road, and many other minor trails. The western destinations of east-west trails running through this area were the Chickasaw towns in the upper Tombigbee River system and then Chickasaw Bluffs (Memphis) on the Mississippi River.

Most of the east-west trails originated from the East on the Atlantic Coast. The eastern hub of Indian trade was Olde Charles Town, South Carolina which became a bustling center of trade with the Chickasaw and Cherokee. Trade with the Indian nations of this area promoted the growth of trails and paths into well-worn roads from Charles Town and other coastal trading centers. The English were at the forefront of trade into North Alabama. The following from *Cherokees of the Old South* by Henry T. Malone (1956) gives a glimpse of Indian trade:

"The English used the consistent support given by the Cherokees to gain not only military and diplomatic advantage but profitable trading privileges as well...The English royal governors and colonial boards of trade spurred themselves to establish and maintain cordial relations with the redskins. In 1690 James Moore, Secretary of the Carolina colony, and Maurice Matthews went into Cherokee settlements in an effort to find gold and to make trading arrangements...Other colonies were also active in promoting better Indian relations. The Trustees of Georgia desired both to regulate and to improve trade and trading conditions, and as early as 1733 had laws enacted for that purpose...The techniques of the white man's commerce in the Cherokee country were probably exemplified in the activities of South Carolina traders. Charles Town was the hub center of this trade with the Cherokees, as with other Indian tribes. It was a common sight during the eighteenth century to see caravans loading up at the warehouses of Charles Town merchants for an Indian venture. The staple commodity which the Cherokees desired was coarse cloth; other items amongst the trader's stock with which he hoped to dazzle Indian eyes were blankets; hoes, axes, and other implements; and such miscellany as brass, kettles, salt, hatchets, guns, knives, powder and bullets, flints, tobacco, pipes, and rum. Especially appreciated were guns and ammunition, which, with the eagerly sought rum, were the most popular items by 1715...The effort of the English to maintain just trading practices was a major phase of their Indian diplomacy, which was generally successful...Cherokees agreed to be allies

of the English in the event of future war with outsiders, to "Keep the Trading Path Clean," to allow only British traders to enter Cherokee territory...The treaty made in England in 1730 brought generally friendly and peaceful relations which lasted some thirty years. Traders consolidated their arrangements with the Cherokees, and individuals, companies, and colonial officials built up a thriving trade between Charles Town and the Indian country" (Malone, 1956).

The Chickasaws began to depend heavily on English trade. In order to ensure trade goods got to the Chickasaw towns on the upper Tombigbee, the Chickasaws established a town on the Coosa River where Indian guides would direct traders by the most secure route. The Indian guides from Breed Town would follow the Coosa Path north toward Chickasaw Island. Along the route, they could turn west along the High Town Path, which followed the Continental Divide, or continue on toward Chickasaw Island where they could turn west on the Coosa Path through the Moulton Valley. The Coosa Path passed the present-day areas of Sommerville, Hartselle, Danville, Oakville, Moulton, Hatton, and westward into the Chickasaw Nation. The guides could continue to the river, where they could travel the South River Road along the Tennessee River toward Colbert's Ferry. In the vicinity of present-day Decatur, they could turn south-west toward Cotton Gin Port along the Old Chickasaw Trail, passing present-day towns of Moulton and Russellville, or continue west by Melton's Bluff on the South River Road.

The following excerpts from Charlotte Hood's (1995) book *Jackson's White Plumes* gives details of Coosa towns established to escort trade goods:

"The years following 1736 were filled with change and upheaval for the Indians as settlers began pouring into their nation. The Allegheny Mountians were a natural barrier, and Britain issued a proclamation making settlement illegal west of the Appalachian Chain (1736). Nevertheless, English, Irish, and Scottish emigrants ignored the proclamation and merged inland from the eastern coast, while Spanish and French affiliates pushed from the south and north. The beleaguered southeastern Indian tribes were caught in a vice of white flesh.

English traders from Charles Town had begun supplying the Chickasaw with Euro/Indian necessities in the late 1600's. Edmond Atkin, an experienced Indian trader and merchant who was appointed British Superintendent to the Southern Indians in 1756, reported that the Indians had been supplied with English goods since the year 1692...Charles Town was one of the first English trading centers, and most who lived there made their fortunes by marketing goods to the Indians...The Chickasaw Nation was 'near 900 miles' from Charles Town. Because of that great distance, Chickasaw warriors lived on the northern portion of the Coosa River between their nation and their trading center. They were there to escort English traders through the sometimes hostile Creek and Cherokee lands. The 900-mile trading distance was shortened by English storehouses that were established near the Coosa River in the Creek Nation. Chickasaw-Natchez settlements gradually became a part of the area around the Coosa and below the Tennessee River. An early eyewitness account of British traders and their Chickasaw escorts was recorded by Antoine Bonnefoy in 1741-42...The Chickasaw nation was west-northwest from the Abekas. Early maps placed the Abekas on the east side of the Coosa River, near present-day Ohatchee, Calhoun County, Alabama...The path that Bonnefoy traveled has been identified as the Chickasaw Path. Bonnefoy came upon it below the southern bend of the Tennessee River, near present-day Guntersville. The Cherokee Chief Pathkiller verified this path in a letter written to Andrew Jackson at the beginning of the Creek War in 1813. Pathkiller informed Jackson that the warring Creek 'army had crossed the Coosee River and they would take the Musle Shoal Path...they crossed the river below the Ten Islands.'

The 'Musle Shoal [Muscle Shoals] Path' led to the Chickasaw Old Fields and the Chickasaw Nation. It was a means of communication between the Chickasaw and the Natchez, who were located in the Ten Island area. This trail was also known as the Creek Path, and from the bend of the Tennessee River, Guntersville, it led south to a crossing at the Ten Island Shoals of the Coosa River and to the island village of 1650-1715....

Another settlement that existed in this same area was called Ooe-Asah, or the Breed Camp. Ooe-Asah was an 'upper western town of the Muskohge,' which was settled by the Natchez and Chickasaw. James Adair, British subject, Chickasaw trader and historian, mentioned this as an established town in 1746...The Chickasaw-Natchez settlement of Ooe-Asah, located in the upper westen section of Creek territory, was evidently abandoned around 1760."

From Breed Town, Chickasaw guides would lead traders working for the English around hostile bands of Spanish or French supported Indians. Since weather also played a role in the selection of the route traveled by traders, the High Town Path played a major role because it was free of creeks, low lands, and other wet weather obstructions.

- **Avery's Trace** or **The Great Wagon Road** ran from the French Lick east through South West Point (Kingston, TN), to White's Fort (Knoxville, Tennessee). The trace was a 300 mile road built on old buffalo trails by Peter Avery in 1787 from South West Point (Kingston, Tennessee) to the French Lick

(Nashville, Tennessee). Forts or stations were built along the route included South West Point, Fort Blount, Bledsoe's Fort, Mansker's Fort, and Fort Nashborough. These forts or stations were built for the protection of white settlers moving into the Cumberland River Valley.

- **The Cumberland Trace** ran from the French Lick east to Cumberland Gap, Kentucky.

- **High Town Path** ran from Charles Town, SC, to High Town (Rome, GA), to Turkey Town, to Cotton Gin Port, and then to Chickasaw Bluffs (Memphis, TN).

- **Coosa Path or Muscle Shoals Path** ran from Ten Islands on the Coosa River, to Ditto's Landing on the Tennessee (south of Huntsville, AL), and then to Tuscumbia Landing (Tuscumbia, AL).

- **Old Chickasaw Trail** ran from Chickasaw Island (south of Huntsville, Al), to Russell's Settlement (Russellville, AL), and then to Cotton Gin Port on the Tombigbee River in Mississippi.

- **Gaines' Trace** ran from Melton's Bluff on the Tennessee River in Lawrence County, Alabama, to Cotton Gin Port on the Tombigbee River.

- **Brown's Ferry Road** ran from Big Spring in Huntsville, Alabama, to Brown's Ferry on the Tennessee River, and then to Gourd's Settlement (Courtland, AL).

- **South River Road** ran from Chattanooga, Tennessee, along the south bank of the Tennessee River to Bear Creek near the northeast corner of Mississippi.

- **North River Road** from Chattanooga, Tennessee, along the north side of the Tennessee River to Florence, Alabama, and then to Waterloo, Alabama.

Chickamauga Trails and Roads

Adjacent to the Warrior Mountains in northern Alabama are numerous Indian trails that have been used during a prehistory of some 14,000 years. These Indian trails usually involved one or more river crossings which triangulate the area of the Warrior Mountains. The river crossings include Chake Thlocko (The Big Ford, Great Crossing Place, or Muscle Shoals) on the Tennessee (Hogohegee) River, Ten Islands located on the Coosa (High Tower) River, and the French Landing (Cotton Gin Port) on the Tombigbee (Chattawatchee) River.

These Indian trails crisscrossed the northern part of Alabama many times and made it hard to clearly differentiate if a particular trail was a minor or major trail, a connecting route, a shortcut of major trails, or a side trail to springs, creek crossings, and other important sites. The trails were utilized for trade, hunting, communications, war, in defense of villages and towns, and to protect territory from the encroaching white settlement. The following Indian trails had an impact on the area of North Alabama and the Warrior Mountains; most trails leading through our area became modern corridors of travel and transportation.

For thousands of years of prehistory to the early 1900s, the shoals of the lower Tennessee (Hogohegee) River have been a barrier to navigation. The hydroelectric dams of the Tennessee Valley Authority have eliminated the Shoals of the Great Bend of the river. Prior to the impoundments, the rapids of the river were found in the southernmost portion of Tennessee and also in Northern Alabama, along a stretch of waters from present-day Chattanooga, Tennessee to Colbert's Ferry where Natchez Trace crosses the river. These two areas of major shoals had dangerous waters, capable of destroying all types of early boats.

The first set of rapids is just west of Chattanooga (Point of Rock or Mountains Facing Each Other) in the Tennessee Valley Gorge, where the river ripped its way through the mountains, creating a stretch of water rushing down a rocky defile of canyon. Early river travelers referred to the gorge's tumbling shoals as The Suck, The Frying Pan, The Skillet, and The Boiling Pot (Govan, Gilbert and James Livingood, 1977). It is at this place the Tennessee Valley narrows in the middle as the sand clock hourglass and is commonly referred to as the 'Narrows.' The Cherokees called the place "Mountains-Looking-At-Each-Other" because of the close proximity of mountains. Lookout Mountain, Signal Mountain, Raccoon Mountain, and other mountains helped create this treacherous stretch of the Tennessee River.

The second set of rapids, Chake Thlocko (Cha Ke' Thloc Ko') -- the great crossing place or Big Ford -- is downstream beginning somewhat near the middle of North Alabama, where the river flows west to northwest through another geological feature of chert outcroppings, creating a series of six tremendous shoals which plunged some 134 feet within a 37-mile stretch. Beginning at the upstream end near Brown's Ferry was the first of six shoals that formed a "River of Death" for many inexperienced water travelers who tried in vain to shoot the Muscle Shoals.

Heading downstream, boaters would encounter some fifty miles of treacherous water from Elk River Shoals, to Big Muscle Shoals, then through Little Muscle Shoals, Colbert Shoals, Bee Tree Shoals, and finally Waterloo Shoals. Bee Tree Shoals and Waterloo Shoals were basically swift areas containing numerous sand bars and islands, though they were passable with boats. The treacherous waters lay between Brown's Island and Tuscumbia Landing. Only experienced Indian guides were able to safely navigate the Muscle Shoals during high water levels and rainy seasons of the year. One such Indian guide was half-blood Cherokee James Melton, son of John Melton, who ran keelboats through the Muscle Shoals for Malcolm Gilchrist, an early land speculator.

Because of the wild and dangerous rapids, the Tennessee River was never a major western migration route of travelers; therefore, Indian people and explorers utilized a series of trails that linked the southern side of the river. Even though the Shoals were extremely dangerous, Indian towns seemed to flourish along the portion of the river for thousands of years due to the abundance of freshwater mussels that provided an inexhaustible supply of food.

Black Warriors' Path

The relationship of the Gaines and Mitchell Traces does not end with a common beginning point at Melton's Bluff but was connected on their southern ends by a trading route from Fort Mitchell to St. Stephens; therefore, an early Indian trading triangle was established in the area that became the State of Alabama long before the area became a state. Beginning near the eastern end of Elk River Shoals on the Tennessee River at Melton's Bluff in Lawrence County was an old Indian trail called Black Warriors' Path and later Mitchell Trace; the trail led south into the foothills of the Warrior Mountains now known as the William B. Bankhead National Forest. The old trail led through the eastern portion of the forest and into the Black Warrior River Valley. To the north, Black Warriors' Path led to Fort Hampton, Bridgewater, Elkton, Columbia, and the French Lick.

The Black Warriors' Path crossed the Mullberry Fork of the Warrior River just northeast of the junction of the Mulberry and Sipsey Forks where it intersected another trail, Black Warrior Road, coming from the Tennessee River at Ditto's Landing near present-day Huntsville. The trails crossed and the Black Warriors' Road proceeded a few miles southwest of the crossing to the Indian village of Black Warrior Town. The Creek Indian town was destroyed by General John Coffee's forces in 1813. Davy Crockett assisted Coffee and his American forces as they burned Black Warrior Town.

Billy Shaw and Dan Fulenwider in Black Warriors' Path at Baltimore Ford of Mulberry Fork

According to William Lindsey McDonald's article on Melton's Bluff, *"The renowned pioneer and soldier, David Crockett, remembered two occasions when his military unit crossed at Melton's Bluff. The first instance was in November 1813. Actually according to Crockett, he crossed the Tennessee River twice on this first occasion in order to maneuver around the local Indians. After crossing at Huntsville, they moved westward to cross the river again at Melton's Bluff. Crockett described the river at this point as being about two miles wide. The rocky bottom of the river was rough and dangerous. While fording the river, several of the horses became stuck in the rocky crevices and had to be left there while military command moved onto their destination. Crockett's second crossing at Melton's Bluff was in October 1814. Payroll and muster records reveal that he was a third sergeant in Captain John*

Cowan's company at the time." According to McDonald, the above information was obtained from the book *A Narrative of the Life of David Crockett*.

Many early travelers from the north followed Black Warriors' Path from Nashville, to Columbia, to Elkton, and then to Melton's Bluff in Lawrence County, Alabama. According to the book *Historic Limestone County,* *"Early in 1818 there was an attempt to sell plots in a community to be called "Bridgewater" near Sims Landing, just upstream from Buck Island (on Elk River)...Bridgewater was located 15 miles below Elkton, 10 miles above Fort Hampton, and opposite the great bend in the Elk that almost circled round bottom near Sims settlements...The prospectus predicted that the nearest road from Melton's Bluff in Lawrence County to Nashville would touch Bridgewater"* (Dunnavant, 1993) .The Black Warriors' Path ran north to slightly northeast from Melton's Bluff toward Nashville.

During the first surveys of the Lawrence County area in 1817, the Black Warriors' Path was noted several times. The route ran basically from the Mallard Creek Road from Melton's Bluff to the old Tennessee Valley School east of Hillsboro approximately one and one half miles. The road then traversed just east of Penny Cemetery where it joined the Hillsboro Road to Fairfield before crossing Elam Creek. Another route traversed due south from Melton's Bluff to the base of the mountain near Penny Cemetery where it intersected the route that followed along the river.

The Black Warriors' Path leading south through Lawrence County passed the area of Oakville. Just north of Oakville, the trail crossed Elam Creek and the West Fork of Flint Creek and appears to have proceeded adjacent to the large ceremonial Indian mound at the present-day Oakville Indian Mounds Park. Remnants of a very old road are still visible on the west side of the mound. After passing the large mound, the trail forked with the West Flint Creek Trail proceeding southwest toward a western portion of the High Town Path. It does not appear accidental that the trail connected areas of

CREEK INDIAN REMOVAL

Black Warriors' Path played a critical role as a route for Creek Removal. On December 19, 1835, some 511 Creek emigrants passed along the path through present-day Oakville Indian Mounds Park. In September 1836, a group of Creeks left Tallassee in a wagon train of 45 wagons, 500 ponies, and 2,000 Indians. This contingent followed along Black Warriors' Path and passed through the present-day Oakville Indian Mounds Park on September 23, 1836. It's ironic that the route used by General John Coffee's army and Davy Crockett to defeat the Creeks, was one of the same routes used in Creek Removal. Alabama remains the home of many Creek Indians today.

ERECTED BY
THE ALABAMA INDIAN AFFAIRS COMMISSION
1995

cultural importance to the Indian people of the Cumberland River Valley, Tennessee River Valley, Black Warrior River Valley, and the Chattahoochee River Valley.

Lamar Marshall, publisher of *Wild South*, and I began hiking the old Black Warriors' Path which can be followed over long distances through Bankhead Forest. From Oakville, the trail appears to pass just east of Speake School in eastern Lawrence County and very near the old Lindsey Cemetery located approximately two miles south of Speake School.

David Miller, whose family was of Cherokee Indian descent, was one of the first settlers in the area. He is buried in the Lindsey Cemetery which is adjacent to the old Indian trail. From Lindsey Cemetery, the trail proceeds south and becomes very visible approximately one half mile south from the cemetery. The remnants of the trail can be followed from the Lindsey Cemetery area through the eastern end of Poplar Log Cove.

The trail passed through an area known as Beaty Hollow which is about one mile south of the Lindsey Cemetery. In Beaty Hollow, David Miller originally entered part of the land along the Indian trail on April 11, 1836, and Asa B. Crosthwaite entered land on November 1, 1847, through which the Black Warriors' Path passed. The Black Warriors' Path crosses a forty-acre tract of Forest Service land, continues through Beaty Hollow and proceeds south across the lowest northern gap of Poplar Log Cove, which is on a secondary dividing ridge between the McDaniel Creek and West Flint Creek Drainage. This secondary ridge also runs east and west and is today known as Buzzard Roost.

The trail again enters U.S. Forest Service property and proceeds into the eastern end of Poplar Log Cove and passes within a few feet of Poplar Log Cove Spring. Poplar Log is one of the most beautiful coves in Bankhead National Forest and is located at the very beginning of West Flint Creek. The old trail runs along the northern slope of the eastern end of the cove. Only the western end of the cove is not surrounded by a beautiful range of mountains. As Lamar Marshall and I were walking the beautiful fields of waving fescue grass in the upper portion of the cove, he reached to the ground where a small drainage had cut into the soil and picked up a beautiful Decatur point. The Decatur style point dates well into the Archaic period as early as 6,000 years ago. In addition, Mr. Billy Henderson who lives in the upper portion of Poplar Log Cove recently found a duckbill uni-faced scraper which is a Paleo artifact dating back some 10,000 years.

The old Indian trail was used for thousands of years, but it also was used during the early 1800s as a wagon road. I first observed evidence of the Indian trail by looking at maps of early Lawrence County. The 1818 John Melish map, 1825 map of Alabama, an 1842 map of Alabama, and other early Alabama maps show the trail running from Melton's Bluff or Marathon, by Oakville, crossing the "C" shaped upper portion of West Flint Creek (Poplar Log Cove), and proceeding southerly toward the Black Warrior Town.

Black Warriors' Path eventually became Mitchell Trace which was a post route that connected Fort Hampton in Limestone County to Fort Mitchell in Russell County, Alabama. Fort Mitchell was a Creek Indian outpost built in 1811 and named after the Indian Agent David Brady Mitchell.

Old maps confirm the route of Black Warriors' Path running from Melton's Bluff in Lawrence County to the Chattahoochee River in Russell County, Alabama. The Black Warriors' Path or Mitchell Trace is clearly shown on the following maps listed by date: 1813, 1818, 1823, 1825, 1831, and 1842. Since the road is not shown after the 1850s, the route probably became part of the vast Wheeler Plantation and the Town of Marathon became one of the dead towns of North Alabama. After the county seat was moved from Melton's Bluff in 1820 and after the railroad around the shoals was opened on December 15, 1834, Marathon and the Melton's Bluff area were abandoned and the road lost importance.

In December 1835, Black Warriors' Path played a significant role in the romoval of Creek Indians. Grant Foreman (1932) in his book *Indian Removal* gives details of the march that traveled along Black Warriors' Path to the area that is now Oakville Indian Mounds Park. At the south edge of the park, the Creek Indian contingent intersected the Old Coosa Path or Muscle Shoals Path which at that time was called "the Moulton to Sommerville Road via Irwin's Mill." At this location, a limestone abutment bridge crossed the West Fork of Flint Creek. Foreman wrote: *"The agent attempted to enroll the Indians of his party in Tallapoosa County, but he 'found it impossible to get a correct roll in the Nation in the vicinity of so many grog shops,' and he was obliged to take them across the Coosa River before he could count them. Traveling about twelve miles each day they passed through Montevallo, and forded the Cahawba River on the eleventh; passed Elyton, crossed two forks of the Black Warrior River, the West Fork of Flint Creek, Moulton on the nineteenth, and arrived at Tuscumbia the twenty-first. Hearing discouraging reports about the condition of the roads, Deas decided to take the Indians from here by boat. Sending their horses in charge of the contractors to be driven through by volunteer Indians, the remainder of the party, their wagons, beef, and corn were embarked December 23 on a small steamboat and two keel-boats that carried them down the river to Waterloo; here they were placed aboard the steamboat Alpha and two large keel-boats in tow for the passage to Fort Gibson, and departed the twenty-sixth" (Foreman, 1932).*

From Oakville to Tuscumbia Landing, the Creek removal contingent followed the Old Coosa Path. From Moulton, the Coosa Path was referred to in early county records as the Old Indian Trace to Big Spring in Franklin County (now Tuscumbia).

It appears that maps published after the 1850s omitted the old Black Warriors' Path, but evidence of its existence is clearly visible. The old route would obviously become rutted out in one location and the road would be moved to the left or right a few feet creating long mounds between the old wagon roads running parallel to each other. The road had a distinguishing feature which was flat sides with stones occasionally laying on the edge of the road. It appears that Indian mixed-bloods and early settlers moved stones out of the old roadway and many are still found where they were placed many years ago. Portions of the Black Warriors' Path became the approximate route of Highway 41 and Old Corn Road. The trail was an early Indian route leading from the Cumberland River Valley to the Tennessee Valley to the Chattahoochee River Valley in Russell County, Alabama.

According to Gaylon D. Johnson, 1982, *Before the German Settlement of 1873: The Land and People That Became Cullman County*, the area along Black Warriors' Path in Cullman County was a heavily occupied prehistoric Indian site. *"Into this greatly varying area first came the prehistoric man most often referred to as the Indian. Evidence of his existence tells us he was here during the Paleo Age approximately 14,000 years ago. (Silent Footsteps, by Howard King & Don Wilbanks) Although there are many sites scattered throughout the county, the earliest ones are located in the southwest area of the county on the Mulberry and Sipsey Forks of the Black Warrior River and in the Ryan's Creek watershed. Many sites, such as the large one near Bethany Church where pottery, burial mounds, and human remains have been found, date from a later period, but show that the Indian frequented this area consistently until the arrival of the white man.*

The territory containing the Mulberry and Sipsey Forks and the Ryan's Creek watershed seem by far to contain more sites than the rest. But there are good reasons for this. In this area there was a plentiful water supply which sustained life and provided fish for food. Later as the Indian developed farming and a resulting partial dependency thereon, the fertile bottoms along these streams furnished the fields which he needed for farming...

At many of these sites, such as the one on Lick Creek near Logan and the two sites on Ryan's Creek near Bethsadia, signs of agricultural activities have been found.

110

At the sites near Bethsadia, mortars and pestles used for the grinding of corn into meal have been found. At the site on Lick Creek near Logan, rounded impressions in a rock ledge near Shady Grove Church shows where corn was ground into meal. These fields that were originally cleared by the Indians were later cultivated by the white settlers when they came into the vicinity. The Indians probably occupied these scattered sites during the growing and hunting seasons for several years. The end of spring flooding allowed the Indians to temporarily settle the sites and remain until the end of the fall hunting season. With the coming of winter the Indians would return with their stores of provisions to the large river valleys of the Tennessee River to the north and the tributaries of the Black Warrior to the south...

In the western part of Cullman County other burial sites have been located. Under the cliffs of Rock Creek, Indian remains have been found. Near Bethany Church in the Wheat Community, mounds mark the site of a burial ground. On Ryan's Creek near the junction of Simpson Creek another large burial ground was located on bottom land now covered by Smith Lake. Further up Simpson Creek, near the junction of Cane Creek or Murphee Branch, another single mound was found. On Dorsey's Creek several mounds have been located. Many of these are accompanied by camp sites which have given up artifacts such as pottery chips, celts, hoes, arrowheads, and hatchets."

Now, after 150 years since the road was last listed on maps, the Black Warriors' Path still exists in areas where the terrain has not been altered by extensive farming or timber harvesting practices. It is hoped that in the future the U.S. Forest Service will be kind to the remnants of the old Indian and early settler trail because of its historical significance. Once evidence of the Black Warriors' Path is completely destroyed, an important part of Lawrence County history will be lost forever.

Black Warrior Road

The Black Warrior Road intersected Black Warriors' Path just east of Baltimore Ford on the

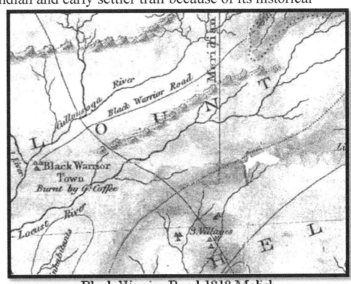

Black Warrior Road-1818 Melish

Mulberry Fork of the Warrior River south of present-day Cullman, Alabama. The Black Warrior Road led from Ditto's on the Tennessee River south of present-day Huntsville to the Black Warrior Town villages on the Mulberry Fork that were located near present-day Sipsey.

The Black Warrior Town Villages were Creek Indian towns that were named in honor of a great Creek Chief Tuscaloosa (*tusca* means warrior, *lusa* or *loosa* means black). During the Creek Indian War, General John Coffee and famous frontiersman Davy Crockett destroyed the Black Warrior Town villages. Later when white settlers began entering Alabama, they named a town on the lower Black Warrior River in honor of Chief Tuscaloosa which is the present-day City of Tuscaloosa.

Browns Ferry Road

Today, you can walk down an old road worn deep into the red clay banks of the Tennessee River on the northeastern edge of Lawrence County. The old road bed eases off into the backwaters of Wheeler Lake directly across the river from Browns Ferry Nuclear Plant. The road bed is some thirty feet wide and eroded into the red earth some fifteen feet at various points. The only noise now heard at the shore is the gentle lapping waves of the backwaters, an occasional four wheel drive vehicle breaking the silence, and boats of all kinds running up and down the river. However, in the not so distant past, Browns Ferry was a busting Cherokee village, and the ferry was utilized as a major river crossing at the head of Muscle Shoals. Over the years, the Indian crossing of the Tennessee River was known by several names: Doublehead's Town, Cox's Ferry, and Browns Ferry; however, Browns Ferry was the name that had the sticking power of the red clay dirt.

On December 18, 2003, I talked to Mr. Bill Sams and Mr. Paul Ausbon whose descendants lived at Browns Ferry. Mr. Ausbon, who was born on October 5, 1925, remembers when the Tennessee Valley Authority flooded his family's farm at Brown's Ferry. He noted that they destroyed some of their very fine farmland along Rocky Branch. Mr. Ausbon in particular noted that the old ferry road went between two islands that were formed by the back water then turned toward the river. Just downstream from the old ferry site, a large island called Knight Island (Brown's Island) was the location of a prison. Many of the farmers were able to get prisoners to help work their crops. When Mr. Ausbon lived in the area the ferry was no longer in service; instead a ferry at Decatur was the only way to cross the Tennessee River in his area.

The Browns Ferry crossing was located between Mallard, formerly known as Mallet's Creek, and Fox's Creek at the head of Elk River Shoals, which was the first upstream shoal of the Big Bend of the Tennessee River. The road crossing at this point connected Big Spring (Huntsville) to Goard's Settlement (Courtland). Early maps show a flip stock style road from Courtland, with one route to Melton's Bluff and the other fork to Browns Ferry. Brown's Ferry and Melton's Bluff are approximately eight miles apart by water, but rapids on each side of Brown's Island at times created hazardous conditions. Flatboats and keelboats would wait at the eastern end of Brown's Island, the uppermost beginnings of Elk River Shoals, for a rise in the river so they could shoot the Shoals (navigate through the rocky outcroppings).

Butch Walker and Charles Borden walking Browns Ferry Road

As early as 1790, maps of the State of Franklin show Browns Ferry as the home site of Doublehead. Also Albert James Pickett's *Alabama History*, written in 1851, states: *"In December 1801, settlers came down the river and stopped at the home of Doublehead at the head of the Shoals. They then traveled over land to the BigBee Settlements."* Therefore, Doublehead was noted as living at Brown's Ferry in present-day Lawrence County until 1802.

During the "Battle of Talledega" in November 1813, Colonel Joseph Brown found out from an old half-blood Cherokee named Charles Butler that, Cherokee Chief Cuttyatoy was living on an island (Gilchrist Island) across from the mouth of Elk River in Lawrence County. Joseph Brown (supposedly no relation to Brown's Island or Ferry) went to General Andrew Jackson and requested help to retrieve his father's slaves stolen by Cuttyatoy in 1788. Brown and ten of Jackson's best men rode to the house of Cuttytoy which was approximately 12 miles west of Brown's Ferry. The next morning Joseph Brown forded the river with the slaves while Cuttyatoy and his people went up river to cross on a large raft which was Browns Ferry. Both Joseph Brown and Cuttyatoy met in the late afternoon at Fort Hampton in present-day Limestone County.

The Browns Ferry Road was the major route leading west from the Tennessee River toward Goard's Settlement, which was a Cherokee town in Mississippi Territory. The crossing by way of Brown's Ferry by Cuttyatoy and his people was one of the first documented river crossings at this site, but the ferry operated much earlier as a river crossing of the Brown's Ferry Road. The Brown Indian family operated ferries from Chattanooga to this Brown's Ferry site in the Big Bend. The family migrated westward with the Cherokees and brought with them their family business of operating river ferries. One of Brown's Indian daughters married a Cox and later ran the ferry with her husband. During their operation of the ferry, it was known for a brief time as Cox's Ferry.

In the first surveys after the Turkey Town Treaty of 1816, the Brown's Ferry Road was already in existence. In June 1817, the area north of the river was surveyed by General John Coffee's men. They noted in their field notes several occasions where they crossed the Brown's Ferry Road leading to Huntsville. Prior to these surveys, the land belonged to the Chickasaw Nation; and, therefore, the Browns Ferry Road was a documented Indian trail running through present-day Madison, Limestone, and Lawrence Counties. General Coffee signed and approved the surveys on October 10, 1817.

During Anne Royall's stay at Melton's Bluff in January 1818, she noted Browns Ferry up river some eight miles in distance. At the time of Anne Royall's stay at Melton's Bluff, General Jackson visited his plantation on several occasions. Andrew Jackson and Captain John Hutchings bought the plantation from Cherokee David Melton on November 22, 1816.

After the Turkey Town Treaty of 1816, which took the Cherokee land claims to the area, Brown's Ferry continued to operate as a river crossing of the Brown's Ferry Road. Settlers begin to pour into the great Tennessee Valley of Lawrence County by way of Brown's Ferry Road from Huntsville, Athens, and points north of the Tennessee River. One of the last crossings documented at Brown's Ferry was by the army of Confederate General Nathan Bedford Forrest during April 1863. He moved his cavalry along the Browns Ferry Road to protect Courtland from Union General Grenville M. Dodge's eight thousand troops. From here, he chased Colonel Streight across Lawrence

County and made the famous capture of some fifteen hundred men with his five hundred cavalry men.

Byler's Old Turnpike

Byler's Old Turnpike became the first authorized road by the State of Alabama and showed progression from an animal trail, to Indian path, then to the first state road. The Byler Road ran through the western portion of the Warrior Mountains from the Tennessee River to Tuscaloosa. The Byler Road was one of the first roads authorized by the Alabama State Legislature meeting in Huntsville in 1819. The road was approved two days after Alabama was admitted into the Union of the United States of America on December 14, 1819. The road was named after John Byler, who was buried in Rock Springs Cemetery at Mt. Hope.

The road ran from the Great Military Road to Bainbridge Ferry on the Tennessee River, passed south through Jeffreys Cross Road (Leighton), across the western border of Lawrence County, and into the Warrior Mountains of present-day Bankhead National Forest. After following the range line between Range 9 West and Range 10 West, the old road meandered up the mountain just east of Steele Hollow to the upper drainage of Bear Creek. The old road continued south along the ridge between the upper tributaries of Bear Creek, then crossed the creek to the Tennessee Divide near Poplar Springs Cemetery. The road then followed the basic route of the Old Buffalo Trail, which was a north-south route for the Creeks and Choctaws to the French Lick (Nashville). The road went southward to the falls of Tuscaloosa River and basically ran the divide (Byler Ridge) between the Tombigbee and Warrior River Drainages.

The mountainous part of the route between the upper portion of Bear Creek and Sipsey River Drainages of Lawrence County was part of the Cherokee and Chickasaw Territories. It appears that the road up the mountain proved to be a great problem. From historical evidence found in old maps and physical evidence of old road beds meandering up the hill, the original route of the Byler Road to the top of the mountain

115

was at a place now called Steele Hollow. The site was the home place of Ms. Byler.

Based on physical evidence, four additional alternate routes up the mountain were utilized. The Ebenezer Martin Gap was just east of the present-day route up Stinson Gap. As you start up the mountain toward the horseshoe bend on Stinson Gap, an old road turns south toward Ebenezer Gap. The old road bed is clearly visible but is no longer in use.

The first ridge, west of the existing Stinson Gap, contains the remains of a deeply rutted road. This portion traverses up the middle of the ridge but has long since been abandon as a road to the mountaintop. Still another old road two ridges west of Stinson Gap has the remains of a deeply rutted road traversing the west edge of the ridge toward the mountaintop. This particular route went up the east side of a hollow toward the valley's beginning on the Tennessee Divide. As the road neared the mountaintop, it passed through a narrow saddle before reaching the summit. All of these old road beds were formerly routes of

the Byler Road. All these old roads joined prior to the toll gate near the Northwest Road. According to an early map of Lawrence County, William McCain, son-in-law of John Byler, ran a toll gate on the Byler Road near its junction with the Northwest Road. The toll gate was located in the southeast quarter of Section 18 of Township 8 South and Range 9 West.

The Moulton Fork of the Byler Road ran from Moulton, skirting the edge of the mountains through Youngtown, and up the mountain at McClung Gap. The two Byler Roads joined at a site known as the 66-mile Tree which was located southwest of the junction of the High Town Path and the Moulton Fork in the southwest one-quarter of Section 33 of Township 7 South and Range 9 West. The 66-mile Tree was thought to be a designated tree at the forks of the two roads. The total distance, from the beginning of the Byler Road at Bainbridge Ferry on the Tennessee River, and the beginning of the Byler Road Fork beginning at Moulton, to the junction on top of Continental Divide south of Mt. Hope, was supposedly marked on a tree designating the 66 miles of the Byler Roads north from that point. Since prehistoric Indian times, the portion of the Byler Road between Poplar Springs Cemetery and Aunt Jenny Brooks' home-place was utilized as an Indian trail. This particular portion of the Byler Road was previously designated using the following various names: The High Town Path, Old Buffalo Trail, or Doublehead's Trace. The road was also the tribal boundary of the Creeks, Cherokees, and Chickasaws.

According to legend, during the Civil War Union troops of Northern Aggression under the command of Colonel Abel Streigh were attacked on the Byler Road near Aunt Jenny's place. In addition, Union General G.M. Dodge's scouting party utilized the Byler Road in the spring of 1864. Later in March, 1865, en route to Tuscaloosa and the Battle of Selma, one division of General James H. Wilson's Cavalry passed through Lawrence County and stayed the night at David Hubbard's Plantation, located at Kinlock.

Chickasaw Path

The Old Chickasaw Path, which passed through the Tennessee Valley portion of present-day Lawrence County, is mentioned in several historical documents, but Captain Edmund Pendleton Gaines in 1807 and 1808 survey notes defines its origin and ending points. According to the _Alabama Historical Quarterly_, Summer 1971, page 142, Gaines states upon marking the old path at mile 28, _"Old Chickasaw Path, which leads from Flint Creek about 20 miles above Mr. Melton's, to the Chickasaw Nation. Ascend the ridge which divided the waters of Bear Creek, from those which empty into [the] Tennessee above the mouth of said Creek."_ Page 137 of the _Alabama Historical Quarterly_ gives the ending point of the trail: _"after reaching the Tombigbee River, they encounter some Chickasaws who expressed pleasure of the prospect of having the government improve their trail between the two rivers."_ Gaines' official report to the War Department recommended that the old trail be expanded into a wagon road and concluded that the Tennessee-Tombigbee route was the most feasible route for supplies for the South Alabama settlements.

Based on historical records, the Old Chickasaw Trail crossed Flint Creek in the Decatur area near where it flows into the Tennessee River. The route ran along the River Road in northern Morgan County just south of the Tennessee River. The following 1819 description on Morgan (formerly Cotaco) County identifies a portion of the Old Chickasaw Path, *"David Ballew appointed overseer of that part of the road leading from Sommersville toward Meltons Bluff to the crossing of the village trace and Christopher Borden appointed to proportion the lands."* Christopher Borden eventually settled in Lawrence County and was an early surveyor in this area.

Lamar Marshall in Chickasaw Path south of Elam Creek on Dragstrip Road

One route of the Chickasaw Path through Lawrence County was the South river Road following the southern valley of the Tennessee River to Melton's Bluff. The main route of the Chickasaw Path ran from Flint Creek, to Moulton, to Russellville, and then to Cotton Gin Port, Mississippi. From Melton's Bluff, Gaines route followed in the same general direction of the Old Chickasaw Trail. At mile 28 from Melton's Bluff, Gaines specifically notes the Old Chickasaw Path ascending a ridge between the Bear Creek and Tennessee River Drainages.

Chisolm Road

Captain John D. Chisolm, who married Patsy a mixed blood Cherokee daughter of Captain John Brown, was a close associate and business partner of Cherokee Chief

Doublehead. Chisolm utilized an old Indian trail that ran north from present-day Florence, Alabama through Zip City, and became known as the Chisolm Road. Today, the route is still known as the Chisolm Road; John died in 1828 and is buried in the Chisholm Cemetery beside the road a few miles north of Florence. His grandson Jesse Chisholm who was the son of Ignatius Chisholm and Old Tassel's daughter blazed the famous Chisholm Trail of the west.

Coosa Path or Muscle Shoals Path

This was an early Indian trail south of the Tennessee River identified as the Coosa Path by Captain Edmund Pendleton Gaines in December 1807 and called the Muscle Shoals Path by Cherokee Chief Path Killer in October 1813. The Muscle Shoals Path or Coosa Path was an overland route around the Great Muscle Shoals in the Big Bend of the Tennessee River. The western portion of the route ran from the Chickasaw Island in the Tennessee River south of present-day Huntsville to Big Spring in Colbert County (formerly Franklin) near the Tennessee River at Tuscumbia Landing. This overland Indian route circumvented Elk River Shoals, Big Muscle Shoals, Little Muscle Shoals, and a portion of Colbert Shoals.

The Muscle Shoals or Coosa Path connected the Indian towns through the Moulton Valley to the Indian Town of Cold Water (present-day Tuscumbia). The western portion of Muscle Shoals Path or Coosa Path ran from Chickasaw Island, to Sommerville, to Hartselle, to Danville, to Oakville, to Moulton, to Hatton, to Wolf Springs, to Cotton Town, and then to Big Spring in Franklin County (present-day Spring Park at Tuscumbia Landing). Evidence exists that an alternate route ran from Wolf Springs, to LaGrange, and then to Tuscumbia Landing. All along the valley route signs of prehistoric Indian occupation exist. Village sites with stone artifacts are indicators of an extensive prehistoric population throughout the Moulton Valley.

The first Cherokee valley town on the eastern edge of Lawrence County was Oakville. Archaeological evidence indicates that Oakville has been an Indian town for some 2,000 years. Based on a Clovis point in the Oakville Indian Museum from this site and a piece of another Clovis found nearby, Oakville has a prehistory of some 12,000 years. Five mounds were located in the vicinity of present-day Oakville Indian Mounds Park according to a 1924 Smithsonian archaeological survey. According to personal communication with Mr. Dee Gillespie, *"I was always told by my folks that a large Cherokee village was located at the mound site at Oakville. The Cherokees at Oakville were known for the extensive trade with settlers and other tribes. I was told this by my ancestors who passed the information down through my family for years."* Mr. Gillespie also reported that a copper celt was removed from the mounds east of the present-day museum.

Moulton was an Indian village located at the junction of the Sipsie Trail, Coosa Path, and Old Chickasaw Trail. According to tradition, an Indian mound was located approximately two blocks from the courthouse. The town square of Moulton is based on a Cherokee-Celtic style village. The courthouse in Moulton is located on a mound in the center of the town square. There is no known evidence that the mound in the center of the town is an Indian mound; however, early historic records say that the courthouse was built on a small knoll. Many believe this small hill was actually an early Indian mound. Moulton was named after Lt. Michael Moulton who was killed at the Battle of Horseshoe Bend while serving under General Andrew Jackson during the Creek Indian War.

Hatton was located at junction of two Indian trails, the Coosa Path and Doublehead's Trace. According to personal communication with Bobbie Gillespie, *"Several Indian sites were located in the vicinity of Hatton, at least two mound sites located near Hatton with one toward Blackground and the other toward Town Creek. From the Blackground mound site, my family possessed a pink turkey tail that was 11.5 inches long. We got the artifact from postmaster Sanderson, who got the point from a local farmer. Another mound site was located northeast of Hatton."* Hatton sits on a prominent hill overlooking vast flatlands to the west.

Wolf Springs was the location of a prehistoric village site based on numerous artifacts from the surrounding areas. A small Indian mound site is located just east of present-day Wolf Springs. Wolf Springs was also located at the junction of the Coosa Path and Gaines Trace. At Wolf Springs, the old Coosa Path forked with one route northwest toward Cotton Town and the other fork west toward LaGrange. The routes rejoined at Tuscumbia Landing in Tuscumbia, Alabama.

In May 1820 and again in June 1820, the early Lawrence County Court records approved work on the old Indian trace from Moulton to Big Spring in Colbert (formerly Franklin) County. In later times, the path becomes identified as the Moulton to Sommerville Road via Irwin's Mill. Today, portions of the path between Danville and Sommerville follow along State Highway 36.

The following text is from Lawrence County Court records of 1820. Notes by this author given in parentheses and bold. *"State of Alabama, County Court Act Lawrence County, May term of 1820. By order of said court, Tobis Isbell, William White, Benjamin Toney, Hiram Hammons, Obidiah Waller, Micheal Beavers, and John*

Patrick were appointed to view and mark out a road to run from the town of Moulton the nearest and best route to intersect the road leaving from Courtland to the Big Spring in Franklin County (Spring Park in Tuscumbia in present-day Colbert County) at Col. Wallers on the east side of Town Creek — They therefore to command you and each of you to meet at Moulton on the 26ᵗʰ day of June — next to act cordially — given at the office of the clerk of said court at office this 8ᵗʰ day of May 1820...J.W. Wright —

Agreeable to do within order we the undersigned signed Juriors met in the Town of Moulton and viewed and marked out the road that your order said May term 1820. Intersect the road leading from the Town of Courtland to the Big Spring in Franklin County N. Lat. On the east side of Town Creek at Obidiah Wallers beginning at the town of Moulton on the public square, thence north to the north part of Burlisons Plantation, thence a north west direction to the Indian Ford of Big Nance, thence on to William Norwood's, thence north of north west direction to the mile stake in range nine, township four sections 24. 23. 14. 13., thence north along the so line down Wolf Creek (Wolf Springs) as near as possible to the line 2 sections in township, thence on so line to the 4 township 4 sections in township, thence on so line to the 4 township 4 sections 35 & 36 keep the middle thence west of north so as to intersect the road that your order laid, through section 26 in said township and range where we think some damage is required on the south part quarter of section 26 township 4 range damage to Bevely Reace on the N.E quarter of the same section damage $10 — to Cordeel Fairecoth no other damage required that we know of. — June 2, 1820 — Benjamin Jones, W. White, O. Waller, John Patrick, Hiram Hammond

Portions of the old road became extremely important during Creek Indian Removal during 1835 and 1836. Creek Indian people were brought from the area around Fort Mitchell along Black Warriors' Path or Mitchell Trace. On December 19, 1835, 511 Creek people traveled along Mitchell Trace to intersect the Muscle Shoals Path in the south entrance of present day Oakville Indian Mounds Park. After reaching the junction of the Muscle Shoals Path, the Creek Indians turned west and crossed the old timbered bridge crossing the West Fork of Flint Creek to Moulton. They followed the Muscle Shoals Path to its termination at Tuscumbia Landing on the Tennessee River. Again in September 1836, some 2,000 Creek Indians followed along the same route during Indian removal. Today, the old limestone abutments are still visible at the West Flint Creek Crossing which was a few yards north of the mouth of Buck Branch.

During December 1807 and January 1808, Captain Edmund Pendelton Gaines surveyed a route from Melton's Bluff to Cotton Gin Port. After crossing Path Killers (Big Nance) Creek at the 16th mile, Gaines notes an Indian road called the Coosa Path from the lower end of the Shoals toward present-day Moulton. The following is Gaines' description as given in his original field notes.

On the rainy day of December 29, 1807, Captain Edmund Pendleton Gaines was beyond the sixteenth mile of his survey from Melton's Bluff to Cotton Gin Port when he made the following note, *"...cross Coosa Path, leading from the lower end of the Muscle Shoals to Coosa-Town, Creek Nation, bearing about S.26 degrees. E.70 miles distance"* (*Alabama Historical Quarterly,* Summer 1971). The surveyed location of the Coosa Path described by Gaines was between Cotton Town in present-day Colbert County and Wolf Springs in Lawrence County. In an examination of Gaines' coordinates, the Coosa Path was traversing toward the present-day Town of Gadsden, Alabama on the Coosa River; therefore, the Coosa referred to by Gaines was the Old Coosa Town near Ohatchee, Alabama. The path was an overland route connecting the Chickasaw Nation on the lower end of Muscle Shoals of the Tennessee River to Creek Indian Nation along the Coosa River.

The Coosa Path or Muscle Shoals Path was an old Indian trail running from the lower end of the Shoals through Lawrence and Morgan Counties to Chickasaw Island south of present day Huntsville. This portion of the Coosa Path was following the old Indian trace described in May and June 1820 court records as running from Moulton to Big Spring in Franklin County (now Spring Park near Tuscumbia Landing in Colbert County). At Oakville, the Coosa Path crosses the Black Warriors' Path then traverses easterly toward Chickasaw Island, then southeast toward the Creek Indian village of the Old Coosa Town on the Coosa River near present-day Ohatchee.

The Coosa Path noted by Gaines and the Muscle Shoals Path written about by Cherokee Chief Path Killer converged with the Creek Path at Ten Islands in the Coosa River. The following as described by Charlotte Hood in 1992 integrates the three paths as the same route, *"...Creek Path-Coosa to Cumberland River Trail noted in history as the Creek Path, led from Coosa Town, but may be considered as starting from Hickory Ground. It ran northward to the present Red Hill in Marshall County...1790 Brown's Village. At this place the trail divided, one branch crossing the Tennessee River at Ditto's Landing...The Creek Path was the noted trail used by the Creeks living at Coosa and the Hickory Ground in their inroads into the Cumberland settlements in Tennessee. The branch of the Creek Path that crossed the Tennessee River at Ditto's Landing was the same path that went to the Chickasaw Old Fields. This Chickasaw Trading Path, or as Cherokee Chief Pathkiller called it in 1813, the Muscle Shoals Path, crossed the Coosa River at the Ten Island Shoals.*

From Pathkiller (To Andrew Jackson)

122

Turkey Town October 22, 1813

Friend and Brother:

I have now to communicate to you..a talk I had yesterday with two of the hostile Creeks who were sent as messengers...(The) messengers said that...three nights ago...the (Creek) army had crossed the coosee river and the(y) would take the muscle shoal path - that they crossed the river below the Ten Islands...

Reevaluated historical facts imply that the site of Taitt and Adair's Coosa Old Town was located on the Coosa River between present day Ohatchee Creek and Cane Creek in Ohatchee, Calhoun County, Alabama...is immediately below the Ten Islands and the old Creek Path, or as Chief Pathkiller called it before Jackson reached the area in 1813, the Muscle Shoals Path."

The Coosa Path, High Town Path, and Creek Path shared a common route from the present day Attalla area (Wills Creek) to the Guntersville area (Gunter's Landing). The paths ascended Sand Mountain and meandered along and crossed the banks of Line Creek through a gorge which is today known as Sheffield Gap.

This segment of the path was described in Lucius Verus Bierce's journal of 1822 when he wrote:

"April 5 Struck our tents and after a journey of three miles crossed Wills Creek, the boundary between the Cherokee Nation and St. Clair County Alabama, which is a deep, clear river, a branch of the Alabama. Here I departed with my company with whom I had traveled through the wilderness sixteen days. ....They were going South West on to the Black-warior where I should probably never see any of them again.

My course from Carolina hath hitherto been a little South of West. I now turned north of west, taking the road Jackson cut out when going to the Creek War. Eight miles from Wills Creek I came to a gap in Mt. Lookout, cut by Queer creek, which I so called from one of that name near Chilicothe in Ohio which in serpentine crooks resembles it. I followed the bed of the creek from the gap to the top of the mountain, which is about six miles, crossing the creek in that distance forty one times.

The scenery on each side of this road is the most sublime than can be well imagined. The huge mountain cut through to its base by the stream - the whole width of the opening not exceeding forty or fifty yards, and the rocks towering above the head seem to threaten distruction to any who attempt the pass. Arriving on the top of the *mountain it is nearly level. On the left of the road is a dismal swamp from which proceeds the creek that cuts through the mountain. This road is on the line between the United States and Cherokees as run by General Coffee - the trees being marked on one side U.S., on the other C. Eight miles from the top of the mountain came to Cox's a kind of pioneer who keeps a tavern on the line - just within the line of Blount County Alabama. One mile from Cox's I again crossed the line into the "Nation," nine miles farther and came to the foot of the Appalachian Chain, on the West side, and put up for the night at Brown's tavern. This Brown is father to Catherine Brown, "the Indian Convert," whose fame resounded so far at this time <u>The Journal of Lucius Verus Bierce, Travels in the Southland 1822-1823</u>*, Ohio State Press).

After the Treaty of Fort Jackson in 1814, General John Coffee determined and marked the true Cherokee-Creek boundary line in order to establish United States government claims taken from the Creek Nation. This line ran along the ancient Indian path that was opened for wagon traffic by Andrew Jackson during the Creek Indian War. By the 1830s, the old Coosa Path, High Town Path or Creek Path became known as the "old army road" and the "Fort Strother Road."

Creek Path

The Creek Path was a north-south Indian trail that crossed the Tennessee River at Guntersville, Alabama. The path traversed south over Sand Mountain along the same route as the Coosa Path and the High Town Path through Sheffield Gap. The Coosa Path continued toward Ditto's south of Huntsville while the High Town Path followed the Tennessee Divide westerly toward Flat Rock.

From Sheffield Gap, the Creek Path ran south through present-day Attalla, Alabama which was the site of a large Cherokee village and home of Captain John Brown. The daughters of John Brown, Catherine and Anna, established the Creek Path Mission School in 1820, some six miles south of present-day Guntersville, Alabama. The path proceeded south to cross the Coosa River at Ten Islands. From Ten Islands, the Creek Path continued south to Fort Toulouse. Fort Toulouse was originally a French outpost that was later named Fort Jackson.

since and had not been reclaimed by the Creeks—
at that day I construed their statement, into an
admittance on the part of the Creeks that the
Cherokees had claim to the Country as low as
Wills Creek, and acting as a Commissioner for
running out the lines of the Country ceded by
the treaty of Fort Jackson in 1814. I run a
line from Wills creek, along an old Indian
path to Gunters ferry on Tennessee river, as
being the line between the two nations, that path
was then called the Creek path, and is yet
known by that name—

General John Coffee identifies Creek Path

Doublehead's Trace or Old Buffalo Trail

The road crossing the Tennessee River at the mouth of Blue Water Creek in the middle of Big Muscle Shoals was an early Indian hunting path known as Doublehead Trace or the Old Buffalo Trail. According to *America! America!*, "*by 1716, the Choctaw and Chickasaw Indians used the Natchez Trace as a main buffalo hunting road*" (Buggey, 1980). In addition, the Chickasaws and Choctaws, in pursuit of buffalo, passed along the Old Buffalo Trail or Doublehead's Trace as well as other north-south routes across North Alabama. Actually this Indian trail traversed south from French Lick and crossed the Muscle Shoals of the Tennessee River to the Tombigbee Valley Towns and the Black Warrior Valley Towns. Jackson's Military Road followed portions of Doublehead's Road or Trace.

The Creeks also traveled the Doublehead's Trace, Doublehead's Road, or Old Buffalo Trail and had befriended Chickamauga Cherokee Chief Doublehead. The road was utilized as a route that passed east of the unfriendly Chickasaw stronghold of the upper Tombigbee River towns and through friendly territory controlled by Doublehead. The Creeks assisted Doublehead in establishing villages along the Great Bend of the Tennessee River. Doublehead utilized friendly Creeks, Chickasaws, Cherokees, mixed-bloods, relatives, and friendly whites to enforce his supreme control of the Great Bend. His followers became known as the Chickamauga; however, after his assassination in 1807, a cloud of impending doom for Doublehead's Creek alliance began to spread over the Tennessee Valley. The tension was also due to an increase in roads as seen in this excerpt from _The Old Southwest_ *"Among the Creeks a deep dissatisfaction stemming from numerous and diffuse sources was seething. In part, the roots of Creek uneasiness related to the opening and expansion of so many roads and trails — activities viewed by many of their leaders as an evil omen. Immigrants were already taking advantage of the widening of the Federal Road from the Chattahoochee River to Mims' Ferry on the Alabama, and the Secretary of War had ordered General Wade Hampton to open a wagon road from Muscle Shoals to Fort Stoddert along a route surveyed by Edmund P. Gaines"* (Clark and Guice, 1989).

The road described ran from the Muscle Shoals on the Tennessee River to Fort Stoddert on the Tombigbee River just north of Mobile. The Old Buffalo Trail or Doublehead's Trace ran from the French Lick across the Muscle Shoals at Shoal Town to the lower Tombigbee River.

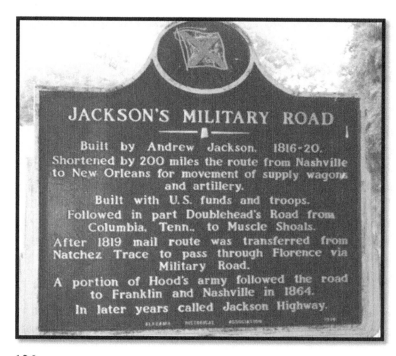

The route of Doublehead's Trace or Old Buffalo Trail ran from the French Lick (Nashville) to the Duck River, to Loretta, to Lexington, Elgin, and then to the eastern mouth of Blue Water Creek. Doublehead and his people made the 100 mile trail into a wagon road from the mouth of Blue Water Creek to Franklin, Tennessee. In this area of the Tennessee River was one of the largest Cherokee towns of the Big Bend of the Tennessee River known as Shoal Town. The trace crossed the river at Shoal Town to the western mouth of Pathkiller Creek (Big Nance) and followed the divide of Pathkiller and Town Creeks in close proximity to present-day Highway 101. The Old Buffalo Trail traversed through Town Creek, Hatton, Old Town Creek Church, McClung Gap, to the Byler Road, and from there south along Byler Ridge to Tuscaloosa.

Shoal Town was the site of an important Cherokee village located some six miles from the eastern end of Big Muscle Shoals. The town lay in the area between Path Killer's (Big Nance) Creek, Town Creek, and Bluewater Creek on the north side of the Tennessee River. Path Killer's Creek and Town Creek are on the south side of the Tennessee River and are separated by a rock wall called Green's Bluff. The mouths of the two creeks are only two miles apart. In this area, some of the largest shell mounds on the Tennessee River were excavated by Gerard Fowke of the Smithsonian in 1924. Three of these shell mounds were over 300 feet in length, over 100 feet wide, and 10 feet or more high. These tremendous aboriginal deposits are evidence of extensive occupation of the Shoal Town area from archaic to the historic period of early Lawrence County. (Forty-fourth Annual Report of American Ethanology, 1928) It should also be noted that the area was also known as "Kittkaski" in early Lawrence County which was named after Doublehead's friend KattyGisky; today, the area is presently the site of Doublehead's Resort. Kittkaski Creek runs into Shoal Town Creek (now known as Town Creek) just west of the resort; upstream from the mouth of Kittkaski Creek is KattyGisky's Spring which is just downhill from the old brick John Johnson home.

Somewhere around 1802, Doublehead moved to the Shoal Town area in Lauderdale County on Bluewater Creek. Even though Doublehead lived at Shoal Town from 1802 until his death on August 9, 1807, the main north-south trail became known as Doublehead's Trace. Earlier the trail had been used by Indian people as a major buffalo hunting route into Tennessee to the Duck River Valley and Cumberland River Valley.

On December 1, 1809, Return J. Meigs wrote the following statement to the Secretary of War and confirmed that Doublehead and the Cherokees had completed Doublehead's Road of 100 miles in length from Franklin County, Tennessee to his home at the mouth of Blue Water Creek in present-day Lauderdale County, Alabama, *"...one road of 100 miles in length, opened by Doublehead, commencing at Franklin County, Tennessee, and runs to the Muscle Shoals, and it is contemplated to be continued to the navigable waters of Mobile."*

In the late 1700s, buffalo were still being hunted in the vicinity of the Duck River as seen in the excerpt from an 1851 article printed in Cornersville, Tennessee. *"In this point of view, the traditional recollections which are detailed in the following sketch of the family of James Brown, connected, as they were, so intimately with some of the most important political events of that period, cannot fail to throw new light upon the pioneer history of the country, and inspire our hearts with renewed gratitude to those hardy, but wise men and women, who built up so goodly a State, amidst, so many troubles, in the dark and bloody valleys of the Shauvanon, Tanasces, and Ho-go-hegee...About the year 1761 or 1762, Miss Gillespie became the wife of James Brown, a native of Ireland, whose family settled in Guildford some years before. At the beginning of the Revolution, Mrs. Brown had a large family of small children, but she freely gave up her husband when his country demanded his services..For his revolutionary services he had received from the state of North Carolina land-warrants, which entitled him to locate a large quantity of lands in the wilderness beyond the mountains...Taking with him his eldest sons, William and John, and a few tried friends, he explored the Cumberland valley. He secured lands on the Cumberland river below Nashville, at the place now known as Hyde's Ferry. He also explored the wilderness south, as far as Duck River, and located a large body of land south of Duck River, near Columbia. The whole country was then almost untrod by the foot of the whiteman. It was the hunting-ground of the Chickasaws, Creeks, and Cherokees, and was full of deer, elk, bears, and buffaloes."*

The Old Buffalo Trail passes within a few yards of Kinlock Spring located about one-half mile west of Hubbard Creek on the Kinlock Road. Remnants of the old trail are clearly visible as it winds its way through the western portion of William B. Bankhead Forest. The Old Buffalo Trail, which later became the Byler Road in its southern portion, led from the French Lick (Nashville) on the Cumberland River to the Indian towns on the lower Black Warrior River and the lower Tombigbee River Valley. The old trail passed by Kinlock Spring that provided many weary Indian travelers a refreshing drink after long trips to the French Lick. Portions of the Old Buffalo Hunting Trail lie along the Byler Road which is on the dividing ridges of upper Sipsey River and Bear Creek.

Until the late 1800s, Lawrence County's western border ran through White Oak, to the Tennessee River on the range line between Range 9 West and Range 10 West. Eventually the western portion of Lawrence County from the mouth of Town Creek to the mouth of Mud Creek (a western tributary of Town Creek) was annexed into Colbert County.

Gaines Trace

Gaines' Trace was one of the earliest federal roads in the Southeast. Gaines' Trace was approximately ninety miles long and extended from Melton's Bluff on the Tennessee River in present day Lawrence County, Alabama to Cotton Gin Port, Mississippi on the Tombigbee River. The Gaines' Trace was the first existing federal road mentioned before our county became a county and before our state became a state. Gaines Trace ran from Melton's Bluff on the Tennessee River, to Russellville, across the Tennessee Divide, to the Cotton Gin Port, and then to St. Stephens Trading Post on the Tombigbee River. The Gaines brothers, George S. and Edmund P., surveyed or negotiated routes in 1802, 1805, 1807-8, and 1810 for a road from the Tennessee River to the Tombigbee River in order to avoid Spanish taxes.

Butch Walker in Gaines Trace near the Spring Creek crossing

According to Rayford Hyatt, (*Old Lawrence Reminiscences*, March 1993) *"The goods for this place came in through Mobile then under control of the Spanish who exacted a heavy tariff on them and the outgoing products. Lt. Edmund P. Gaines, U.S. Army, and brother of George, was ordered to explore the region between the Tennessee and Tombigbee and investigate the possibilities of transporting goods by that route. This he did in the summer (actually winter) of 1807.*

The best route selected was from Melton's Bluff to Cotton Gin Port on the Tombigbee, and since it was to be a pack horse path, was probably marked by blazes on trees. Goods were to be shipped down the Tennessee River by flat boat to Melton's

Bluff, thence by packhorse to Cotton Gin Port, then down to the present Courtland, up Blackground Mountain, near the intersection of Highways 101 and 157, Beavers Crossing, Wolf Springs, King Cemetery, forded Town Creek just below the mouth of Masterson Creek, then across Franklin County to or near Saints Crossroads, Tharptown, Russellville, Belgreen, Old Nauvoo, thence southwest into Mississippi and to Cotton Gin Port near the present Amory, Mississippi" (Hyatt, 1993).

Gaines' Trace was authorized in 1805 by Article IV of the Wafford Settlement, a treaty with the Cherokees which primarily ceded Cherokee lands in central Tennessee and Kentucky. The road was named and eventually laid out by General George Strother Gaines beginning in October 1810. Gaines' Trace began approximately eight miles west of Mallard Creek at Melton's Bluff near the head of Elk River Shoals and proceeded southwest where it forked at Russellville. One route continued northwest to Eastport, Mississippi, with the other route passing southwest through Russellville to the Cotton Gin Port on the Tombigbee River. This trace route joined or crossed a route laid in 1802 by Edmund P. Gaines that ran from Colbert's Ferry to the Cotton Gin Port on the Tombigbee River.

Gaines' route was described by Captain Edmund Pendleton Gaines in a letter to the Secretary of War on January 29, 1808. As requested by the Secretary of War on July 31, 1807, Captain Gaines surveyed and marked a way for a road from the head of Muscle Shoals to Cotton Gin Port on the Tombigbee River. Gaines said in his letter, *"I have also explored the route. From the head of the shoals to the northeast sources of Bear Creek, distance 35 miles, is as nearly level as could be wished, either for making good road for carriages by going near a straight course; but by waving the course in conformity of the slopes of the ridges all will be crossed without ascent or decent of more than 13 ½ degrees...The route for the greater part of this distance, is on the dividing ridges, between the waters of the Tennessee and Mobile...Several Cherokees have designated different places, where they promise to settle in the course of the present year, along the way as far as Bear Creek Ridge, which they call their south boundary...."*

As given in the *Territorial Papers of the United States* compiled and edited by Clarence E. Carter, the description above describes the dividing ridge between the Bear Creek drainage which flows to the Tennessee River and the Sipsey River drainage which flows to Mobile. The High Town Path which was the Chickasaw's southern boundary defined by the Treaty of January 10, 1786, also follows the same dividing ridge. In his letter, Captain Edmund Gaines states that the Cherokee claim the Continental Divide of Bear Creek Ridge as their southern boundary. In addition, Edmund Gaines identified two routes from the Shoals that joined on the ridge near the headwaters of Bear Creek and proceeded southwest along a divide toward Cotton Gin Port.

Gaines Survey

The article, "Surveying the Gaines Trace, 1807-1808," <u>Alabama Historical Quarterly</u>, Summer of 1971, is so significant to the route of Gaines Trace through Lawrence County that the majority of text follows. This author identifies important text and notes in parentheses.

"In late 1807, Captain Edmund Pendleton Gaines undertook what was, for a young army officer, an extremely important mission — to save from extinction the American settlements on the Tombigbee River in what is now south Alabama. At that time, Spanish taxes imposed at Mobile were virtually strangling such centers as Fort Stoddert and St. Stephens. Aside from government officials and army troops, the population of the raw south Alabama frontier region consisted of a very few hardy pioneers. These Americans, who began to populate the lower Tombigbee area as early as 1791, earned precarious livelihoods by raising indigo in the rich creek bottoms, by herding cattle on the prairies, or by trading trinkets, blankets, arms, and ammunition with the Indians for honey, bees wax, bear oil, groundnuts, tobacco, skins, and pelts.

When the American traders, operating out of the government trading post at St. Stephens, began to cut deeply into the Spanish-Indian trade in the first years of the nineteenth century, the Spanish at Mobile objected strenuously. Because they controlled Florida, which extended at that time all the way to the Mississippi River, the Spanish possessed the strategic advantage in the struggle for the Indian trade. Florida officials began to delay American vessels at Mobile and to harass American officials who were connected with the trading post at St. Stephens. More ominously, they placed heavy duties on American goods passing through Mobile. An American settler could buy, for example, a barrel of Kentucky flour for four dollars at Natchez, but by the time it reached St. Stephens, due largely to prohibitive Spanish taxes, a barrel of the same flour cost sixteen dollars.

From the American point of view, the situation on the lower Tombigbee was intolerable, but for several reasons a direct military confrontation with the Spanish was out of the question. In 1806 George Strother Gaines, the Factor at St. Stephens, and his older brother Edmund Pendleton Gaines, the Commandant at Fort Stoddert, began to devise methods of circumventing Spanish control of transportation facilities. The Gaines brothers were apparently aware of an old French scheme to connect the Tennessee and Tombigbee Rivers by canal, thus providing a direct water link between the Tennessee and the lower Tombigbee area. Realizing that a canal was impractical at that time, they reasoned that a wagon road connecting the two rivers, though less convenient than an all-water route, would serve their purposes almost as well.

The War Department agreed that such a road was a practical solution. The government hoped to be able to ship goods by way of the Ohio and Tennessee Rivers to Muscle Shoals, over the proposed wagon road to Cotton Gin Port, located in what became Monroe County, Mississippi, Cotton Gin Port developed into a thriving trading town and river port in the first half of the nineteenth century. Its success was due to its fortunate location at the southern terminus of the Gaines Trace where it met the Tombigbee River at the head of navigation. Cotton Gin Port became a ghost town in 1887, the victim of rail construction in the area and down the Tombigbee to the settlements, thus avoiding Spanish taxes. Accordingly, in the summer of 1807 General Henry Dearborn, the Secretary of War, ordered E. P. Gaines to survey a route from the Tennessee to the Tombigbee. Gaines was well equipped for the job. Having been one of the surveyors of the Natchez Trace, he was experienced in such matters, and some considered him the best surveyor in the army. Also, his experiences at Fort Stoddert had convinced him that the Tombigbee settlements could not survive without a new supply route.

Following Dearborn's orders, Gaines conducted a survey between the Muscle Shoals on the Tennessee and Cotton Gin Port on the Tombigbee during December 1807 and January 1808. Gaines and his small party traveled the well-known Chickasaw trail connecting the two points. After reaching the Tombigbee River, they encountered some Chickasaws who expressed pleasure at the prospect of having the government improve their trail between the two rivers. Gaines' official report to the War Department recommended that the old trail be expanded into a wagon road and concluded that the Tennessee-Tombigbee route was the most feasible route for supplies for the south Alabama settlements.

In October 1810, William Eustis, the Secretary of War, appointed George S. Gaines to negotiate a treaty with the Chickasaws for the right to build the road. Gaines was only partially successful. The Chickasaws were much less enthusiastic about the road than they had been in 1808, and they refused to allow Gaines to build a wagon road over their trail. However, they did sign a treaty allowing the Americans to use it as a horse path. George S. Gaines opened the route in late 1810, and it became known as the Gaines Trace because of his efforts. The trace connected the two rivers provided considerable savings on freight, perhaps saving the settlements from extinction. It also helped insure that the Americans would eventually vanquish the Spanish in the struggle for political and commercial control of the area.

E. P. Gaines was a meticulous man who maintained extensive records of his activities. Fortunately for students of Alabama history, the diary Gaines kept on his survey through northwest Alabama during the cold wet winter of 1807-1808 has been preserved. The Right Reverend Dr. Charles Todd Quintard presented it to the Tennessee Historical Society in 1867. Gaines entitled it "Notes of a Survey from the head of Muscle Shoals, Tennessee River, to the Gin-Port, on the Tombigbee, East of the Chickasaw Nation; and down the last mentioned River to the mouth of Oaknoxaby Creek. By Edmund Pendleton Gaines, Captain 2. U.S. Infantry, and by order of the Honorable Henry Dearborn, Secretary of the War Department of the United States. Completed in January 1808." In this document Gaines recorded what is probably the most detailed description of the northwest Alabama frontier in the period before permanent white settlement.

(Gaines' Notes)

Having completed a Survey of the Muscle Shoals, and the route, by land, from the lower end to the head thereof, commence a survey from thence to the Navigable Waters of the Tombigby River, route (December) 26th 1807.

Begin at the house of Mr. Melton (Melton's Bluff), on a bluff, left or south bank of the Tennessee River (present-day Lawrence County), near the head of the Muscle Shoals.

Width of the Tennessee at this place 280 chs. or 1 m. 120 chs. A chain is normally considered to be sixty-six feet. Gaines, however, used a chain thirty-three feet in length, making 160 chains to the mile.

Mark the route with two chops & a blaze on all trees near the line, front and rear; — and a chop on small growth, so as to make it bend to the ground, & leave it alive (Marker trees develop from bent saplings).

We travel South 45E West for 50 chains thro' Mr. Melton's (Irishman John Melton established his home between Spring Creek and Mallard Creek on the Tennessee River) lane — Upland of the first quality.

S. 50E . W. 110 chains. At 100 chains cross a path (South River Road) — Oak & Hickory timber...

S. 45E . W. 9 miles & 145 chains....At 110 chs cross a path (Brown's Ferry Road to Doublehead's Town at Brown's Ferry) leading N. & S. — At this place is a skirt of thin land, lightly timbered with Hickory and Oak: — grassy.

2nd Mile....Strong upland, nearly level. Hickory growth.

4th Mile....At 64 chs. Cross a small path (Cuttyatoy's Trail to Swoope Pond then to Wheeler) leading N. & S. — At 68 chs. Cross Big-Spring-Creek, 2 ½ chs. Wide — runs N.N.W. — About 70 chs. South of this place is the big Spring (Big Head Spring located at SE corner of NW 1/4 of NW 1/4, S16, T4S, R7W), which is about 100 yards wide, & 300 yards long. Encamp near the big Spring.

December 27th 1807 — Our pack-horses missing until 2 P.M. when we proceed, same course, on rich upland, open and nearly level; with small Hickory & Black-oak timber.

5th Mile....Land & timber as last noted. No under-wood to this place.

6th Mile....At 28 chs. Cross a path (Sipsie Trial to Lamb's Ferry crossing) N.W. & S.E. Land nearly level, with Post-oak and Hickory timber. — No underwood. — Small patches of strong land.

At 47 to 100 chains, best 2nd rate upland. Large Black-oak & Hickory timber. — Nearly level.

At 104 chs. Timber mixt with Post-oak. Small ledges of rocks near the line. — Land nearly level.

At 111 chs. Cross a path (Doublehead's Trace to Shoal Town) nearly at right angles.

At 116 chains Path. Killer's Creek (now known as Big Nance's Creek), 3 chains wide from tops of banks, — 2 ½ chs. At low water, 6 to 8 feet deep; gently, silent current. Banks 12 feet high; firm and well adapted to bridging. We go down the creek, which continues too deep to ford, for about a mile, where it makes a considerable turn to the right — thus at which we find a convenient Crossing-place. The banks, on both sides, to this place continue high and firm, as at the place where the line strikes the creek, to which place we return and encamp.

December 28th 1807 Depart at 7 O clock A.M. same course.

7th Mile....Beautiful land, nearly level: — Oak & Hickory timber.

8th Mile....At 119 chs. Cross the path (South River Road) which leads from the Shoal-Town, eastwardly, to the Goard's Settlement, about 3 miles distance.

9th Mile, Land and Growth as last noted.

10th Mile....At 68 chs. Growth mixed with Pine.

At 70 chains cross a branch running to the left.

At 145 chains change course.

11th Mile....Rocks....Strong upland.

12th Mile....down a Branch. Land nearly level, and of good quality. Oak and Hickory timber....

13th Mile....Thin Cane-brake, near a branch, to the left. Encamp. Rain during the afternoon. On reconnoitering the route and adjacent grounds back to the 10th Mile, I find the ridge between the 11th & 12th Miles may be surrounded without much inconvenience, by bearing about a mile to the N.W. but is deemed unnecessary to deviate from the present line so much, as the distance around the point of the ridge would be too great to justify such an alteration; especially where no serious obstacles to a good road, are found crossing it.

December 29th Rain.....Beautiful, level, firm land; tall Oak & Hickory, with some Ash and Poplar growth....

14th Mile....cross Lick-fork of Town-Creek (presently Wolf Creek), 5 ½ yards wide....A high hill to the left....a Cliff to the left....a fine Spring. Rich firm Land. Timber as last noted....A small Creek, a few chains to the right, runs N.

15th Mile....cross a small creek, runing to the right....A rocky hill to the left. Rich, firm ground, nearly level. Narrow Cane-brake to the right....Small creek a few chains to the right....cross a small creek, 5 yards wide, runing to the right....a rocky knobb....to the right....a ledge of Rocks.

16th Mile....cross a small branch, runing to left. Good upland: Oak and Hickory timber....a low ridge....cross a branch runing to the left....cross Coosa path (Old Indian Trace near Iron Bridge from Tuscumbia Landing, to Cottontown, Wolf Springs, Hatton, Moulton, Oakville, Danville, Hartselle, to Ditto's Landing) leading from the lower end of the Muscle-Shoals to Coosa-Town, Creek Nation, bearing about S. 26E .E. 70 miles distance (Old Coosa Town at Ohatchee).

17th Mile....Waving ridges — Strong upland — Oak timber....descend a short hill, which has a rocky base. Firm land of good quality....

18th Mile....cross a branch runing west (King Branch runs west and parallel to Wolf Springs Road). Strong upland; — low ridges. — Oak and Hickory timber....top of a ridge, 14 chs. Across, & 6E . Ascent & descent....Through rich Cane-brake-low-grounds, to the right bank of Town-Creek.

Encamp early in the Afternoon, in order to examine the Creek and adjacent ground, so as to ascertain the most suitable crossing place. I find the low grounds from 30 to 50 chs. Wide; generally dry and rich; with considerable skirts of cane-brake.

The timber consists, principally, of Oak, Poplar, Beech & Hickory. The banks of the Creek, at this place, are high and firm; and appear never to have been overflowed. Find an excellent ford a short distance above our Encampment.

December 30th 1807. Clear & Cold....19th Mile....cross the creek (very close to Bean Bridge), 3 chs. Wide; 2 ½ feet deep; strong current; stony bottom; and high, firm banks. We experienced considerable inconvenience, from the cold, in wading this creek. We found no tree near the ford that would reach across; and our Horses being all packed, left us no other means of geting over....a gentle ascent out of Cane-brake....Open woods. — Ascent continued....Along a low ridge. Strong upland....cross a branch runing left....A steep bank and creek, 12 to 15 chs. To the left....

20th Mile....Second rate land — low ridges, nearly level. Small oak and Hickory timber. No under-wood....cross a small creek runing to left....cross a Branch runing to the left....Strong upland; nearly level, and firm....

21st Mile....Ditto land & growth....touch the bank of the creek to our left, near an Indian Camp (This Indian village near the junction of Mud Creek and Town Creek may have been know as Vandiver's Mill on Old Byler Road. The Vandiver's were Cherokees of mixed ancestry. Also, the Mehama Post Office was located near the site from 1908 to 1917), on the side of a low ridge....

December 31st 1807....22nd Mile....27 mile....a small path....28th Mile....along the top of a ridge....large rocks project above the surface. Growth as last noted; intermixt with Cedar. Ascent 4E ....top of Cedar-hill. — Descent 3E ....to good land....old Chickasaw path, which leads from Flint-Creek, about 20 miles above M. Meltons, to the Chickasaw Nation. (If drawn on a straight line, the Chickasaw Path would run from Decatur, Moulton, Russellville, then to Cotton Gin Port.)....Ascend the ridge which divides the waters of Bear-Creek, from those which empty into the Tennessee, above the mouth of said creek. Ascent 6E . — Find, at several places on the ridge, considerable
136

quantities of Iron-ore, in small lumps, on top of the ground....First rate upland: — Large Hickory and Black-oak timber: — No underwood: — Long grass: — Dark-brown Soil, of a reddish cast a few inches below the surface; loose, rich and deep.

29th Mile....42nd Mile....Encamp

January 2nd 1808....45th Mile....right bank of Bear Creek

46th Mile....Cross Bear-Creek, or Just-like-a-River; as the Cherokees term it, 34 yards wide; strong current; and, at this place, Knee-deep, and gravelly and strong Bottom.

48th Mile....At 46 chs. Cross Laurel-Branch (of Bear Creek) a beautiful rivulet runing to the right. We cross a few yards above a Cliff, which extends across the valley and branch, about 60 feet over the top, and 30 feet from top to bottom; shelving over, and forming a large semicircular concave, which would afford shelter to an hundred men. The bed of the rivulet, for a few perches above the rock, is horizontal, and 6 feet wide; from which the ascent on either side does not exceed 6 degrees.

About the middle of the rock, at its summit, is a small gap, from which the whole of the stream has a clear fall of 30 feet perpendicular. From this cataract, Laurel-Branch meanders, north-westerly, through a deep valley bordered by perpendicular cliffs Encamp...January 3rd 1808....52nd Mile....Dividing-Ridge. Leave Tennessee waters (The Tennessee Continental Divide which runs through Lawrence County).

54th Mile....58th Mile....

January 4th 1808....63rd Mile....cross a rivulet, runing to the right, near a very small Path, leading towards the Chickasaw Nation — west....66th Mile....cross a creek, 5 yards wide, runing to the left....Low grounds, rich and well timbered, near a Creek....cross a creek, 16 yards wide, runing to the left. This creek is supposed to be a fork of Tuckaloosa, or Black-Warrior, which, by the Chickasaw Hunters, is called Sipsey. It runs, for several miles, in a S.E. direction.

Encamp near the right bank of the Creek.

January 5th 1808....71st Mile....cross a plain path, leading W.N.W. & E.S.E. from the upper part of the Chickasaw Nation to the upper Creeks....72nd Mile....Encamp....on the dividing ridges betwixt the main forks of Tombigby, & the waters of the Black-Warrior.

January 6th 1808....82nd Mile....We encamp at dark.

January 7th 1808....Reconitre....Along the Path....83rd Mile....To a plain path near an Indian Camp....84th Mile....Find the low grounds of Lunecisto, the principal fork of Tombigby....Encamp....

January 8th 1808....Follow an old path to the River Lunecisto, a few miles in front of our Survey, at a ford, at which we cross....I explored this river, in 1802, from a few miles above this place to the mouth of Twenty-Mile-Creek, about 25 miles N.N.W. from hence.

The mouth of 20 Mile-Creek is about 45 Miles from Colbert's Ferry,on the Tennessee, and about 23 miles from the highest point of navigation on Bear Creek; and is deemed the highest navigable branch of Tombigby; and is the head, or highest part, of what the Indians call Lunecisto, or Alli Swamp. It is about 28 yards wide, where it receives 20 Mile Creek, and increases in width to the mouth, where it is 50 to 55 yards, and is generally as above described. It receives two large creeks, and several small ones, below the mouth of 20 mile....

January 9th 1808....

January 10th 1808....Descend the river, on board our perogue, to the Cotton-Gin-Port, where we encamp....

January 11th 1808, at Cotton-Gin Port....this may be considered the highest point of navigation of the waters of the Tombigby River....The road from Natchez to the State of Tennessee, might be much improved by passing from the head waters of Big-Black, at the Pigeon-Roost, The Pigeon Roost was a popular inn on the Natchez Trace. It was located in central Mississippi, about half way between Natchez and the point where the trace intersected the Alabama-Tennessee line, north-

eastwardly direct to this place; and thence along my new survey to the Muscle-Shoals; and thence through the Cherokee Nation to SE -west-point, Tennessee; as by this means the distance from Natchez to SE . -west-point would be shortened nearly an hundred miles; and a much drier and better road be made, than the one now in use; for betwixt this place and the Tennessee River, there is not a Water-Course but may, at all times, be crossed without danger or great Difficulty; even in times of the highest freshes, by the help of Foot-logs; and none of them bordered by Swamps that will require a Causeway, except a Branch of Sipsey, which may, for 60 or 70 Perch, require it. In dry weather, or when the rains are not immoderate, these creeks will not, any of them, take a Horse above the knee.

In 1802, I reconoitred a considerable part of the country betwixt the Gin-port, and the head Waters of Big-Black, and am of the opinion that it will admit of an excellent road.

January 12th 1808, at Gin Port.....Explore the left side of the River in the neighborhood of the Gin-Port....Obtain from the Chickasaw Indians, a few miles up Town-Creek, a small supply of Provisions; for which we are compelled to give our Blankets, as they refuse money.

Several Chickasaw Indians visit our Camp, and appear much pleased to find that a road, from the Tennessee, is likely to be opened to this place. One of the Indians, called John Lewis, has determined to make a settlement at this place; and several other design settling at different places towards Bear-Creek, for the purpose of raising corn, and other necessaries, for travellers, when the road shall be completed.

January 13th 1808....88th Mile....cross a Path leading N. 58E . W., for about 45 chs. To the low grounds of Lunecisto, thence S. 80E . /w, for100 chs. To the River, at a good ford, before noted.

89th Mile....To a path near the River Tombigby, leading to a ford near the Cotton-Gin bluff....To Tombigby River, at upper end of a beautiful bluff, nearly opposite to, and a few chains above, the Cotton-Gin-Bluff where we are camped.....on Cotton-Gin Bluff, on right bank.

January 14th 1808....In order to ascertain the course and distance from this place to a Survey which I made, in 1802, from Bear-Creek to the head waters of Big-Black, — the point where the said survey crosses Town-Creek, Near Levi Colbert's, in the early nineteenth century, Levi Colbert or Itawamba was one of the more wealthy and powerful Chickasaw chiefs. He owned 4,000 cattle, 500 horses, large herds of

139

sheep and swine, and forty Negroes. Settlement — Proceed to the said point, near the 60th Mile from....Colbert's Ferry, on the Tennessee, and run....southeast to Camp on Cotton-Gin Bluff. Distance 8 miles & 158 chs. Through an excellent body of upland, near the low grounds of Town-Creek.

January 15th 1808. We this day build another Perogue, and make preparations for descending the River. Send the Pack-Horse party back to Muscle Shoals for the Baggage.

January 16th 1808. Very cold.

Send Corporal Jacobs and one man with four Horses by land to St. Stephen's, and at a half past 7 O'clock A.M. depart, on board two perogues lashed together, A popular design for small river craft in the early nineteenth century was two perogues (or two dugout canoes) connected in the middle by a sturdy cane platform designed to carry baggage. This was, no doubt, the type craft the Gaines party constructed from Cotton-Gin-Port, down the Tombigby River.

Gaines; course, by land, from the head of the Muscle Shoals on the Tennessee to Cotton Gin Port on the Tombigbee. The total distance by this course was 14,390 chains (33 feet each) or 89.9375 miles. The Gaines Trace was built over this route (Stone, 1971).

Finally, the Gaines Trace was opened in October 1810. Rayford Hyatt stated, *"The Trace was apparently used very little for the purpose it was laid out, because George Colbert pressured for most of the goods to come across his ferry on the Natchez Trace. Gaines Trace was used extensively though by others including merchants and traders shipping goods; and, by settlers going to the lower Tombigbee. It later developed into a road, and parts of it are still in use today."* The old Gaines' Trace is still visible today in sections of the Courtland to Russellville Road which still exists. In addition, west of Russellville, the old Cotton Gin Road is a small unimproved highway in Franklin County, Alabama.

After the completion of the early 1830s railroad around the Muscle Shoals from Decatur to Tuscumbia Landing, the importance of Gaines Trace began to fade very rapidly. The second federal road through Indian lands of North Alabama was initially viewed as a great American trade route but failed miserably with the evolution of the iron horse; however today, the Gaines brothers' dream of this great trade route lives on in the form of the Tennessee-Tombigbee Waterway.

Old Huntsville Road or Great South Trail

Madison County became one of the first counties of North Alabama as part of the Chickasaw treaty of December 1801. U.S. President James Madison moved the land office from Nashville, Tennessee to Huntsville, Alabama during his term of presidency from 1809-1817. In September 1818, James Madison entered some twenty large tracts of land in Lawrence County, Alabama. During his quest as a land speculator, he and his staff as well as other land seeking settlers utilized the Huntsville Road south from Nashville to present-day Huntsville, Alabama. The Huntsville Road was known as the Great South Trail and/or the Great Tennessee Trail.

Huntsville Road-Billy Shaw and Dan Fulenwider

Prior to becoming a road of great importance during the early settlement period, the Huntsville Road was an Indian trail leading from the French Lick (Nashville), to Huntsville, crossed the Tennessee River at Ditto's, passed south through Jones Valley, by Elyton (Birmingham), to Tuscaloosa, by the Falls of the Warrior, then on to Mobile. All portions of this route became a principal immigrant trail from Nashville through the central portion of Alabama from the Tennessee state line all the way to Mobile. The Huntsville Road intersected the Old Chickasaw Trail, the Coosa Path, the High Town Path, and Black Warriors' Path all of which traversed through the Warrior Mountains of Lawrence County, Alabama. The route also passed an important Indian site in North Alabama known today as Bear Meat Cabin at Blountsville, Alabama.

Jackson's Old Military Road

After the Treaty of Fort Jackson ended the Creek Indian War and the British were defeated at the Battle of New Orleans in 1814-15, General Andrew Jackson turned his attention to land speculating. Probably as part of his efforts to improve his holdings in Lawrence, Lauderdale, and Colbert County, Jackson constructed the Old Military Road through Northwest Alabama from 1816 to 1822. Some three hundred workers helped improve earlier Indian roads which passed through the downtown portion of Florence, Alabama. Settlers and military troops could move south from Nashville along Natchez Trace to Columbia, Tennessee, where the Old Military Road started, then south through the City of Florence toward Mississippi.

GENERAL JACKSON'S MILITARY ROAD

Andrew Jackson returned victorious from the Battle of New Orleans along this path to Tennessee after the War of 1812. Already in use by 1812, it was improved with federal funds in 1816. The road handled foot, horse, wagon, and stagecoach traffic and attracted settlement along its New Orleans to Nashville route for much of the nineteenth century.

From Columbia, Jackson's road branched off the Natchez Trace and became a route east of the Trace heading in a southwesterly direction toward Florence. The Old Military Road crossed the river at Florence and continued southwest through Russellville and Franklin County, through Marion and Lamar Counties, to Columbus, Mississippi, then on to Madisonville, Louisiana.

During this time, the route was passing along the eastern portion of the Chickasaw Nation and followed old Indian trails and paths that were already in existence. The area of Northwest Alabama through which the old road passed had been Indian lands until the Turkey Town Treaty of September 1816; however, after the Chickasaws and Cherokee ceded their land holdings, the Old Military Road promoted the settlement and trade of the general area of Northwest Alabama and Eastern Mississippi. Some folks would probably consider Jackson's Old Military Road as an eastern side branch of the Natchez Trace used in order to pass through the developing City of Florence, Alabama.

Jasper Road

In the early days, Jasper Road was an old Indian trail that traversed by present-day towns of Nashville, Columbia, Athens, Decatur, Danville, Addison, Arley, Jasper, and Tuscaloosa. Today, the old road is referred to as the Danville Road and follows the present-day corridor of Highway 41. My dad referred to the road as the Jasper Road.

When I was a young boy, I remember the route being a dirt road that passed my granddaddy Dan Walker's final homeplace approximately one fifth mile south of present Highway 157. When I was a baby, I lived just south of Granddaddy Walker's on the east side of the road. Every Sunday afternoon, the family was expected to be at Granddaddy Walkers to sit on the front porch to listen to him tell stories and eventually get to preaching. After giving up making wildcat whiskey in Tar Springs Hollow, he became a hellfire and brimstone Baptist preacher in his older days.

The Jasper Road passed the foothills of the Warrior Mountains at Grandpa Walker's home and headed south toward the Tennessee Divide. Prior to reaching the divide, the old Indian trail forked, forming two parallel routes to the mountaintop and rejoining near Piney Grove. The eastern route passed by present-day Andrew's Chapel, while the western route traversed up the mountain to Cave Springs Cemetery and Cave Springs Rock Shelter. The rock shelter was a long-term Indian habitation and water supply immediately adjacent to the west edge of the old trail.

From Cave Springs Cemetery, the High Town Path, Black Warriors' Path and the Jasper Road followed along the same trail to Piney Grove where the High Town Path and the Black Warriors' Path turned east along the Old Corn Road. Cave Springs Cemetery is the burial site of my great, great, great, great-grandmother Martha Welborn, which makes me a seventh generation descendant in southeastern Lawrence County.

My great, great, great-grandparents Lockey B. Welborn and Mary E. Welborn Segars Naylor, children of Martha, were one quarter Cherokee Indian. Other Indian ancestors are buried in the old cemetery with present-day Echota Cherokee Chief Billy Shaw's folks buried near my Indian people.

On south toward Upshaw at Old Friendship Cemetery on the Jasper Road, my Walker grandparents and kinfolks are buried. To the west of the Jasper Road, just north of Upshaw at the source of Soakingwater Creek was the homesite of my granddaddy Walker's brother William (Will) Walker. William was named after his granddaddy, great-granddaddy, and great, great-granddaddy, all of whom were named William. The

first William (three quarters Cherokee Indian) was the son of John Walker (one half Cherokee) and Catherine Kingfisher (full Cherokee) and is buried in Blount County. To the east of the Jasper Road and south of Upshaw at the headwaters of Boone Creek and Indian Creek, was the homesite of my granddad Dan Walker. Will and Dan were the only two children to make their home in Alabama. James, Will and Dan's brother, was brought back from Oklahoma and buried next to his daddy Sidney and his great granddaddy William A. Walker at Old Emeus Cemetery at Logan in Cullman County. The rest of the children remained in the Red River area of Texas, Oklahoma and Arkansas.

Butch Walker in old Jasper Road near Inmanfield

The Old Jasper Road became a historic landmark because of the Looney's Tavern gathering at the beginning of the Civil War. The old tavern was located at Brown Springs near Inmanfield Church and was the site for an 1862 meeting of some twenty-five hundred folks from Winston County claiming neutrality from the Confederacy and the Union; however, Winston County eventually became a Union

144

County. Both my great, great, great-granddaddy William A. Walker and my great, great-granddaddy William B. Walker fought with Company I of the 1st Alabama Cavalry of the Union Army. After the war, both signed the loyalty oath to the Union on August 12, 1867.

The Jasper Road followed the old Indian trail along the dividing ridge between Rock Creek and Brushy Creek all the way from Piney Grove to the crossing of Sipsey River north of Jasper. For nearly twenty-five miles in this area, the road does not cross a creek or stream; it created a route across present-day Winston County that was passable year round. The route continued from the crossing of Sipsey River near present day Duncan Bridge to Jasper and then to Tuscaloosa. North of Piney Grove, the route crossed the West Fork of Flint Creek a few miles north of present-day Neel and continued to the Decatur crossing of the Tennessee River at or near Rhodes Ferry. Prehistoric sites are found all along the route, indicating an Indian trail that was used for thousands of years.

McIntosh Road or Georgia Road

William McIntosh was a mixed blood Creek Indian trader; he was born about 1775 to a Creek woman known as Senoya of the Wind Clan and Captain William McIntosh, a Scots Irish Savannah planter. The young William McIntosh was known as Taskanugi Hatke or White Warrior. He fought with Andrew Jackson at the Battle of Horseshoe Bend against the Red Stick Creeks in March 1814 where Menawa escaped; William was promoted to Brigadier General at the end of the Creek War. William McIntosh became a wealthy plantation owner with many black slaves

William McIntosh

The McIntosh Road was initially developed by mixed blood William McIntosh, and it ran from north Georgia to Talladega Alabama. The alternate route built by the Cherokees passed by Running Water Town located near present-day Hale Town, Tennessee; it then followed along the same route as the South River Road running south through Nickajack and Crow Town prior to reaching Talladega. From Talladega, McIntosh graded the route to his ferry located on the Chattahoochee River.

William McIntosh signed the Treaty of Indian Springs on February 12, 1825, that ceded Creek lands in Georgia. McIntosh was later sentenced to be executed by the

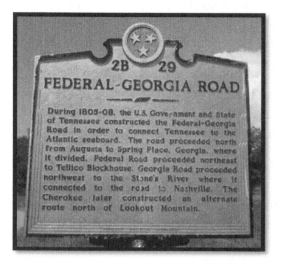

FEDERAL-GEORGIA ROAD

During 1803-08, the U.S. Government and State of Tennessee constructed the Federal-Georgia Road in order to connect Tennessee to the Atlantic seaboard. The road proceeded north from Augusta to Spring Place, Georgia, where it divided. Federal Road proceeded northeast to Tellico Blockhouse. Georgia Road proceeded northwest to the Stone's River where it connected to the road to Nashville. The Cherokee later constructed an alternate route north of Lookout Mountain.

Creek Indian Council for selling Creek territory. Even though he was chief of the friendly Lower Creeks, the assassination of McIntosh was carried out by Menawa and other Creeks on April 30, 1825; a party of Creek Warriors was sent specifically for that purpose. Menawa set his house on fire, but he escaped and was killed later that day. William McIntosh was buried at the McIntosh Reserve in Carroll County, Georgia.

In later years, the route became known as the Georgia Road. The road was built from 1803 to 1805 through the Cherokee Nation under the terms of the Treaty of Tellico; it was opened in 1805. In 1819, the road was improved and renamed the Federal Road. Eventually, white settlers began passing along the road and some settled near the road in Cherokee Territory. In 1830, the State of Georgia took the remaining Cherokee lands and gives it to the white settlers in 1832; the road continued as a major transportation route into the 1940s with some portions still in use today.

Ken Wills in section of McIntosh Road, Talladega NF

Natchez Trace

The Natchez Trace was one of the earliest federal roads through the northwestern corner of Alabama. Beginning in the late 1700s, the road was known as Mountain Leaders Trace and was used primarily as a route for boat guides and crews to come overland from Natchez, Mississippi on the Mississippi River and return to Nashville, Tennessee on the Cumberland River. Trade goods were floated down the Cumberland River to the Ohio, then to the Mississippi River and on to New Orleans. The flatboats were sold as lumber and the boat crew would then return overland to Nashville along the old trace which crossed the Tennessee River at the mouth of Bear Creek. Eventually, the government established the new crossing up river and Chickasaw Chief George Colbert ran Colbert's Ferry on the Natchez Trace; settlers began using the Natchez Trace as a migration route south.

Lamar Marshall in Natchez Trace, NW Alabama

Initially, a ferry on the Tennessee River at the mouth of Bear Creek would transport travelers across the river; however, the area around Bear Creek's mouth was subject to periodic flooding. When the government negotiated a treaty with the Chickasaws in 1801, the ferry site was moved upriver to higher ground. George Colbert negotiated for a house and other facilities to be built by the government. He and his Chickasaw family ran the ferry on Natchez Trace for many years. Some seven miles south of George Colbert's Ferry, Levi Colbert built a house at Buzzard Roost Spring just west of Cherokee in Colbert County, Alabama. Colbert County was named after the two half-Scots and Chickasaw brothers-George and Levi Colbert.

Nina Leftwich (1935), in her book, *Two Hundred Years of Muscle Shoals*, gives a nutshell look at the eventual development of the Natchez Trace:

"William (Colbert) gave most valuable aid to Capt. Isaac Guion when he was sent to take possession of the Spanish military posts in the Southwest in 1798. Major General William, Colonel George and Major James Colbert led 350 Chickasaws to join General Jackson in the Battle of New Orleans in 1815. It is not known whether the brothers held these titles when they went into the War of 1812 or that the titles were conferred by their great commander in recognition of their services.

The next step in the relations of the white man with the Indian was the opening of public roads and mail routes through the vast area of undisputed Indian country

which separated the white settlements in the Natchez District from those of Tennessee and Kentucky. The most famous of these was the Natchez Trace. From time before there were records kept by the whites there had been a trail from the northeast to the far southwest by the way of the mouth of Bear Creek, known as the Mountain Leader's Trace. Intercourse between the United States and the Natchez District was by way of the difficult ascent of the Mississippi and Ohio or by way of this lonely trail, a mere bridle path for 500 miles. Since 1797 the government's mail carrier had been carrying the mail between Nashville and Natchez over the dangerous old trail.

And so, immediately after the organization of the Mississippi Territorial government in 1798 the Federal authorities empowered General Wilkinson in command of the United States troops at Natchez to enter into negotiations with the Indians in reference to opening a road. As the result, in October, 1801, a "Treaty of reciprocal advantages and mutual conveniences between the United States and the Chickasaws" gave leave to cut and open a wagon road between Nashville, Tennessee and Natchez, Mississippi. Governor Claiborne appointed commissioners and *the road was laid out in 1802. In 1806 congress appropriated $6,000 for opening the road through the Indian country and in 1815 made a larger appropriation "for repairing and keeping in repair the road from Natchez to Nashville." The road, which had now become definitely known as the Natchez Trace ran by way of Columbia, Tennessee, crossed the Tennessee River at Colbert's Ferry thence southwest by the present Allsboro into Mississippi and on by old Pontotoc southwest to Natchez. Under the treaties the Indians expressly reserved rights to establish public houses of entertainment along the route and to control the necessary ferries across the water courses. Levi Colbert and his son-in-law, Fitzpatrick Carter, kept such a house at Buzzard Roost (Chisca); while George Colbert kept the house of entertainment and controlled the ferry where the Trace crossed the Tennessee River in the present Colbert County."*

North River Road

The North River Road traversed east to west along the north side of the Tennessee River. It ran from Bridgeport, to Scottsboro, to Huntsville, and through present-day Florence, Alabama; the route followed the corridor of Highway 72 across North Alabama. Portions of this old Indian trail ran concurrent routes that became the Brown's Ferry Road from Athens to Huntsville. At Elgin Crossroads, the North River Road (also known as the east to west Huntsville Road or present-day Highway 72) intersected Doublehead's Trace or the Old Buffalo Trail which is present-day Highway 101. The North River Road ran portions of Jackson's Old Military Road from Killen toward Florence. The trail intersected the Old Huntsville Road (known as the Great South Trail from Nashville to Huntsville to Tuscaloosa which passed Bear Meat Cabin), the Brown's Ferry Road, Black Warriors' Path or

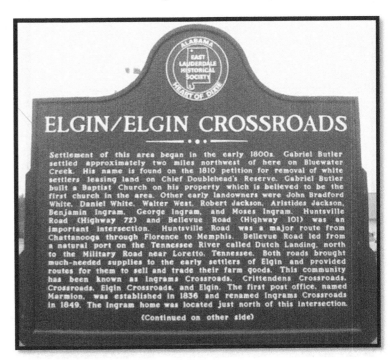

Mitchell Trace, Sipsie Trail, Doublehead's Trace or Old Buffalo Trail, Byler's Turnpike, and Jackson's Military Road.

The North River Road was the major Indian route along the north side of the Tennessee River in North Alabama. The road ran from Crow Town near Stephenson, to Sawtee Town near Scottsboro, to the Flint River Settlements east of Huntsville, to Rogers' ville, and to Shoal Town. Shoal Town was located on the Tennessee River near present-day Wheeler Dam; it was one of the largest Lower Cherokee towns along the North River Road route. Talohuskee Benge and Cherokee Chief Doublehead lived in the Shoal Town area. The North River Road passed through Doublehead's Reserve and by Doublehead's home just east of Blue Water Creek and north of the Tennessee River on Doublehead's Trace.

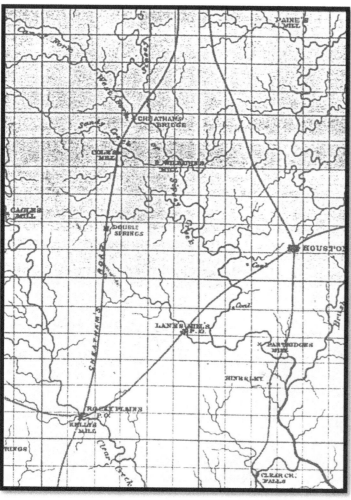

Sipsie Trail

According to early Alabama maps, the Sipsie Trail became the Cheatham Road or Wilderness Parkway, and crossed Lost Creek several miles south of the Sipsey River crossing. At the Sipsey River crossing, an old log timber bridge is still seen bolted to the sandstone bottom of the river. The trail ran from the French Lick (Nashville) to Tuscaloosa. From the French Lick, the trail traversed south to Pulaski, Minor Hill, Rogerville, to the head of "Big Muscle Shoals," where it crossed the Tennessee River. From the river, the route passed through Courtland to Moulton, and proceeded to the Wren Mountains at the southern edge of the

150

Moulton Valley.

Later, the Cheatham Road crossed the Tennessee River at Lamb's Ferry located in Lawrence County. Lamb's Ferry was a early ferry between Elk River Shoals and Big Muscle Shoals just south of Rogersville. The following excerpt identifies its use as early as 1820. *"Another early family in the Rogersville area was that of Joshua James, a Baptist preacher. Mr. James was sent from Boston to help minister to the spiritual needs of the Indians in the area. He and two sons, one of whom had a fifteen-year-old wife, travelled by oxcart, preaching along the way until they reached Chattanooga. There they took a flat boat down the Tennessee River to Lamb's Ferry near Rogersville arriving in 1820. Along the way the family wove colorful coverlets from scraps and threads given them by settlers they met. By the time they reached north Alabama they had woven fifteen or sixteen of these coverlets. They had few contacts with the Indians, who had vacated most of the area"* (Cagle, 1977). From Lamb's Ferry, the route traveled south to Moulton and continued on to Tuscaloosa.

Wyatt Cheatham was authorized to upgrade the trail and build the road by an 1824 Act of the Alabama Legislature. The act specified *"That a public road beginning at a point on Payne's Road, about seven miles south of Moulton in Lawrence County, and running thence in a direction toward Sipsey Creek and thence on the nearest and best way until it crosses Lost Creek and thence on the nearest practicable route, for a good road, to Tuscaloosa, be and the same is hereby established"* (Elliott, 1972).

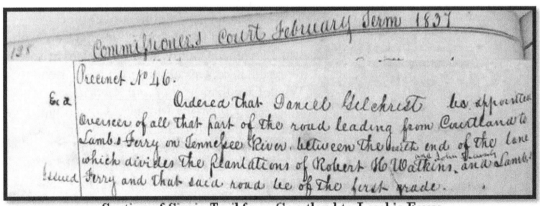

Section of Sipsie Trail from Courtland to Lamb's Ferry

A portion of the Indian route known as the Sipsie Trail became the Cheatham's Turnpike, since Wyatt Cheatham was authorized to upgrade the trail and build the road. The actual upgrade of the trail began seven miles south of Moulton and is the approximate location of the existing junction of Leola Road and Highway 33. The roadway was to be cleared eighteen feet wide with twleve feet of roadway clear of

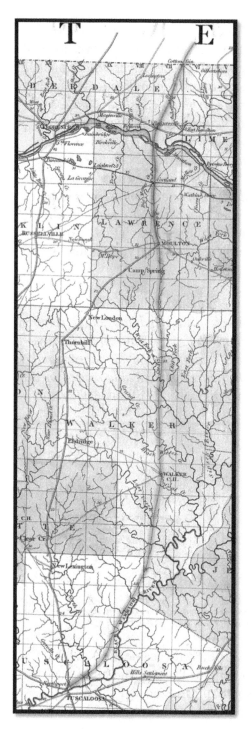

stumps. The old horse and wagon road through the mountains is still visible in many places. The original road ascended Wren Mountain along the west side of the valley, west of present-day Highway 33. The old road reaches the mountaintop some two hundred yards east of the junction of Ridge Road with Highway 33. South from Ridge Road on Highway 33, old roadbeds exhibit existing signs of the original trail and run adjacent to the eastern edge of the Wilderness Parkway.

According to the *Annals of Northwest Alabama* by Donald and Wynelle Dodd, Cheatham was directed by the Act to build the road toward Tuscaloosa. The point of beginning would be the approximate junction of the Leola Road with State Highway 33, presently known as the Wilderness Parkway. This point would be the same as the High Town Path's junction with the Brushy-Sipsey Dividing Ridge.

It appears that Wyatt Cheatham had assistance in his appointment over the construction of the roadway. Joseph Coe, who was Lawrence County's state legislative representative, was obviously a good friend to Wyatt Cheatham. *Old Land Records of Lawrence County* by Margaret Cowart indicates that Joseph Coe (originally from Tennessee) had entered land some three miles south of Courtland in Section 7 of Township 5 South, Range 7 West on September 11, 1818. Cowart states that Wyatt Cheatham originally entered 160 acres of land at Wren and 160 areas near Spivey Gap on September 12, 1818; therefore, both owned land adjacent to the old Indian trail. Cheatham also entered an additional 160 acres near Wren after moving to Winston County. On February 12, 1825, Wyatt Cheatham and Joseph Coe jointly entered 80 acres of land in Winston County where the (their) road crossed Clear Creek in Section 30 of Township 11 South, Range 8 West, according to the Dodds. Earlier on January 26, 1825, Wyatt Cheatham had entered 80 acres near the same location in Winston County.

Wyatt Cheatham is listed in the 1820 Census of Lawrence County, but is not found after that time in the county census records. However, Wyatt entered the additional 160 acres of land at Wren on September 28, 1831, some six years after entering land in Winston County. According to the Lawrence County Census of 1820, Wyatt Cheatham and wife had nine boys under the age 21 and 2 girls under 21, along with the ownership of two slaves. In the 1830 Census of Walker County, Wyatt Cheatham is listed as being 55 years old with six boys under age 20, 3 boys over age 20, one female under age 20, and one female over age 20, and in addition, two slaves. It is obvious that Cheatham lost a daughter or his wife between 1820 or 1830. Again in the 1850 Census of Winston County, Wyatt Cheatham is listed as being a 72 year old native of Virginia. At the time of this census, Wyatt lived with Lamina, 29; George, 16; Francis, 12; Thomas, 11; and an infant girl, Elizabeth, 1. All are listed as being born in Alabama.

Cheatham served in the War of 1812 as a sergeant in John A. Allen's Madison County Company. After the war, he moved to Wren where he entered a total of some 320 acres of land. Wyatt Cheatham had a strong alliance with Andrew Jackson (Dodd, 1974). Wyatt Cheatham moved from Madison County and lived at Wren in Lawrence County from 1818 until he was authorized to build the Cheatham Road. By 1825, he had moved to Winston County and entered land at the Clear Creek crossing of his road. In later years, he profited in trade from folks who traveled along his road and stopped by his tavern on Clear Creek.

On January 13, 1826, an election precinct was approved at the home of Wyatt Cheatham on Clear Creek where said Cheatham's Turnpike crossed the Sand. In 1828, Wyatt Cheatham obtained a license to sell liquors at his place at the Clear Creek crossing. Wyatt and his son, Wyatt D. Cheatham, renewed their liquor license for $10.00 in 1833.

The route through the middle of Bankhead Forest was known for many years as the Cheatham Road. The road officially changed to Wilderness Parkway after the establishment of the Sipsey Wilderness Area. The present-day route of Highway 33 going to the top of Wren Mountain is in its third location since the original road was built. The Cheatham Road was improved and parts were re-routed up the Wren Mountain in the late 1920s. The road was eventually paved and re-routed again during the late 1940s. Many portions of the original Sipsie Trail and Cheatham wagon roads are still visible today along Highway 33 south of Wren.

The original trail and road up Wren Mountain is still clearly visible as it traverses up the west slope of the long valley directly south of the intersection of present-day Highways of 36 and 33 at Wren. The old route traversed to the flat top of the mountain at its junction with the High Town Path or the present-day beginning of the Ridge Road.

South River Road

During early historic North Alabama, a series of Cherokee Indian towns were located along the Muscle Shoals that were connected by the South River Road. These Lower Cherokee villages included Moneetown or Mousetown, Doublehead's Town at Brown's Ferry, Melton's Bluff, Cuttyatoy's Village (Gilchrist Island), Goard's Settlement (Courtland), Shoal Town (present site of Doublehead's Resort), Colbert's Ferry, and others.

Portions of the Black Warriors' Path, Gaines' Trace, Old Chickasaw Trail, the Coosa Path or Muscle Shoals Path, the Creek Path, the Great War and Trading Path, Desoto's Route, and other Indian trails knitted a South River Road from Hiwassee to Colbert's Ferry. Along the route, many small shoals, fords, and later ferries provided crossings of the numerous creeks and streams flowing from the south side of the Tennessee River. Later the English and French traders utilized the South River Road in setting up trade alliances with the Cherokee and Chickasaw.

By the 1700s, the South River Road was coming into prominence: "*....Jean Couture....who had deserted the French to become a free-lance trader....cultivated the*

154

reputation as the "greatest Trader and Traveller amongst the Indians for more than Twenty years," and had encouraged Moore's party with political intelligence concerning the interior. After a chance meeting with Couture, Blathwayt's prospectors gained a strong impression of the strategic importance of the Tennessee River to continental competition with France, a geographical idea which was to firmly graft itself on the minds of both colonists and English officialdom.

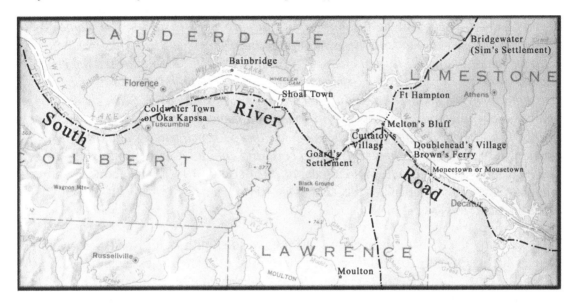

To prove that the Tennessee linked up with the Ohio, and to demonstrate its importance in driving a "wedge" between the French territories in Louisiana and Canada, Couture in 1700 led a group of Englishmen down the Tennessee river to its confluence with the Ohio and then west to the Mississippi. A year later, alarmed by the news of the English incursion, Iberville in France commissioned a "reverse reconnaissance" of the Tennessee River. Eventually the French party found a portage near the Cherokee Valley towns linking the Tennessee with the Savannah drainage, and progressed downriver to Charlestown, where they discussed with Governor James Moore the possibility of establishing a trading pact.

This <u>river road</u> was scarcely traveled in the years before 1715, because of the intercolonial and intercultural hostilities especially in the direction of Spanish Florida — which engaged the English during the first decade of the century....Though the colonists may have overestimated the bindings of trade, there is no doubt that joint Cherokee and Carolina trade expanded greatly, along with the burgeoning commerce of Charlestown, right up to the 1750's. Though rice had supplanted deerskins in export value, deerskin loadings remained high at the Charlestown docks, and a significant *percentage of these were of Cherokee origin. During 1747 — 48 the value of shipments of deerskins (and other tribal commodities) roughly equaled the combined total of indigo, beef and pork, lumber, and naval stores....On the other hand a Charlestown alliance with the tribe would finally give Carolinians access to the long-sought Tennessee River road to the Mississippi"* (Hatley, 1995).

Portions of the South River Road in this area were used to attack Indian towns as early as 1787. According to the *Journal of Muscle Shoals History*, *"Col. James Robertson was selected to lead the expedition to the Tennessee River...left Nashville with one hundred and thirty men on the 1ˢᵗ of June 1787. He safely reached the river, found the cabins empty...early next morning the guns, ammunition, and fifty men crossed over in the boat. The remainder with the horses swam over. Scarcely had they reached the south bank...Col. Robertson's men commenced a rapid march down river...the battle was begun...many were killed...three French traders and a white woman who would not surrender, fled to a boat and entered it with twenty-six Indians. The Americans with one volley killed them all"* (Sheridan, 1974). The above documents villages along the south bank of the Tennessee River connected by a road or trail which aided the rapid movement of Robertson's forces.

During the early historic period, the area of the South River Road was occupied by the Cherokees on the eastern upper reaches of the river in Tennessee, the Yuchi in the middle of the Great Bend Region of North Alabama, and the Chickasaw in the western portion of the river system into Mississippi. The Yuchi Indians were located in the northern portion of Alabama along the Muscle Shoals and were visited by five Canadians who ascended the Tennessee in the summer of 1701. It is highly probable that the Canadians utilized portions of the South River Road during their visit. John R. Swanton (1946) notes that the Yuchi were living near a Chickasaw Town and later moved to the Hiwassee River in Tennessee.

According to the *Journal of Muscle Shoals History*, *"...the Cherokees were not the first Indians to live at the Muscle Shoals on the Tennessee River. This honor belongs to the mound builders who were followed by the Euchees (Yuchi), a tribe having a unique language and no migration legend. They may have lived at the Shoals in pre-historic times. The Euchees were probably living at the Shoals when Desoto (1540) came through Alabama and were definitely there in 1700 when discovered by some traveling Canadians...Shortly after they were discovered by the Canadians in 1700, the Euchees departed from the Shoals and moved to the mountainous regions of what is now East Tennessee"* (Watts, 1973).

156

After conflicts over the Muscle Shoals with the Shawnee, the Chickasaws were given the land east to Chickasaw Island just south of present-day Huntsville by the Chickasaw Boundary Treaty of January 10, 1786. Later, Cherokees under the leadership of Doublehead were living among the Chickasaws along the Muscle Shoals; therefore, the Cherokees and Chickasaws controlled most of the South River Road until the Turkey Town Treaty of September 1816.

Today, the old trail on the south side of the Tennessee is known as the River Road or Old River Road in Colbert and Morgan Counties. In Lawrence County, the South River Road is a series of roads made up primarily of the Mallard-Spring Creek Road, which follows sections of both the Black Warriors' Path and Gaines' Trace.

In addition, the road which passes International Paper to Red Bank, then to Town Creek was along the corridor of the South River Road. In Morgan County, the Old River Road runs east-west and lies between the river and the present-day town of Priceville. Ironically, the path crosses Town Creek at Joe Patterson (formerly Fosters') Bridge at a place called Doublehead's Resort on the western edge of Lawrence County. As the old road proceeded west along the Tennessee River in Colbert County, it is called the River Road.

The portion in Colbert County connected the Indian villages along the south bank of the river westerly from Shoal Town. The incident of Robertson's forces identifies Indian villages prior to reaching Cold Water. At Cold Water, the French had operated a trading post from which raids were made against Cumberland settlers. *The French established a fort on the Cerstates River (the Tennessee) sometime around 1715. They maintained successful trade relations with the Indians of the area for almost seventy years. In 1785 the French had a trading post at Cold Water (Spring) Creek. In June 1787, Colonel James Robertson, seeking to end the Indian raids originating in this area, led a party of white soldiers out of Tennessee into Cold Water. Many Indians were killed, and the French traders were taken captive"* (Johnson, Kenneth, 1976).

HIGH TOWN PATH

The High Town Path, one of the most famous Indian trails in the Southeastern United States, traversed across the Continental Divide portion of William B. Bankhead National Forest in Lawrence County, Alabama. The Indian trail completely crossed the Southeastern United States in an east-west direction and traveled through Alabama along the dividing watersheds of the Tennessee River to the north and the waters that drain into Mobile Bay to the south. The long Indian trail was some 1000 miles in length with the Indian village of High Town (Rome, GA) located near the middle of the route.

The focal point of The Path as well as other westerly trails was the Chickasaw Towns in the upper Tombigbee River System.

The High Town Path was probably most heavily used as an Indian foot path in prehistoric times and was free of creek crossings and other water and wet weather barriers. Major portions of the High Town Path followed ridge top divides which appear to be the general routes of early Indian trails. According to the _Natchez Trace Parkway_, *"these traces, or trails, showed a marked tendency to follow watershed divides in an effort to avoid stream crossings and swamps, even though the distances were greater"* (Chapman and Demaray, 1951). Also, _The Story of Alabama_ gives, *"the trails were always along lines where there were the fewest physical obstacles or obstructions often going along on the watershed of two streams, when these watersheds pointed in the right direction"* (Owens, 1949). In addition, the _Manual for Writing Alabama State History_ says, *"Among the Indian Nations, boundary lines between tribes and divisions of tribes were dividing ridges or water sheds, water courses, and sometimes a trail connecting two well-known towns. Either water or a ridge with no water, was a boundary line easily understood by the aboriginal mind."*

The Continental Divide through North Alabama lay along an east-west line which contained the fewest physical obstacles to year-around travel such as creeks, streams, and lowlands. The _Territorial Papers_ also indicate the trail ran easterly along one continuous chain of mountains. According to a letter written by Edmund P. Gaines to the Secretary of War on January 29, 1808, and printed in the _Territorial Papers_, *"the route for the greater part of this distance, is on the dividing ridges, between the waters of Tennessee and Mobile, and consequently not subject to the inconvenience of crossing water courses, save one small creek, and a few rivulets, which will require little*

158

bridging or causeway" (Carver, 1938).

Some information about the famous Indian route known as the High Town, High Tower Path, Ridge Path, or The Path was obtained from many historical sources. The following accounts of the long Indian trail that completely crossed northern Alabama is based on several old maps, Indian treaties, books, census records, local Indian traditions, family legends that have been passed down through the years, and personal testimony. The Path evidently served early Indian people as a trade route, long distance travel from east to west, tribal boundaries, and political purposes including both war and peace with neighboring tribes.

It is easy for one to conjure up ideas of how Indian life might have been when the notorious east-west Indian route called the High Town Path, Ridge Path, High Tower Path, or The Path crossing the northern portions of Georgia, Alabama, and Mississippi was highly used by Indian people. The High Town Path ran from Charles Town or Charleston, South Carolina to Chickasaw Bluffs at the junction of the Wolf River and the mighty Mississippi at what is today known as Memphis, Tennessee.

Indian people, including Indian mixed-bloods, and early settlers moving into Lawrence County from east Tennessee and north Georgia, came in contact with the High Town Path and followed along its course. The Indian trail crossed Georgia just north of Atlanta and another route traversed diagonally across Tennessee toward the southwest from the Knoxville area and through the area east of Chattanooga. Portions of The Path crossed Lookout Mountain and Sand Mountain as it proceeded toward the dividing ridges of the Warrior Mountains in the southern portion of Lawrence County.

High Town, which was present-day Rome, Georgia, and Turkey Town, which was near present day Gadsden, Alabama, were important Indian towns along the eastern portion of the route. It was by this route that numerous Indian mixed-bloods, settlers of the Warrior Mountains, and many North Alabama families can trace the western movement of their ancestors.

EUROPEAN EXPLORERS

The High Town Path was not only an Indian footpath of trade among the prehistoric and historic Southeastern Indian people but also to early Europeans. The east-west land route, connecting the Atlantic Ocean to the Mississippi River and Gulf of Mexico, was a trail of least resistance to our Indian ancestors and also to early historic European travelers. The Path connected overland two areas extremely important to the early navigators of the Spanish, French, and British fleets. Many early European travelers either crossed or traveled along portions of the High Town Path. Some of the most noted Europeans crossing or traveling along portions of the early Indian trail included the Spanish during the 1500s and late 1700s (with DeSoto being the first Spanish explorer in 1540), the French in the early 1700s, and the English in 1698 along with other British traders through the early 1800s.

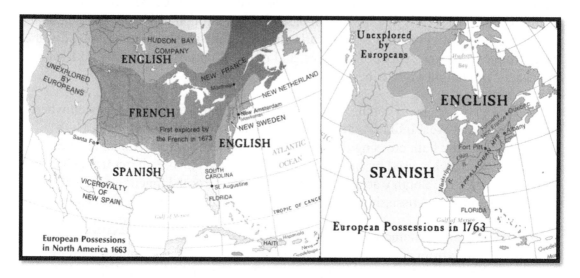

After DeSoto came through North Alabama in 1540, Spanish influence was limited in the Tennessee Valley. Some of the Creek Indians traded with the Spanish and developed a strong alliance toward the late 1700's. By the late 1600's, Britain and France competed heavily for trade alliances with the Cherokee and Chickasaw in the areas of northern Alabama and Mississippi. Many battles were fought between the British and French for control of trade with the Chickasaws and Cherokees. Spanish influence and trade extended through Florida to the Pensacola with the French trying to extend their control of trade in the Gulf panhandle area. Eventually the French King ceded the colony of Louisiana to Spain in 1762. A general peace between Spain, France, and England was finalized on January 1, 1763. France ceded all of Louisiana east of the Mississippi River to Mobile and Canadian possessions to England. Spain ceded all their Florida possessions to England; therefore, the British gained control of the Southeastern portion of this country. By 1764, the English authorities were encouraging emigration along Indian trade routes causing a flood of people pouring into the lands of the Cherokee, Creek, and Chickasaw; however, English control was short-lived due to the signing of the Declaration of Independence on July 4, 1776. Finally, the American colonists claimed all the area along the High Town Path.

These European traders and travelers intermarried with Indian people as they followed portions of the High Town Path along its eastern and western ends. The traders used the dividing ridge portion of The Path through Lawrence County, as well as other trails such as the Coosa Path and Chickasaw Trail. The southern portion of The Path through Oakfuskee appeared to receive greater use by early Europeans. However, many early mixed-blood settlers traveled along The Path and other Indian trails into the northern portions of Alabama and the Lawrence County area. These were largely Celtic-Indian mixed-bloods looking for isolation and trying to avoid removal to the west.

The United States took the area along The Path from the Southeastern Indians by the 1840s. The Treaty of Fort Jackson in 1814 took the lands south of the High Town Path through Lawrence County. In September 1816, the Turkey Town Treaty took the northern side of the Lawrence County portion of the High Town Path; therefore, by 1816, the Warrior Mountains portion of The Path belonged to the United States of America.

SPANISH

After DeSoto traveled through northern Alabama and Mississippi, Spanish influence in these areas was greatly diminished until the 1770s. Desoto's route through the Southeastern United States during 1540 crossed or passed along eastern and western portions of the High Town Path. DeSoto's traveled along or adjacent to the western portion of the High Town Path to the Chickasaw towns; the fight with the Chickasaw contributed to his eventual death. Desoto was placed into the Mississippi River as his final resting place (Swanton, 1985).

According to the *Final Report of the United States Desoto Expedition Commission*, *"Memphis' claims to the point of discovery of the Mississippi were patriotically maintained by J.M. Young in his 'History of Memphis' in 1888 and by Judge J.P. Young in a 'History of Memphis' published in 1912, but the cudgels in its behalf were most vigorously wielded by Mr. James H. Malone. From Pontotoc, he supposes the Spaniards marched northward on the main trail to New Albany and regards it as possible that they kept on to the Fourth Chickasaw Bluff, namely Memphis, on the 'Long Trail' indicated in Lushey's map of 1835 which followed the high land between Wolf and Coldwater Rivers."* It should be noted that the "Long Trail" is referring to the western portion of the High Town Path since both trails followed the same route along the divide from Copper Town to Memphis. Copper Town was located in the area of Pontotoc Ridge in Pontotoc County, Mississippi (Swanton, 1985).

According to a map in the book *America! America!*, the Spanish possession in North America during 1663 followed along the same general route as the High Town Path, from near Charles Town, South Carolina to the Mississippi River near Memphis, Tennessee. The 1663 Spanish boundary through North Alabama followed an east-west route south of the Tennessee River along the Continental Divide and was basically the same route as the High Town Path. The Spanish tried for years to establish a strong alliance with the Creek Indian people to the south of the High Town Path. The Spanish-Creek Alliance eventually was as strong as the French-Choctaw or British-Chickasaw Alliances.

The transfer of Louisiana by France to Spain in 1762 created tremendous problems for the newly established United States Government. In 1779, Spain declared war on Great Britain and took west Florida on May 9, 1781; therefore, Spain effectively controlled trade along the Gulf Coast and up the Mississippi River. At the end of the American War of Independence, both the Spanish and American governments were seeking treaties with the Chickasaws. Through efforts of Creek Chief Alexander McGillivary, the Chickasaws signed a treaty with Spain in Mobile in June 1784. Spanish agents immediately began sending trade goods from Pensacola and Mobile by way of the Tombigbee and Mississippi Rivers into the Chickasaw Nation. On the other hand, the United States negotiated a treaty with the Chickasaws on January 10, 1786, which established the boundaries of the Chickasaw Nation; therefore, the Chickasaws became a key player in westward migration of American settlers.

Spain was attempting to block the movement of American settlement of the West by using the Chickasaw Nation as a barrier. Spain used Alexander McGillivary of the Creek Nation to influence the Chickasaws; however, the Creeks, who were robbing and killing traders bringing American goods from the East, killed Piomingo's nephew. Chickasaw Chief Piomingo, who favored American traders, convened his council and declared war on the Creeks. In 1793, the Americans delivered five hundred stands of guns along with powder, lead, and flints to Piomingo for defeat of the Spanish-supported Creeks. In addition, the Spanish-Creek alliance began to fall apart after the death of Creek Chief Alexander McGillivary in February 1793. However, Piomingo continued his vicious war against old McGillivary faction of Creeks. Finally, after much bloodshed, the Creeks and Chickasaws agreed to a lasting peace in July 1798.

Spain signed a treaty in 1795 giving the United States title to the territory to the Mississippi River. By 1802, the United States established a trading house at Chickasaw Bluffs. This trading house required continuous use of trading paths from the east and prompted the establishment of a trading route from the Tennessee River to Cotton Gin Port on the Tombigbee River. The trading route, which would eventually be called

Gaines' Trace, was established to avoid Spanish taxes that were to be paid by the Lower Tombigbee settlers bringing goods from Mobile.

FRENCH

The French published a southeastern United States map in 1733 and referred to a trail which follows portions of the High Town Path as the Chemin de la Caroline. The Chemin de la Caroline is interpreted as a route to and from the Carolinas. The Chemin de la Caroline map shows a trail passing through Oakfuskee then proceeding northwest through the center of Alabama to the Chickasaw towns on the upper Tombigbee River System. The western portion of the Chemin de la Caroline appears to travel westerly along the High Town Path route from Flat Rock Camp to the French Landing on the Chattawatchee River (Now Cotton Gin Port of the Tombigbee River).

According to the 1663 map, the French land claim boundary was south of the Tennessee River in Alabama and followed along the same line as the Spanish. The French Territory lay to the north of the divide with the Spanish claims to the south of the Tennessee Divide (Buggey, 1980). The French tried to control most of the Indian trade in the Mississippi River Valley (which included the Tennessee Valley) and had an established trading post located at the Muscle Shoals by 1715. In addition, French officials regarded it as essential to establish French presence and power in that region to thwart the English thrust which had nearly reached the Mississippi. Reports from French traders in the Northwest warned that "the English are coming," confirming the English traders' relentless march from their base at Charleston to the West. French and English traders inevitably were the vanguard of troops, fortifications, and settlements. Their daring and intensively competitive attempts to establish commercial relations with tribes in the lower Mississippi Valley prompted the early incidents in the long and bloody contest for control of this region which lasted from the 1680s to 1763. At times, Spain was a reluctant participant in this power struggle which centered on the Chickasaws (Gibson, 1971). However, the British maintained greater influence with the Chickasaws and Cherokees than did the French. The British goods were half the price of French goods and usually much better. The French had a much greater alliance with the Choctaw than either the Chickasaws or Cherokees.

French troubles with the Chickasaws began in 1698 because of the undermining influence of the English from Carolina. The French tried to block the Carolina trader paths using Choctaw Indians, with whom they had a strong alliance. The French were unable or unwilling to supply the amount of trade goods desired by the Chickasaws; therefore, they turned to the English who delivered large pack trains and caravans ladened with quality goods to the Chickasaw Nation. By 1720, the first French-

Chickasaw War broke out with the killing of a French trader. The first Chickasaw-French War ended early in 1725 when French officers led their Choctaw companies from ambush positions on the Carolina trader paths back to the Choctaw Nation (Gibson, 1971).

The second French-Chickasaw War started in 1731 because of the burning of three captured Chickasaws and refusal by Chickasaws to release Natchez refugees to the French. Bienville, French Governor of Mobile, methodically plotted his major offensive against the Chickasaw Towns in the upper Tombigbee. In 1736, Bienville was determined to defeat the English supported Chickasaws. Allied with Choctaws, Bienville camped his army six miles from the upper Tombigbee Chickasaw Towns ready for an assault. The following account from Albert James Pickett's _History of Alabama_, 1851, pages 156-160 gives the situation, *"May 24, 1736: His intention, at first, was to march to a circuitous direction, around the Chickasaw villages...The Chickasaws had fortified themselves with much skill, and were assisted by Englishmen, who caused them to hoist a flag of their country over one of their defenses. The French troops, as they advanced, were not a little surprised to see the British Lion, against which many of them had often fought in Europe, now floating over the rude huts of American Indians, and bidding them defiance...The brave Chickasaws maintained their positions in the fortified houses, and, from loop holes, riddled the French with their unerring rifles...When the French had retreated some distance towards Bienville's headquarters, the Choctaws, by way of bravado, rushed up to the Chickasaw fortifications, as if they intended to carry them by storm, but receiving a general volley from the enemy, they fled in great terror over the prairie...Night now shrouded the scene with its sable mantle, and the French troops reposed behind some trees which had been felled for their protection. The Chickasaws remained quiet within their entrenchments. At length day dawned, and exhibited to Bienville a painful sight. On the ramparts of the Chickasaws were suspended the French soldiers and officers, whom Beauchamp was forced to leave upon the field. Their limbs had been separated from their bodies, and thus were they made to dangle in the air, for the purpose of insulting the defeated invaders. Many of the officers wished to rush again upon the villages, but Bienville was determined to retreat, as the Choctaws were of no assistance to him, and he was without cannon to batter down the fortifications...If the Chickasaws had followed up the French, they could easily have destroyed Bienville's army at this time. At length the army reached Fort "Tombechbe," now Jones Bluff. Bienville, sending on a portion of the troops, and the sick and wounded to Mobile, disembarked at the fort. He remained there, however, but one day...the governor entered his boats, and continued the voyage until they were moored at the town of Mobile."*

The French under command of Bienville suffered this bitter defeat at the hands of the Chickasaws. The second French-Chickasaw War ended in February 1740 with both sides agreeing to end hostilities and exchange prisoners. After serving as Governor of Mobile for forty years, Bienville was returned to France because of being unable to defeat the Chickasaws. Trouble between the French and Chickasaw continued with raids occurring at frequent intervals. Again, a third French-Chickasaw War began in 1752, and the French decided to annihilate the Chickasaw Nation. Marquis de Vaudreuil, the new French Governor of Mobile, organized seven hundred French regulars and a large number of Choctaws to invade the Chickasaw Nation. The invasion force followed the route of Bienville up to the Tombigbee and met with the same fate as his predecessor. Therefore, after three bloody wars the French were unable to defeat the English supported Chickasaws. France finally relinquished the area to the English on January 1, 1763.

According to *Two Hundred Years at Muscle Shoals*, "*Oka Kapassa was established as a Cherokee village about 1770 on the west bank of Coldwater, or Spring Creek, at its confluence with the Tennessee, about one mile west of the present Tuscumbia. This site was resorted to by neighboring Indians for the purpose of trading with the French who still persisted on the Wabash, and became the source of great vexation and numerous outrages to the Cumberland settlements about our present Nashville*" (Leftwich, 1935). Eventually, the French were defeated in several battles by the British Alliance with the Chickasaws and Cherokees; however, toward the end of the 1770s, French influence greatly diminished. Cumberland settlers organized a campaign against the French Trading Post at Coldwater in present-day Tuscumbia and wiped them out.

BRITISH

Beginning in the late 1600s, indentured servants of Celtic origin became the traders for the British to the Indian Nations of Northern Alabama. By 1736, the British made it illegal for their subjects in the colonies to travel westward and settle beyond the Appalachian Mountains; therefore, British traders utilized Celtic people to conduct their trade and commerce with the native people to the west of the colonies. These Celtic traders rapidly intermarried with the native people of this area and eventually developed a culture unique to the Warrior Mountains and Southern highlands. The Chickasaws actually formed mixed-blood towns such as McIntoshville in Mississippi and Breed Camp on the Coosa River in Alabama. Breed Camp was actually a Chickasaw outpost in eastern Alabama established to guide British and American traders around hostile locations and direct them to the Chickasaw Towns in the Cotton Gin Port area of the upper Tombigbee River System. These mixed-ancestry people rose in prominence among the local tribes and dominated the ruling factions of the southern Indian Nations.

These Celtic traders intermarried with Indian women and contributed to the mixed-ancestry in the area. By the 1800s, all three local tribes, of Cherokee, Chickasaw, and Creek were controlled by Scots-Indian mixed-bloods. John Watts, Jr. (half Scots, half Cherokee), Chief of the Cherokee Nation, was the son of Scots trader John Watts and Cherokee Chief Doublehead's sister. He was the brother to Wurteh Watts, the mother of Sequoyah (George Gist). George and Levi Colbert (half Scots, half Chickasaw), Chiefs of the Chickasaw Nation, were the sons of Scots trader James Logan Colbert, who came into the Chickasaw Nation during the late1730s and married three Chickasaw women. George Colbert married two of Doublehead's daughters. Alexander McGillivary (half Scots, one quarter French, one quarter Creek), Chief of the Creek Nation, was the son of Scots trader Lachlan McGillivary and Sehoy Marchand, a half-blood French-Creek lady of the most powerful family in the Creek Nation known as the Wind Clan.

The British traders traveled extensively through the Southeastern United States during the 1700s. The British traders of Scots and Irish origin operated pack trains loaded with goods in order to undermine French and later Spanish influence. The British goods were twice as good and sold at half the price. By the early 1700s, the British Lion was flying over Chickasaw towns. The alliance of the British and Chickasaws led to several victories over the French during the three French and Chickasaw Wars.

The English route of Colonel Welch to Mississippi, in 1698, appears to pass some distance south of the High Town Path along its western course. The eastern portion of Welch's route follows the High Town Path from Charles Town and proceeds to Oakfuskee, thence to the old Chickasaw crossing at Cotton Gin Port, and then appears to travel through the southern portion of the Chickasaw Nation in Mississippi. Afterwards Welch's route was used by English traders (Mitchell Map, 1755).

The Purcell Map of British Indian Trade was developed not later than 1770. The British route traveled from the upper drainage of the Oconee River through the dividing ridges of Alabama to the towns of the Chickasaw Nation in the upper portions of the Tombigbee River System. (Purcell Map, 1770) Portions of this particular route passed along the dividing ridges of the High Town Path in the Bankhead Forest portion of Lawrence County, Alabama. According to a note on the Mitchell Map of 1755, *"the country of the Cherokee which extends westward to the Mississippi and northward to the confines of the Six Nations was formally surrendered to the Crown of Britain at Westminister 1729."*

Another British route passed north from Charles Town to Tellico in east Tennessee. Still another British route passed southeast from Charles Town to Oakfuskee through the Creek Towns then westerly to the Choctaw Nation. In addition, the route referred to as "formerly ye Common Road of ye English Indian Trail" began at Charles Town on the Atlantic Coast and traveled westward to the Chickasaw Bluffs on the Mississippi River.

The British became a strong trading ally to the Chickasaw and Cherokee. Toward the latter part of the 1770s, the British wiped out villages of Celtic people, many of which were of mixed-ancestry, along the eastern edge of the Appalachian Mountains. The vicious nature of the British turned the Indians of mixed-ancestry against their once strong ally.

After the Declaration of Independence was signed on July 4, 1776, and the Revolutionary War began, Celtic traders and their families of mixed-ancestry were caught in the middle of bloody battles. British forces still saw their Celtic traders as barbarians and their mixed-blood Indian families as savages. This tragic turn of events would eventually lead to a bloody confrontation of "Scots Irish Over-the-Mountain Men" and one third of the British Army. In 1780 after the British wiped out several Celtic villages, some three thousand of these "Scots Irish Over-the-Mountain Men" crossed the Appalachians in search of revenge. Many of these mountain men were of mixed-Indian ancestry, wore buckskins, shot long rifles, and fought as their Indian forefathers, using guerrilla warfare.

Ferguson was in charge of one division of the British's three divisions that were going to split the colonies and then conquer each. Ferguson and his division was cutting off South Carolina and Georgia along the border of South and North Carolina when he learned of the Scots-Irish army. Ferguson chose "Kings Mountain" to defeat the rag-tag army of men. Needless to say, Ferguson's battle plan was to fight the old English style with his men in rank and file firing volleys of shot; however, they were not expecting this new Indian style of warfare brought over the mountains. During the Battle of Kings Mountain, one third of the British Army was wiped out, allowing General George Washington to muster his troops into winning the Revolutionary War. By the Treaty of Paris in 1783, Great Britain ceded to the United States the territory west to the Mississippi and north of thirty-one degrees (Gibson, 1971).

British influence did not stop at the Battle of Kings Mountain or the ending of the Revolutionary War. After defeating the Creek Indians at Horseshoe Bend with the assistance of Cherokee Indians in 1814, General Andrew Jackson turned his attention to the British in New Orleans. Again the British were soundly defeated by Jackson's crack shot long-rifle men from Tennessee. The Battle of New Orleans ended most of the British aggression in the Southeastern United States.

HISTORIC SIGNIFICANCE

From the early 1700s, the Chickasaw Indians living in Northern Alabama and Mississippi became of primary interest to four nations -- Spain, France, England, and later the United States. The Spanish were the first to test the fury of Chickasaw warriors when DeSoto's expedition fell to ruin at their hands. Next, the French tried unsuccessfully to defeat the Chickasaws in three wars during the 1700s. The British won Chickasaw favor in trade as did the American Government after the War of Independence.

Since Spain and France controlled the Gulf Coast, British goods had to be shipped over land from their primary trade center at Olde Charles Town, South Carolina. French and Spanish forces allied with the Choctaw Indians tried for over a century to disrupt these east-west Carolina trading routes of the British and later of the Americans. To get goods to the Chickasaw Towns in the upper Tombigbee, traders of the British and later American Colonies had to use many paths and trails running east to west. Since France in the early 1700's was strongly allied with the Choctaws, and Spain in the late 1700s was strongly allied with the Creeks, the most used Carolina trading paths to the Tombigbee Chickasaw Towns was through north Alabama, south of the Tennessee River.

Of five east-west trading routes in North Alabama, four ran through present-day Lawrence County: Old Chickasaw Trail, Coosa Path or Muscle Shoals Path, South River Road, and High Town Path. The Old Chickasaw Trail ran through the Tennessee Valley parallel and south of the Tennessee River. The Old Chickasaw Trail ran from Ditto's, to the mouth of Flint Creek on the south bank of the Tennessee River near Decatur, to Moulton, to Russellville, then to Cotton Gin Port, Mississippi on the Tombigbee. The Coosa Path or Muscle Shoals Path ran through the Moulton Valley between the Tennessee River and Warrior Mountains. The Coosa Path ran from Coosa, to Ditto's, to Sommerville, to Hartselle, to Danville, to Oakville, Moulton, Hatton, Wolf Springs, and then Tuscumbia Landing. The South River Road ran along the south bank of the Tennessee River. The High Town Path ran the Continental Divide in the southern portion of Lawrence County. A fifth path, the Chickasaw Nation- Little

Oakfuskee Trail ran south of the High Town Path but joined it at Flat Rock, around the Haleyville area.

In order to avoid French-Choctaw or Spanish-Creek raiders along the paths, guides from Breed Town on the Coosa would direct pack trains and caravans of goods along the different routes through North Alabama. French and Spanish mercenaries kept watch for isolated trading parties. These hostile forces lurked along the routes to disrupt English or American trade and plunder the goods. The effect was opposite of the outcome the French and Spanish desired; the Chickasaw were driven into strong alliance with the English and later the Americans. Probably the greatest impact was the fusing of Chickasaw and Cherokee bloodlines with that of Scots, Irish, and English traders. These mixed-ancestry Celtic Indian people had a more compelling desire to rid their country of both the French and Spanish.

The American Government persisted in establishing roads through Cherokee Country to the Chickasaw Towns on the Tombigbee. In October 1805, portions of the High Town Path were upgraded by treaty as a route from Tellico to the Tombigbee. On October 27, 1805, the Cherokees granted the free use of a road through their country for the carriage of the mail, which stated: *"The Cherokees agree that the citizens of the United States, shall have, so far as it goes, through their country the free and unmolested use of a road leading: from Tellico to Tombigbee, to be laid out by viewers, appointed on both sides, who shall direct it, the nearest and best way; and the time of doing the business, the Cherokees shall be notified of. In consideration of the above cession and relinquishment, the United States agrees to pay to the Cherokee Indians, sixteen hundred dollars in money, or useful merchandise, at their option, within ninety days after the ratification of this treaty."* The articles were agreed upon by Return J. Meigs and Daniel Smith, appointed commissioners of the U.S. to hold conferences with the Cherokee Indians at Tellico (Gentry, 1962).

According to the *Annals of Northwest Alabama*, *"The High Town Path was an Indian trail that extended from near the present site of Atlanta, Georgia, westward through the Cherokee Nation south of Sand Mountain, through the Creek Nation, and into the Chickasaw Nation and the present counties of Lawrence, Franklin, and Marion in Alabama prior to entering Mississippi. Settlers from North Georgia and South Carolina could migrate to Winston along this route having good roads until they turned southward to cross the mountains. After the building of the Cheatham Road and Byler's Road, they could have fair roads all the way"* (Elliott, 1972). It should be noted that the High Town Path entered Winston County only in the northern portion and passed through the present town of Haleyville. It is very probable that the Indian town of Flat Rock was on the site of the town of Haleyville. Settlers traveled from The Path along present-day Highway 41, the Cheatham Road (present-day Highway 33), and the Byler Road to get into Winston County.

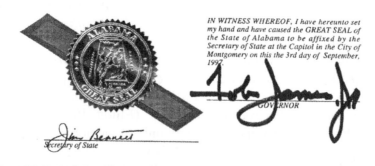

State of Alabama

House of Representatives

MONTGOMERY, ALABAMA

Resolution

HJR 84

By Representatives Neal Morrison, Mike Millican, Jack Page, Jim Murphree, Nelson Papucci, Joe Ford, Blaine Galliher, Johnny Mack Morrow, Howard Hawk, Paul Parker, Ralph Burke, Ken Guin, Tom Hogan, Sam Collins and Bill Dukes

DESIGNATING THE HIGH TOWN PATH

WHEREAS, the High Town Path is the most famous east-west Indian trail and tribal boundary in the Southeastern United States, traversing the Continental Divide across North Alabama. The High Town Path passes through the North Alabama Counties of Cleburne, Calhoun, Cherokee, DeKalb, Etowah, Blount, Marshall, Cullman, Morgan, Lawrence, Winston, Marion, and Franklin prior to entering Mississippi. The High Town Path was officially designated by Governor Fob James as a state historic district through William B. Bankhead National Forest in Lawrence County, Alabama, on November 17, 1996; and

WHEREAS, the Indian trail completely crossed the Southeastern United States in an east-west direction from Charleston, South Carolina, to Memphis, Tennessee, and traveled primarily through Alabama along the dividing watersheds of the Tennessee River to the north and the waters that drain into Mobile Bay to the south. Portions of the High Town Path became the tribal boundary of the Creeks to the south and the Cherokees and Chickasaws to the north; and

WHEREAS, the Indian trail was some 1000 miles in length with the Indian village of High Town (Rome, Georgia) located somewhat near the middle of the route; now therefore

BE IT RESOLVED BY THE LEGISLATURE OF ALABAMA, BOTH HOUSES THEREOF CONCURRING, That the High Town Path in Alabama is hereby designated such, in recognition of the greatest known east-west Indian trail and tribal boundary in the Southeastern United States.

RESOLVED FURTHER, That the State of Alabama Department of Transportation and Alabama Historical Commission in conjunction with the leaders of the Echota Cherokee Tribe are authorized to erect signs in appropriate places within the counties of North Alabama where the path crosses state highways to recognize the greatest east-west Indian trail and tribal boundary of the Southeastern United States.

IN WITNESS WHEREOF, I have hereunto set my hand and have caused the GREAT SEAL of the State of Alabama to be affixed by the Secretary of State at the Capitol in the City of Montgomery on this the 3rd day of September, 1997.

GOVERNOR

Secretary of State

170

Following are two descriptions of the High Town Path as reported in *The Story of Alabama*, *"High Town Path, from High Shoals on the Apalachee River to High Town in the fork of the Oostenalla and Etowah Rivers, the site of the modern Rome Georgia, thence to Turkey Town of the Cherokee Country, to Coosa, thence to Flat Rock in the northwestern part of the state, thence to Copper Town of the Chickasaw Nation. Two great trails from the east united at Flat Rock in Franklin County, Alabama, and thence continued west to the Chickasaw Nation. One of these trails come from the Chattahoochee to Little Oakfuskee thence to Flat Rock. Since Haleyville is located at the junction of several divides and also lies along the Tennessee Divide, Flat Rock is near or located at Haleyville. The other, the High Town Trail, started from Tellico in Monroe County, East Tennessee, thence southwest to Coosa Town, and from it to Flat Rock"* (Owens, 149). Flat Rock was an Indian village located on the High Town Path and was mostly likely the present-day town of Haleyville.

The book *Alabama History for Schools* also describes the trail: *"One example of a long Indian trail was the High Town Path. This was named for the Creek Indian village of High Town in present day Etowah County. This trail ran all the way across Alabama from the land of the Chickasaws in the west, through the Creek Country to Turkey Town. From Turkey Town it ran through the Cherokee Country and across the Chattahoochee River into Georgia"* (Summersell, 1981).

According to the book, *History of Alabama*, *"The Creeks had numerous paths radiating from eastern Georgia into Alabama, along which Carolina and Georgia traders, and later settlers, penetrated the interior of the state. The most notable of these were the 'High Town Path' and the 'Southern Trail.' The former crossed the Chattahoochee at Shallow Ford, just north of the present city of Atlanta and extended by way of High Town (Etowah), Turkey Town, and other villages along the Cherokee border to the Chickasaw Country"* (Moore 1951).

According to the book *The Chickasaws*, *"In early historic times three heavily traveled trails crossed the Chickasaw Nation. The Big Trading Path from Mobile along the Tombigbee, later used as a horse path by traders; The Great Chickasaw Trail which crossed the Savannah River near Augusta and coursed westward to the Chickasaw Crossing on the Tombigbee; and a diagonal trail connecting the Ohio and Cumberland with the lower Mississippi near the mouth of the Yazoo River, which became The Natchez Trace"* (Gibson,1974).

According to the sesquicentennial edition 1819-1969 of the *Franklin County Times*, *"Indian trail was first county road: The first account in history of a traveled pathway through Franklin County is of an Indian trail that came from the east and intersected another trail from the north at "Flat Rock" in Franklin County. The first authentic story of a road or 'trace' made by white men is the 'trace' made by General Gaines which is found in the field notes of both Lawrence and Marion Counties. The Indian trace and trace branch appear in some of the field notes in the southern part of Franklin"* (*Times*, 1969). Portions of the pathway and Indian trace follow the High Town Path. The High Town Path formed the fourth diamond trail pattern starting at Flat Rock.

HIGH TOWN PATH VILLAGES

Some very important Indian towns west from Charles Town lying along the east-west Indian path included High Shoals, Tellico, High Town (High Tower), Turkey Town, Coosa, Brown's Village, Flat Rock, and Copper Town. Many other smaller Indian towns and villages lay along the prehistoric and historic Indian trail. Many minor or major Indian trails and European routes intersected, or crossed portions of The Path as it traversed an east-west route across the Southeastern United States.

SOUTH CAROLINA

Early maps show the two western routes, both of which became known as the High Town Path, originating at Olde Charles Town on the Atlantic Coast. According to the book *Slavery and the Cherokee Society,* from 1670-1732, an English trading trail ran from Charleston, South Carolina to the Cherokee village of Tellico (Perdue, 1981).

Olde Charles Town was an important center for English trade with the Cherokees and Chickasaws. Pack trains loaded with British goods traversed the High Town Path to the Chickasaw Nation on the upper Tombigbee River. When Lachlan McGillivary, father of Creek Chief Alexander McGillivary was visiting Old Charles Town, South Carolina, he observed large pack trains that consisted of many horses. He saw hundreds of pack horses, pack saddles, and curious looking pack horsemen, in demi-civilized garbs, together with packs of merchandise, ready to be carried to the wilderness (Pickett, 1851).

The book *Stolen Continents* records a million deerskins were shipped from Charleston, South Carolina, during the years between 1700 and 1715. The British made several trips from Charles Town to the Overhill Towns on the Little Tennessee River during the middle 1700s establishing trading ties with the Cherokees. In 1756, the British built Fort Loudon near the forks of the Tellico River and Little Tennessee River (Wright, 1992).

172

From Charles Town, one trail lead northwesterly to Tellico and one trail lead westerly to High Shoals. According to *The Story of Alabama*, the trails from Tellico and High Shoals united at High Town in the fork of the Oostenalla and Etowah Rivers near the present-day site of Rome, Georgia (Owens, 1949).

TENNESSEE

Tellico was an important Cherokee town located near the forks of the Tellico River and the Little Tennessee River in Monroe County, Tennessee. Tellico was an overhill Cherokee town which was near the site of Fort Loudon and later the Tellico Blockhouse. Several treaties with the Cherokee were negotiated at the Tellico Blockhouse which was also located near the junction of Tellico and Little Tennessee Rivers.

A map of the Cherokee Nation prior to removal shows a road leading from High Town (near present day Rome, Georgia) and extending northward along the east side of the Oostenalla River to New Echota, Georgia located south of the forks of the Connasauga and Coosawattee Rivers. From New Echota, the High Town Path crossed the Coosawattee River and traversed north parallel to the east bank of the Connasauga River, passing Spring Place and J. Vann's place.

From Georgia, The Path entered Tennessee east of Red Clay at McNair's and continued north to the Hiwassee River crossing near present day Calhoun, Tennessee. From the Hiwassee River, the trail continued north to the Overhill Towns located on the Little Tennessee River in Monroe County, Tennessee.

GEORGIA

According to a map of Georgia, High Shoals was on the south fork of the Apalachee River, which is a tributary to the Altamaha River that flows into the Atlantic Ocean. (Georgia, 1810) High Shoals was an eastern hub for both Indian and European travelers. High Shoals appears to be the first major Indian town west of Charles Town. According to the territorial papers and old maps, a portion of the High Town Path follows the boundary line of the Cherokee and Creek land claims for the greater part of the distance from High Shoals on the Apalachee to Turkey Town on the Coosa then to Flat Rock. From north of present-day Atlanta, Georgia to Coosa, the Path turned northward into the Cherokee Nation to High Town.

The trail divisions appear to form diamond patterns which are repeated from east to west at least four times (Southeast, 1850). *The Story of Alabama* indicates two

173

diamond shaped divisions of the trail with one from High Town. At High Town, one trail traversed a northeasterly route to Tellico and the other a southeasterly route to High Shoals (Owens, 1949).

At High Shoals, another diamond pattern emerges with the northwesterly route to High Town and a southwesterly route to Little Oakfuskee. According to a southeastern map, the river crossing of the trail from High Shoals was at the Creek Indian village of Little Oakfuskee. The crossing at Little Oakfuskee was located on the Tallapoosa River near Sawyer's Ferry north of the mouth of Ketchepedrakee Creek.

Actually, Indian trails from Georgia lead to two Oakfuskee towns with the southern and greater town located near the forks of the Coosa and Tallapoosa Rivers. The area of the Great Oakfuskee town has been known by several names such as Fort Jackson and Fort Toulouse.

From Little Oakfuskee, the northwestern portion of the second trail diamond is formed by the Little Oakfuskee-Chickasaw Path traversing northwesterly and rejoining the High Town Path at Flat Rock near Bear Creek in Franklin County, Alabama (Owens, 1949).

ALABAMA

From High Town, the Indian route proceeded westerly into Alabama to Turkey Town where it intersected the Great Cumberland River War Trail. According to *The Story of Alabama*, *"The Great Cumberland River War Trail lead from the Hickory Ground up the east side of Coosa River up to Turkey Town, thence to the well-known Creek crossing on the Tennessee River, near the mouth of Town Creek, above Guntersville, thence to the Cumberland settlements in Tennessee"* Owens, 1949) .

174

The Great Indian War Trail System to the Cumberland settlements in the northern portion of middle Tennessee actually forked to three major Tennessee River crossings each of which intersected the High Town Path. For a short distance from Coosa, the Creek Path, Cumberland River War Trail, Muscle Shoals Path or Coosa Path, and High Town Path followed the same route as the war trail toward Ditto's at Huntsville. The Great Indian War Trail intersected the Upper Creek Path and crossed the Tennessee River near Guntersville; the trail passed Bridgeport and once again crossed

the Tennessee River at the Creek Indian crossing just down stream from the Lower Cherokee town of Long Island. The war trail intersected the Cisca and St. Augustine Trail that ran to Nashville, Tennessee.

At Brown's Village, the High Town Path turned westerly along the dividing ridge toward Flat Rock and the war trail continued north. The other Tennessee River crossing of the war trail was also used as major river crossing at Town Creek upstream from Guntersville. At Ditto's, the Creek Path crossed the river and the Muscle Shoal Path or Coosa Path turned westerly toward the lower end of the Shoals.

From Turkey Town, the High Town Path ran westerly to Coosa where it intersected the Creek Path. According to *The Story of Alabama, "Creek Path, Coosa to Cumberland River Trail: this trail, noted in history as the Creek Path, lead from Coosa Town, but may be considered as starting from the Hickory Ground. It ran northward to the present Red Hill in Marshall County, which was founded about 1790, Brown's Village, a well known Cherokee Town. At this place the trail divided, one branch crossing the Tennessee River"* (Owens, 1949).

The Creek Path and High Town Path actually joined two of the Cumberland routes crossing the Tennessee River; therefore, the Creek Path ran along the same route as the High Town Path from Turkey Town, to Coosa, and to Brown's Village. From

Coosa to Brown's Village, the High Town Path ran the same route as the Muscle Shoals or Coosa Path.

From Coosa, the High Town Path traversed northwesterly and crossed at the headwaters of Brown's Creek at Brown's Village. Brown's Village was on the south end of Brown's Creek near the Marshall County and Blount County lines. The Cherokee village was established by a Cherokee Indian who fought at Horseshoe Bend in the Creek Indian War, Colonel Richard Brown. According to the Brown family legend, Richard was recruited by Andrew Jackson to fight the Creeks. According to an early colonial period map of the trail system of the Southeastern United States, Jackson's route led him to Brown's Village. Jackson camped for some two weeks awaiting supplies and recruiting Cherokees for the Battle of Horseshoe Bend.

Richard was one of the sons of a half-blood Cherokee named John Brown. Half-blood John Brown's Cherokee name was Drowning Bear, or "Yonaguska." Drowning Bear had three wives and many children including William, John, Hugh, and Nancy in addition to Richard (Manasco, 1981).

At Brown's Village, the Creek Path and the Muscle Shoals Path or Coosa Path turned north and the High Town Path continued west along the Continental Divide. The Creek Path crossed the Tennessee River at present-day Huntsville, Alabama with the Muscle Shoals or Coosa Path turning westerly toward the lower end of the Muscle Shoals.

From Brown's Village, the High Town Path followed the Continental Divide through Marshall and Cullman Counties and later The Path in this area became known as the "Old Corn Road." The Old Corn Road traverses along the Continental Divide crossing present-day Highway 31 near Vinemont and crossing present day Highway 157 at Battleground on top of Battleground Mountain in Cullman County.

From Battleground, the Continental Divide continues west to an Indian crossroads of the High Town Path intersecting the Black Warriors' Path. The area of this intersection became known as Basham's Gap. Basham's Gap was located near the present-day site of Piney Grove in the southeast corner of Lawrence County.

At Basham's Gap, the High Town Path intersected the north-south Indian path, known as the Black Warriors' Path which traversed from the Tennessee River at Melton's Bluff to the Black Warrior Road crossing north of Black Warrior Town which was located east of Jasper. From junction with the Black Warrior Road, Black Warriors' Path continued southeast toward Fort Mitchell in Russell County, Alabama.

The Black Warriors' Path later became known as the Mitchell Trace which connected Fort Mitchell on the Georgia-Alabama line in Russell County to Fort Hampton in Limestone County.

From Basham's Gap, the High Town Path traversed westerly along the Leola Road portion of the Continental Divide to the Wren Mountain area, where it intersected another southerly divide, an Indian path known as Sipsie Trail. The trail from Muscle Shoals, on the Tennessee River, through the Bankhead Forest to Tuscaloosa became the Cheatham Road (present-day Highway 33).

From the Wren Mountain area, The Path continued on westerly along the Ridge Road portion of the Continental Divide to Kinlock. Near Kinlock, The Path intersected an Indian trail known as Doublehead's Trace or the Old Buffalo Trail from the French Lick (Nashville). Portions of the Old Buffalo Trail later became known as the Byler Road.

Flat Rock

It should be noted that a third diamond pattern of the High Town Path begins at the path's junction with the Old Buffalo Trail or Doublehead's Trace. One fork turned northwest along the Old Bulah Motorway with the other fork traversing southwest by Haleyville, Alabama along the Continental Divide between Bear Creek and the upper Tombigbee River System. To continue west along the Old Bulah route would require at least one stream crossing on the western portion of the Bear Creek System. Some early maps of the Turkey Town Treaty of 1816 do indicate a Flat Rock Corner on Little Bear Creek. It appears that both routes were used and probably rejoined at a point on the divide southwest of Bear Creek. From that point, evidence exists both in text and maps that one trail lead to Copper Town and on to Chickasaw Bluffs. Another route of The Path traversed from Bear Creek on nearly a straight course to Chickasaw Bluffs at present-day Memphis, Tennessee.

Along the southwest route from Kinlock, The Path proceeded along the county line of Franklin to Flat Rock which is at or near the Town of Haleyville. According to _The Territorial Papers of the United States_ dated March 12, 1817, Flat Rock was noted twice as being on Bear Creek. According to these papers, Flat Rock appears to be located on a direct line drawn from the mouth of Caney Creek in Colbert County to Cotton Gin Port, Mississippi to a point where the line crosses the Continental Divide in southwest Franklin County (Carter, 1952). According to the Cherokee Treaty, March 22, 1816, _"The Cherokee Nation extended as far west as a place on the waters of Bear_

Creek, (a branch of the Tennessee River,) known by the name of the Flat Rock, or Stone" (Kappler, 1904) .

A controversy has existed for years over the exact location of Flat Rock as evidenced in the following, *5th Annual Report Bureau Ethnology,* pp. 194 and 272: *"As to the origin, location, and purpose of the true Flat Rock corner, historians have been unable to learn with certainty. In a communication from the Secretary of War to Major Cocke, the Chickasaw agent, dated April 16, 1816, it is stated that from an examination of the Chickasaw Treaty of 1786, it appeared that a point called Flat Rock was considered a corner of the lands belonging to them, and that it had since been considered as the corner to the Creek, Cherokee, and Chickasaw hunting grounds. The Chickasaws, however, professed ignorance of any place on Bear Creek called Flat Rock, but claimed there was a Flat Rock on the Longleaf Pine, a branch of the Black Warrior, which was a corner of their territory.*—5th Annual Report Bureau Ethnology. *pages 207-8, 271. The earliest reference I (Royce) find to any place called Flat Rock is in this Chickasaw Treaty of 1786, and it would seem but fair that they be allowed to define it. They always defined it as being on the Longleaf Pine. This location fits the description of it as being where the Choctaw line joined with the Chickasaws, better than does that on Bear Creek. I (Royce) conclude that the Flat Rock on Bear Creek was never a corner between any Indian tribes until it was arbitrarily, or by misapprehension, made such by the Cherokee Treaty of March 22, 1816."*

The author of this book contends that Flat Rock was at or near the community of Haleyville, which was a hub of crossroads. Evidence of Haleyville being Flat Rock is based on old maps, treaty discription and historical text. The southwest drainage from Haleyville in the upper portions of the Buttahatchee River has been called Stone or Gravel Creek. Small tributaries of the river were called Big Stone or Big Gravelly and Little Stone or Little Gravelly. The area around the Stone Creek and Gravelly Creek drainage is noted for gravel pits and is a source of Tuscaloosa gravel which was used for making projectile points and stone tools.

Old maps show the Flat Rock Creek draining to the southeast into Sipsey River (probably Clear Creek or Blackwater Creek). In addition, Flat Creek forms the northwestern drainage in the City of Haleyville and flows into Bear Creek.

Prior to 1816, Haleyville formed a corner of Indian lands with the Cherokee and Chickasaw land claims to the north and west and Creek land claims to the south and east. A corner of land was located in the area of Haleyville according to the 1786 Chickasaw Treaty. Not only do the drainages indicate Flat Rock at or near Haleyville, but two major dividing ridges cross in the city: the Tennessee Divide, which divides the

Warrior and Tennessee River Drainages, and Byler Ridge, which divides the Warrior and Tombigbee Drainages.

Another major divide in the direction of the Coosa Town near Oakfuskee also traverses southeasterly from the Town of Haleyville. Another major piece of evidence is from an early settler who reported that Haleyville was the site of an Indian town. According to an *Alabama Historical Review* article reprinted in a Haleyville newspaper on April 11, 1983, an Indian village was located at or near Haleyville, Alabama. *"Marion S. Bingham, of Montgomery, who in 1912 designed and built a state-aid road extending about five miles from Haleyville toward Double Springs...became acquainted with...Mr. Dodd...in his early eighties...who told his guest the story about the lost Indian gold mine...When he was a small child living in Nashville, Mr. Dodd recalled that the Indians used to come to Nashville from Alabama to trade, bringing with them gold...three friends of the Dodds, left Nashville and accompanied the Indians back to their village...several years passed and the Dodds came to Alabama intending to settle near the <u>Indian village which was at or near Haleyville</u>...after reaching manhood, Mr. Dodd used to wander through the hills of Winston County looking for this mine. He never discovered it but did find the hills contained coal and other minerals which made him a wealthy man."*

The Indian village that was talked about by Mr. Dodd was very probably that of Flat Rock, which was noted as an early Indian town in the area of Haleyville. According to the article, Mr. Dodd lived in Nashville during the early 1830s. Friends of his family followed Indian traders back to their village at Haleyville but attempted to steal their gold. Only one of Dodd's friends made it back to Nashville but died of exposure before identifying the location of the gold mine. Later Mr. Dodd's family moved to Haleyville and brought with them the story of the Indian village and gold. Archaeological evidence from the area provides supporting confirmation that the town site of Haleyville was a long term Indian site. This highland Indian town had easy access in many directions as a major focal point of the area.

The High Town Path forms a fourth diamond pattern starting at Flat Rock with one fork turning northwesterly to the Chickasaw Bluffs, and the other fork to Copper Town then to Chickasaw Bluffs. An early map shows the northwesterly fork from Flat Rock on Bear Creek to the Chickasaw Bluffs on the Mississippi River.

The southern fork from Flat Rock turned south and westerly again through Marion County to Copper Town in Mississippi. The southwesterly portion of The Path from Flat Rock appears to run the same general route as Gaines Trace.

According to Article 2 of the treaty with the Chickasaw in 1816, *"The Chickasaw Nation cede to the United States all right or title to lands on the north side of the Tennessee River, and relinquished all claim to territory on the south side of said river, and east of a line commencing at the mouth of Caney Creek, running up said Creek to its source, thence a due south course to the Ridge Path, or commonly called Gaines's Road, along said road southwesterly to a point on the Tombigbee River well known by the name of the Cotton Gin Port, and down the west bank of the Tombigbee to the Choctaw boundary."* (Kappler, 1904:135)

MISSISSIPPI

According to *The Story of Alabama,* under the treaty with the Chickasaws of September 26, 1816, *"it* (Gaines Trace or the old High Town Path) *became the eastern boundary of that tribe. It was originally a horse path used for bringing merchandise from the Tennessee River to the Tombigbee River, whence it was carried by boats to the Indian trading house at St. Stephens"* (Owens, 1949).

The major stream crossing to the heart of the Chickasaw Towns was the French Landing (Cotton Gin Port). Nearly all trails in the area intersected at the well-known Indian crossing of Cotton Gin on the upper Tombigbee (Chactawhatchee) River. According to *The Appalachian Indian Frontier*, the Cotton Gin crossing was within thirty miles of the seven major Chickasaw towns of the upper Tombigbee River System (Jacobs, 1967).

At Copper Town, the High Town Trail intersects the Chickasaw or Natchez Trace. The Natchez Trace was an old Indian trail known as the Chickasaw Trace. The trail was upgraded to one of the earliest southeastern highways. The following is a description of the Natchez Trace in *The Story of Alabama*, *"Natchez Trace, the oldest of these is what is known in southern history as the Natchez Trace, or the great Columbian Highway. Its northern terminus was Nashville, Tennessee; its southern, Natchez, Mississippi Territory. It was not only the earliest of the highways projected by the federal government in anticipation of and as part of its policy of opening up the lower Mississippi and the old southwest, but it is to be compared with the old Federal Road only in historic importance. Its route was southwest, passing the present towns of Franklin and Columbia, Tennessee, and crossing the Tennessee River a few miles below Muscle Shoals at Colbert's Ferry. The authorization of the road is to be found in treaties with the Chickasaws and Choctaws dated October 24, 1801, and December 17, 1801, respectively. This road constituted the first post route in the southern country. It entered Alabama in the northern part of Lauderdale County, crossed the Tennessee*

180

River at Colbert's Ferry, and passed through the northwest section of the present Colbert (formerly Franklin) County" (Owens, 1949).

It should be noted that at the time the U.S. government entered into the Treaty with the Chickasaws for Natchez Trace, the Cherokees under the leadership of Doublehead controlled the western bend of the Tennessee River. According to *Dead Towns of Alabama*, *"Doublehead's Cherokee village was established in 1790 with the*

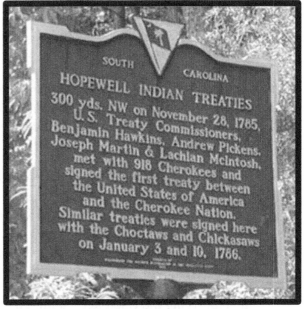

aid of forty Creek and Cherokee warriors near the Natchez Trace River Crossing. Doublehead's Village was on the south side of the Tennessee River, near the place where the Natchez Trace crossed the river at Colbert's Ferry, in Colbert County" (Harris, 1977).

The Turkey Town Treaty of 1816, which favored the Chickasaws, moved the eastern boundary of the Chickasaws to Caney Creek in Colbert County. At the time of the treaties in 1801 and 1816, the federal government recognized the Hopewell Treaty that was negotiated with the Chickasaws on January 10, 1786. The Hopewell Treaty defined the southern boundary of the Chickasaws on the Tennessee Divide running along the High Town Path to the west of a north and south line passing Chickasaw Island near Huntsville, Alabama; at the time of the treaty the area was occupied by Cherokee Indian people. Doublehead and the Cherokees were living in the area by permission of Chief George Colbert who married two of Doublehead's daughters -- Tuskiahooto and Saleechie.

Copper Town appears to be near the center of the Chickasaw Nation in the upper forks of the Tombigbee River System. From Copper Town, the trail turns northwesterly to the Chickasaw Bluffs near modern day Memphis, Tennessee. According to *Indian Trails of the Southeast*, the road from Copper Town and Cotton Gin Port to Chickasaw Bluffs was known by the name of the Middle Memphis-Pontotoc Trail. The trail ran from the Chickasaw towns in the upper Tombigbee to Chickasaw Bluffs at present-day Memphis, Tennessee. The continuation of the High Town Path to Chickasaw Bluffs from Copper Town was along the same route of the Middle Memphis-Pontotoc Trail (Myer, 1923).

HIGH TOWN PATH BOUNDARIES

In addition to traders and early settlers, the High Town Path was not only a path along a geographic boundary of the Tennessee Divide of North Alabama, but also used as a tribal boundary and a political boundary. The ridge was a prominent feature or landmark through North Alabama noted in early history as the dividing boundary of the waters draining south into Mobile Bay and the waters draining north into the Tennessee River.

Tribal Boundaries

According to a report of the Alabama Historical Commission, *"the true Cherokee southern boundary, after following the divide separating the waters of the Tennessee and Black Warrior to the headwaters of Caney Creek, ran thence down Said Creek to the Tennessee River."*

According to the *Annals of Northwest Alabama*, *"before the coming of the white man, the ridge generally separated the lands of the Chickasaws on the west from those of the Creeks to the east and the lands of the Cherokees on the north from the Creeks to the south"*(Elliott, 1972). During the late 1700s and early 1800s, the Ridge Top Path and the Continental Divide was referred to in treaties with the Chickasaw and Cherokee Indians. Later, The Path was used to divide early counties in Mississippi Territory.

In identifying the Cherokees' southern boundary the *Manual for Writing Alabama State History* states, *"Consequently we may conclude in a general way that from the lower end of Ten Islands the line followed the most prominent dividing ridge butting on the river in that vicinity, around the headwaters of Canoe Creek, until it reached the height of Blount Mountain, thence northward with said mountain along the ridge dividing the waters of the Coosa from those of the Black Warrior to the top of Raccoon or Sand Mountain near the town of Boaz in Marshall County. From this point westward to the Chickasaw boundary, wherever that lay, it is quite clear that the line was the ridge dividing the waters of the Tennessee from those of the Black Warrior."* Gov. Blount in 1794, writing to the chiefs and headmen of the Creeks said: *"In the original division of land amongst the red people, it is well known that the Creek lands were bounded on the north by the ridge which divides the waters of the Mobile and the Tennessee."* Judge Haywood, criticizing a Mr. Barnard for some erroneous statements the latter had made to the Governor of Georgia in 1793, says, *"And he (Barnard) ought to have known that the Creek claim to lands was bounded by the ridge which divides the waters of the Tennessee and Mobile."*

Treaty Boundaries

The High Town Path, in addition to an Indian trail, became the line of the Chickasaw Land Claims under the Treaty of January 10, 1786. According to a map of Chickasaw boundaries, the Chickasaw claims line followed the Continental Divide through Lawrence and Cullman Counties and turned north from the Tennessee Divide to east of the Chickasaw Oldfields on the Tennessee River near Huntsville.

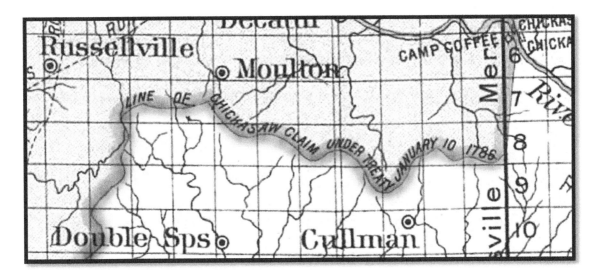

In the Turkey Town Treaty of 1816, which ceded land from both the Chickasaws and Cherokees, the Ridge Top Path (High Town Path) was used as the southern boundary for the land cession of both Indian Nations including Franklin, Lawrence, and Morgan Counties (Jones, 1972). Article 2 of the treaty with the Cherokee, 1816, states, *"The Cherokee Nation acknowledge the following as their western boundary: south of the Tennessee River, commencing at Camp Coffee, on the south side of the Tennessee River, which is opposite the Chickasaw Island, running from thence a south course to the top of the Dividing Ridge between the waters of the Tennessee and Tombigbee Rivers, thence eastwardly along said ridge, leaving the head waters of the Black Warrior to the right hand, until opposed by the west branch of Will's Creek down the east bank of Said Creek to the Coosa River, and down Said River"* (Kappler, 1904).

According *Myths of the Cherokee*, *"failing in this, pressure was at once begun to bring about a cession in Alabama, with the result that on September 14 of the same year a treaty was concluded at the Chickasaw council-house, and afterward ratified in general council at Turkey Town on the Coosa, by which the Cherokee cede all their claims in that state south of the Tennessee River and west of an irregular line running from Chickasaw Island in that stream, below the entrance of Flint River, to the junction of Wills Creek with the Coosa, at the present Gadsden"* (Mooney, 1982) . It should be noted that the irregular line to the west was on the High Town Path along the ridge top and followed the Chickasaw claims of January 10, 1786. The line ran south from Chickasaw Island to the Continental Divide then west along the dividing Ridge Path.

Political Boundries

In addition, several references indicate the Continental Divide was not only a geographic boundary between major watersheds but also an important political boundary in separating the counties of Blount and Shelby in the Mississippi Territory. The county to the north included what is now the Tennessee Valley portion of Lawrence County in North Alabama.

On page 70 of the *Journal of Muscle Shoals History* (1977) the following is given, *"All that tract of country lying south of the Tennessee River, east of the Chickasaw boundary line, north of the highlands that divide the waters of the Tennessee from the water of the Mobile Bay and west of the Cherokee boundary line shall form one other county to be called and known by the name of Blount, the courts of justice where of will be held at Melton's Bluff."* Melton's Bluff is on the south bank of the Tennessee River between Spring Creek and Mallard Creek in Lawrence County, Alabama.

The *Franklin County Times,* reporting on the history of Franklin County, included the following, *"It seems from Ramsey's* Annals of Tennessee *this section was at one time included in the proposed borders of the State of Franklin as laid out by Colonel Campbell, the originator of the idea of a state separate and apart from all other states of the union. Colonel Campbell began to agitate for the headwaters of the Tombigbee River, thence east posed a boundary for the new state to begin at a point on the Holston River and "run west to the Shoals of the Ohio, thence south across the Cherokee River to the headwaters of the Tombigbee River, thence east to the top of the Appalachian Mountains, where the waters divide and then north to the beginning"* (*Times*, 1969).

It should be noted that the ridge along the top of the Appalachian Mountains is the Continental Divide through Lawrence County which separates the water that drains south into the Black Warrior and Tombigbee River Systems and then into Mobile Bay from the water that drains north into the Tennessee River. Along this dividing ridge lies

184

the High Town Path which was a clearly marked geographic division for tribal boundaries and political entities, as well as an east-west route across North Alabama.

The Route Across Lawrence County

The High Town Path passed through Cullman County along the route that became the Old Corn Road to Basham's Gap (Piney Grove). Basham's Gap, located in the southeast corner of Lawrence County, is the beginning of the William B. Bankhead National Forest portion of the trail traversing through Lawrence County. The following is the route of the High Town Path through Lawrence County along present day roads. The Path traveled north from Piney Grove, along Highway 41, to the Leola Road and west along Leola to Highway 33. From the west end of the Leola Road, The Path turned north down Highway 33 to the Ridge Road and west along the Ridge Road to the Byler Road.

Along the dividing ridge of Lawrence County, from Basham Gap to Kinlock in the northwest portion of Bankhead Forest, old segments of the High Town Path are still highly visible. According to the _Annals of Northwest Alabama, "In the spring of 1864, Brigadier General G.M. Dodge was asked to give a scouting report on all roads from the Mississippi line to the Coosa Valley. Dodge described the road as "an old road, well-settled, well watered, fair for forage, crosses the streams high enough up to avoid much difficulty, and is one of the best roads over the mountains"_ (Elliott, 1972).

Warrior Mountains Route

Early settlers of Lawrence County rapidly populated the area along the High Town Path shortly after the treaty with the Cherokees in September 1816. They homesteaded the lands from Piney Grove on the county's eastern border to Kinlock on the western border.

The ability to traverse overland along the High Town Path was the primary reason the areas in Bankhead Forest along the divide were quickly settled. According to county records, the first day land could be homesteaded from the U.S. government was on September 12, 1818.

Piney Grove was an early settler community located on the eastern edge of Bankhead National Forest. The community had a school, store, church, and cemetery. Just north of Piney Grove is Cave Springs Cemetery located near Basham's Gap at the junction of the Leola Road and Highway 41. My great, great, great, great-grandmother, Martha Welborn, is buried in Cave Springs Cemetery.

In Basham, just some twenty-five feet from the High Town Path stood the old cabin of Matt Pearson, whose family was Cherokee mixed-bloods. Matt's sister had married Jock McWhorter; Matt Pearson lived in the cabin on Jock's land for a few years. The log cabin was some fifty feet from stone steps leading to the Basham Rock Shelter. The shelter contains a natural spring, a waterfall, and a large mortar used by early Indian inhabitants for grinding nuts. The old High Town Path lies within some twenty feet along the edge of the shelter as does the Leola Road today.

West along the Leola Road is Center Church and Cemetery. Center School was located at the church. This place is the burial site of several early settlers, many of mixed-blood Indian families. Located just west of Center on the High Town Path was the community of Templeton.

In the Templeton Community were an early school, post office, and small cotton gin, located near the junction of the Flint Creek Road and the Leola Road. The area was probably named for the postmaster, Jackson Templeton.

Continuing west from Templeton along Leola Road, an old steam operated sawmill was run by the Wesley Hampton family. The old sawmill was near the junction of the Hickory Grove and Leola Roads. Ephriam S. Hampton, a patriarch of the Hampton family, entered much of the land in Poplar Log Cove just north of Templeton. He married a Cherokee Indian lady by the name of Lucinda Doss.

The Lindsey Hall Community is west of the Leola-Hickory Grove Road junction. Lindsey Hall Community had Poole Post Office, Lindsey Hall School, Looney Grist Mill and Store, Lindsey Hall Church, and the Old Friendship Cemetery. Brown Spring, which is the start of Brown Creek, is some three hundred yards southeast of Lindsey Hall Church and is named after the Brown Indian Family. About one mile west of Lindsey Hall Church is Shiloh Church and Cemetery.

Continuing west from Shiloh approximately one mile, Poplar Springs School was located near the junction of the Rogers Road and Leola Road. Poplar Springs School was a small one-room log school, which was abandoned as a school sometime around the 1930s.

Within one half mile of Poplar Springs School was Old Bulah Church. The church is located on the Bulah Ridge which separates the canyon of Indian Tomb Hollow into the northern and southern forks. Old Bulah was near the junction of the Pinhook Gap Road and the Leola Road. At Old Bulah was Poplar Springs School, a church, cemetery and the Naylor Sawmill. Naylor Sawmill was first operated by George Washington Naylor.

The High Town Path continued west to the Cheatham Road which was thickly settled. The north portion of the original Cheatham Road traversing up Wren Mountain is still visible. Mountain View School was located on the Cheatham Road section of the High Town Path. The area around Mountain View School was heavily populated in the early settlement days prior to 1900.

After traversing north along Highway 33, the High Town Path turned west along the Ridge Road toward the Penitentiary Mountain area. Along the old Ridge Road were early coal mines which eventually passed completely through the mountain under the High Town Path.

The Mountain Springs Community is located west of Penitentiary Mountain. The community included the area from the road junction to Mountain Springs Church, Mountain Springs School, and cemetery some two miles south of the path. Many early settlers made their home on the Mountain Springs portion of the High Town Path.

Continuing west on the Ridge Road along the High Town Path is the Youngtown section of the trail. Here once stood the old Ridge Road School which served the children south of the ridge in the area known today as McDowell or Wilkerson Cove. The Cove was also known by the names of Wallis and Flanagin after the families who settled the area in the early 1800s. Children from Youngtown on the north side of the Cove also attended the Ridge Road School. After the early school burned, the children attended Mountain Springs School or Youngtown School.

Westward along the trail was the Stephenson Spring Area. Stephenson Spring was a mountain source of water just south of the High Town Path some one hundred yards. The Cole Cemetery is located east of Stephenson Spring on the Path's southern slope. Just east of Cole Cemetery was Jones Grist Mill, which was located at the upper end of Mattox Creek. Living along The Path in the Stephenson Spring area was the Boyles family and the Borden family, who owned the land near the present-day junction of the Ridge Road and Braziel Creek Road.

After continuing west along The Path from Stephenson Spring, the intersection of Doublehead's Trace or the Old Buffalo Trail and the High Town Path forms another diamond pattern. Near the junction of the two routes, the High Town Path has been eroded some five feet deep and runs adjacent to the original road. Near this site was an important marker tree referred to in the Byler Road history as the 63-mile Tree. The

187

original Byler Road ascended the mountain just east of Steele Hollow. After reaching the mountaintop, The Byler Road traversed a ridge between the upper drainages of Bear Creek. The road ran south toward the end of the ridge, where it descended into the Bear Creek Canyon. After fording Bear Creek, it joined the High Town Path north of Poplar Springs Cemetery. An Indian marker tree, which indicates the original Old Buffalo Trail, was located north of the trail junctions, but has been cut.

Aunt Jenny Brooks

One fork of the road turns south at the junction of the High Town Path and the Old Buffalo Trail (Byler Road). Along the south fork of the road about one and a half miles is Poplar Springs Cemetery where a Cherokee lady and part of her Indian family are buried. Her name is Jane 'Aunt Jenny' Bates Brooks Johnson and she was one half Cherokee.

On south of Poplar Springs Cemetery is the mountain Community of Kinlock. Macedonia Church and Cemetery, Kinlock and Gernada Post Offices, Kinlock School, and old toll gates of the Byler Road were located at Kinlock. From Kinlock, the High Town Path's southern fork exits the Lawrence County portion of the William B. Bankhead National Forest.

The northwestern fork of the High Town Path continues toward the west Old Buelah Community, along the Buelah Motorway into Franklin County. The western Old Buelah Community was a fairly populated settlement in the early days. Near the Franklin County line, the northwest fork of the High Town Path exits Lawrence County's Bankhead Forest.

Early Path Settlements

Scattered across the High Town Path portion of the Warrior Mountains were numerous settlements many of which were located near mountain springs. Most of the area along the route was settled by mixed-blood settlers of Scots-Irish and Cherokee Indian descent. Many of these mixed-blood people claimed to be Black Dutch or Black Irish if they contained a high degree of Indian blood in order to avoid removal. All Indian mixed-bloods had to deny their race and choose to be and live as white people.

188

As this mixing and blending crossed many generations, the outward appearance became less and less obviously Indian but the sacred fire still flowed in their veins.

These forsaken Indian people of the Warrior Mountains held to their traditional farming methods and most sought out a meager living by growing small patches of cotton and corn. Many mountain farmers of mixed-ancestry measured the corn patches by the gallons of whiskey they could produce, but most wound up drinking up their profits. The soils along the mountain trail were of poor sandy loam providing only enough nutrients for a small amount of the crops to survive. Most of these mountain people were extremely poor and lived as an old-timer Jake Feltman recently stated, *"We did not have a lot of money or make a lot of money, but back then you could not starve a family out."*

Piney Grove Area

On the eastern side of the High Town Path in Lawrence County an early community developed near the Piney Grove area, known as Beaham's, Gasham's, or Basham's Gap. Basham's Gap was near the western end of the Old Corn Road which traversed along the Continental Divide through Cullman County. The area, first known as Beaham's Gap, was located near the corners of present day Lawrence, Morgan, and Cullman Counties, but is now known as Basham's Gap. Basham's Gap was located at the junction of the High Town

Butch Walker at Basham Shelter and mortar

Path and a fork of the Black Warriors' Path which led south from Melton's Bluff, by Black Warrior Town or Old Warrior Town east of present-day Jasper, Alabama, then to the Chattahoochee River in Russell County, Alabama.

Adjacent to the High Town Path at Basham Gap is a large rock shelter and spring which could be used by early travelers of The Path as a place to rest as well as quench a thirst. The shelter contains a large rock with a mortar hole and several nutting holes. The shelter area appears to have been used extensively by early Indian people.

Just downstream from the shelter is Tar Springs Hollow, which contains two mineral tar springs. These springs were known as Double Springs and the road leading from Poplar Log Cove into Tar Springs Hollow was known as the Double Springs Road.

It appears the two early cemeteries in the Basham's Gap area are the final resting place of many mixed-blood Indians. From examination of the tombstones in the Cave Springs and Center Cemeteries, several of the people were descendants of the Creek and Cherokee Indians who a few years earlier claimed the land of the Warrior Mountains. Many of the family names of those who presently make up the Lawrence County Indian population are found in the old cemeteries.

During historic times my ancestors settled along Lawrence County's eastern portion of the High Town Path. I, Rickey Butch Walker, am the seventh generation from my great, great, great, great-grandmother, Martha Welborn, who was born on June 21, 1797, and is buried along the High Town Path in Cave Springs Cemetery. Her children were one quarter Cherokee Indians of Scots Irish ancestry. Cave Springs Cemetery is located at the junction of Highway 41 and the east end of Leola Road in the northeast corner of Bankhead National Forest. Just a few yards southwest of the cemetery are an Indian shelter and the Cave Spring.

Indian Tomb Area

The Indian Tomb area lies adjacent to the north side of the dividing ridge of the High Town Path. The Path's northern drainage is the beginning of Gillespie Creek, which flows through the center of Indian Tomb Hollow. The Indian Tomb area provided our early Indian ancestors springs of fresh water and many rock shelters from which they could find protection during severe or inclement weather.

The southwestern fork of Indian Tomb Hollow begins at the junction of the Pinhook Gap Road and the High Town Path (Leola Road). Indian Tomb Hollow and the High Town Path were connected by way of the High House Hill Trail, which was the southwestern fork of the West Flint Creek Trail.

In "The Battle of Indian Tomb Hollow," which details that legendary conflict between the Creeks and Chickasaws, the Creeks had nearly made their way into their ancestral homeland south of the High Town Path. The Creeks and their Chickasaw captive were camped in the Indian Tomb Hollow when the battle occurred (WHG, 1856 and Waters, 1967). The Creeks' northern boundary through most of North Alabama was south of the High Town Path, which passed along the Continental Divide (Elliott, 1972).

Within the canyon of Indian Tomb stands an Indian marker tree that was probably shaped at the time "The Battle of Indian Tomb Hollow" was published in the *Moulton Democrat*. It is believed that the marker tree was made by local Indian

Butch Walker at Indian Marker Tree

descendants to mark the importance of the site as was the custom. At the entrance of the trail leading to the tree, two additional forked trees stand adjacent to either side of the trail as sentinels offering a gateway to this most significant Indian marker tree. The tree remains special to Indian people who regularly visit the site to behold the symbolic division of people from a common beginning.

Just southeast of the Indian Tomb Hollow area, along the High Town Path, lies the Lindsey Hall Community where the John Brown family settled. John Brown was a friend of James Havens. According to Havens' family history, James Havens was buried near his Indian friends on the side of the Warrior Mountain in the Pinhook Community. The site where Havens and his Indian friends were buried was where the magnolia blooms in the spring. Based on the description of the mountainside and magnolias, it is highly probable they were buried in the Indian Tomb Cemetery.

John Brown settled on the High Town Path in Lawrence County near present day Lindsey Hall Community in the north portion of Bankhead National Forest. John Brown, who was 61 in 1850, and his son William are found in the Lawrence County census records from 1820 through 1850. According to the Lawrence County Census (1850), William's family includes a John, William and Nancy, which are the same names as those found in his father's and grandfather's family.

Brown Creek and Indian Creek, both of which originate at Lindsey Hall Community in Bankhead Forest are named for the Brown Indian family. The High Town Path lies on the Continental Divide between the upper drainage of Brown and Indian Creeks and a few yards from Brown's Spring. Brown Spring provided the weary a place of rest under its large shelter and thirsty travelers of the High Town Path fresh cool water. Brown Spring is some 150 yards southeast of present-day Lindsey Hall

Church. It should be noted that three Brown Creeks exist in North Alabama with two in Bankhead Forest. The three creeks are named after the Brown Indian family.

Also, Norman Minor's Cherokee Indian family lived about one mile north of the High Town Path at the mouth of Indian Tomb Hollow. Many of the Minor Indian grandchildren still live within a mile of the Indian Tomb area.

Mary E. Welborn

I, Rickey Butch Walker, have a great, great, great-grandmother, Mary E. Segars Naylor, buried just one fourth mile north of the High Town Path at the Old Bulah Cemetery. Mary Elizabeth Welborn Segars Naylor was one quarter Cherokee of mixed Scots Irish ancestry. Her husband, Pascal Sandy Segars, of one quarter Cherokee ancestry, was killed fighting for the Confederate States of America and was my great, great, great-grandfather. Old Bulah is located on the ridge dividing Indian Tomb Hollow into the southern and northern forks and is just north of the intersection of The Path with the Pinhook Gap Road.

Nearly all of my ancestors are buried within a few miles of Lawrence County's eastern part of the High Town Path. My parents and maternal grandparents are buried one mile north of Indian Tomb Hollow in the Wilburn-Alexander Cemetery.

My seventh generation Creek, Cherokee, and Scots-Irish ancestors lie buried within the eastern portion of the Bankhead Forest, which contain both their remains and the haunts of their spirits. From within the heart of Indian Tomb Hollow, I am surrounded by my ancestor's spirits whose remains lie to the north, to the east, to the south, and to the west. As I travel west into the Hollow toward the end of life, I know my spirit will eventually join with those of my grandfathers and grandmothers and will dwell in the safety of the sacred canyon from whence I receive strength: INDIAN TOMB. -- Rickey Butch Walker.

Wren Mountain Area

Near Bankhead Forest's central segment of the High Town Path was the legendary Robert's Inn on Penitentiary Mountain. According to *Life and Legend of Lawrence County, Alabama*, "*The date, 1734 inscribed on a chimney of the old Roberts*

192

Inn on Penitentiary Mountain, is believed by heirs of the Matthew and John Roberts property, to be correct as to when the old penitentiary building and stage coach stop, was built" (Gentry, 1962).

According to the Lawrence County Census (1850), it appears that one John Roberts, who lived in Lawrence County, was born in North Carolina in 1774. According to Lawrence County Census records from 1820 through 1850, there were four John Roberts of different ages which may have been sons and grandsons of a John Roberts born prior to 1770. It should also be noted that the Penitentiary Mountain portion of the High Town Path was Indian country until July 1817 when the Turkey Town Treaty of September 1816 was ratified; therefore, if the Roberts settled in the area prior to the Treaty of 1816, they were either Indian people or squatters on Indian lands.

According to family members, the Roberts were Indian people who operated the Wayside Inn. *"The house, located on a mountain, elevation 1,074 feet, has native limestone pillars, set on stone bases"* (Gentry, 1962). The inn was on the ridge top divide where the High Town Path passed. According to Indian treaties, taverns and inns were operated along treaty-designated roads.

Kinlock Area

On the western edge of the High Town Path in Lawrence County, an important mountain community was known as Kinlock. According to several early maps, Kinlock was located in the area of the present-day Macedonia Church near the junction of the Kinlock and Byler Roads.

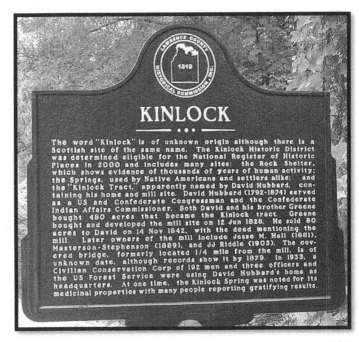

Since Kinlock Rock Shelter and Spring were approximately one mile southeast of the dividing ridge along which the High Town Path ran, the Kinlock sites were heavily used by both prehistoric and historic Indian people. The Kinlock site provided early travelers of the northern portion of Bankhead a source of water and also shelter during severe weather. The Kinlock Shelter is a premier petroglyph site in the State of Alabama.

According to *Two Hundred Years at Muscle Shoals,* *"the first state highway provided for by the legislature meeting in Huntsville in 1819 was built through Bainbridge. It started from the Great Military Road on the west side of Shoal Creek in Lauderdale County, crossed the river at Bainbridge and passed south through Jeffers Cross Roads (Leighton) on through old LaGrange, Kinlock, Haleyville, Eldridge, Bankston to Tuscaloosa. While John Byler and his associates were authorized to build only a portion of the road south of Franklin County, the old turnpike, short sections of which are still in use, was known as Byler's Turnpike Road. The road was directed to be twelve feet wide, clear of stumps and roots, and good causeways were planned for all soft places. The Byler Road was to facilitate travel from Nashville to Tuscaloosa, and, after the latter became the Capital of Alabama, in 1826, was a much used way, for many of our early settlers were from Tennessee and Virginia and used this route"* (Leftwich, 1935).

The Byler Road and the High Town Path ran along the Continental Divide in the western portion of Bankhead Forest for some five miles. Both roads lay along the dividing ridges and east of the upper watershed of Bear Creek. The Byler Road turned south with the High Town Path traveling west along the Continental Divide south of Bear Creek to Flat Rock in Franklin County. The High Town Path became less important as river ferries and passage through Indian lands were obtained through treaties.

The Byler Road portion of the High Town Path, built by John Byler and associates, was one of the first legislative acts of the State of Alabama. According to Lawrence County Deed Book C, pages 28 and 29, John Byler in March 1824 deeded Jacob Byler the undivided third part of the road known as Byler's Turnpike Road.

The Byler Road portion of the High Town Path saw a great deal of action during the Civil War. Supposedly a detachment of Colonel Able Streight's regiment was sent to Kinlock to take the grain and destroy the grist mill. Somewhere along or near the High Town Path portion, the Yankees of Northern Aggression were ambushed with the aid of a Cherokee family -- Jane "Aunt Jenny" Bates Brooks Johnston and her family. Also during the Civil War, Aunt Jenny's husband Willis and son John were killed by some soldiers. Some accounts say that three to seven Yankees were killed in the ambush and were buried in the slave cemetery at Kinlock.

194

Later in the War of Northern Aggression during March 1865, General J.H. Wilson organized the world's largest cavalry of 13,480 horses at Gravely Springs in Lauderdale County. Wilson's cavalrymen eventually engaged the Confederates at the Battle of Selma. One of the three divisions of the Wilson's Civil War Cavalry rode along the High Town Path portion of the Byler Road with the division staying at Hubbard's Plantation (Elliott, 1972). On March 24, 1865, Union General Winslow with a portion of General James H. Wilson's 14,000 men passed along the Poplar Springs area of the High Town Path in route to Selma via Kinlock and Hubbard's Mill.

David Hubbard House at Kinlock in 1930's

Major David Hubbard, who had a plantation home and mill near Kinlock Falls, was appointed Federal Commissioner of Indian Affairs of the Confederate States of America by President Jefferson Davis (Graves, 1985). Major Hubbard had a cotton factory on the High Town Path south of Bear Creek. According to an early Alabama map, Hubbard's cotton factory was located west of his plantation home on the High Town Path. Hubbard's home and grist mill were located at Kinlock Falls and Spring in Lawrence County's southwest portion of Bankhead Forest.

During historic times, one of the most colorful Cherokee Indian ladies to ever settle in Bankhead Forest lived at Kinlock on the historic High Town Path and Byler Road. She went by the name of "Aunt Jenny" and many times she aided weary travelers of the High Town Path. Aunt Jenny deeded some of her Kinlock land for the location of Macedonia Church. All five of her sons and some of her grandsons were shot and killed. Aunt Jenny along with some of her children are buried in Poplar Springs Cemetery, a few yards west of the High Town Path.

Mary Tennessee Garrison Spillers was another Indian lady of historic times whose family settled along the High Town Path in the Kinlock area. Her son, Amos Spillers, who lived for awhile at Kinlock, became the first conservation officer of Bankhead National Forest and is buried in the forest at Mt. Olive Cemetery (Manasco,

1981). Many children who are descendants of Aunt Jenny and Mary Tennessee have been in the Lawrence County Schools' Indian Education Program.

PERSONAL TESTIMONY

After the author spent much study in historical records and old maps, four well-known Warrior Mountain residents were asked to share, in their own words, their knowledge, legends, family traditions, and personal experiences of the High Town Path. Their statements were not edited but printed as they presented the information. Since their statements were taken, the High Town Path Historic District has been recognized by the Alabama Historical Commission as a significant Landmark and added to the Alabama Register of Landmarks and Heritage on November 17, 1995. In addition, the High Town Path was officially recognized across the State of Alabama in the Alabama House of Representatives (Resolution HJR84) and signed by Governor Fob James, Jr. on September 3, 1997.

Rayford Hyatt, Lawrence County Historian, Lawrence County Historical Society, July 22, 1992

Conservation Officer Rayford Hyatt

"High Town Path - This writer has studied the history of the Bankhead National Forest area for over thirty years, and believes this path followed the mountain divide between the Tennessee and Warrior River drainage. The trail entered southeast Lawrence County at Piney Grove via the Old Corn Road; thence north on Highway 41 to Cave Springs Cemetery; then west on the Leola Road by Center Church, Lindsey Hall, to Highway 33. Then north to the Ridge Road following it west to the Byler Road; then north to Bulah Road, west on it into Franklin County; the Bulah Church, Oak Grove, Spruce Pine, to Flat Rock. (Some say the trail turned south on Byler Road to Haleyville, then to Flat Rock).

I have no doubt of the route of the trail through Lawrence County being the Leola and Ridge Roads. This was a walking path and this route avoided climbing the steep hills, cliffs, and fording icy, flooded streams. There may have been some travel by

196

horseback in later times, and a few white traders probably traveled it. Although this trail was probably traveled from long, long ago, it does not today show signs of extensive use. The scattered deep eroded signs this writer has seen may have been made after the white people came in because roads follow this route. Foot travel would not have left many signs that would be visible to us today."

Lamar Marshall, Editor and Publisher *Bankhead Monitor*, Inc. July 27, 1992

"High Town Path - A thousand years ago there were no bridges on which to cross the myriad of streams and waterways in North Alabama. But even by then, man, as well as beast, had long ago discovered the backbone of North Alabama, the Tennessee Divide. It rises above the plain to its north and overlooks the ragged canyons to its south.

By the time the modern dozers straightened out the ancient meandering roadway, it was worn deep into the ground by the moccasin feet of Indian hunters, travelers, traders and eventually the white settlers. I have stood in the narrow trench where it is still intact on the saddles and mountaintops of Bankhead.

I have followed the worn side trails that lead to the springs that erupt from the pores of the mountainside and the rock overhangs that served as the roadside inns of the first Alabama travelers. Their mark is left as a reminder that they were here. Our mark must not erase their marks, for they passed by here first."

Lamar Marshall

Dr. Charles Borden, President Bankhead Trail Riders Association, July 27, 1992

"High Town Path - I am a 45-year-old, lifelong resident of the Bankhead National Forest of American Indian ancestry, who is among the seventh generation of Bordens to live in the Bankhead. Oral tradition describes an ancient Indian path crossing the northern Bankhead along the general route of the Leola and Ridge roads. This tradition is confirmed in historic accounts I have read of the High Town Path.

Charles Borden

Evidence of Indian habitation in the Bankhead dating back perhaps 10,000 years would seem to indicate that this path may have been an important route for travel, for hunting and commerce, for thousands of years. Perhaps it was the path taken by the Bordens to this area.

On a more poignant and personal note I have often reflected upon the plight of the men, women and children of my Indian ancestors who tread this path for the last time as they were rounded up for removal. The High Town Path is significant to me for both cultural and historic reasons."

Bobbie Gillespie, former chairman of the Blue Clan of the Echota Cherokee Tribe, Dec. 22, 2004

High Town Path - *"I remember even as a child, it has been a traditional family pilgrimage, for the Gillespie clan to go to certain, special places in the Bankhead Forest and hear how these places were visited and used by my direct ancestors. One of*

Bobby Gillespie

these places that my father, Dee Gillespie, took me was on the High Town Path which was also known by my family as the Old Stage Coach Road. He called the site we visited the Old Stagecoach Inn. No buildings were left standing but we did find evidence of the site and an old coin was found there.

The old road was used by James Richard Gillespie on the way to the Creek War when he traveled through the Bankhead along the High Town Path. He evidently was so impressed by its beauty that he came back after the war and settled in Indian Tomb Hollow around 1820. James and other family members are buried there. His son is buried just south of the High Town Path behind Charles Borden's present home place.

Today, I continue to share these places with my children and grandchildren in hopes that the significance of these places will never be lost by my descendants."

High Town Path Conclusion

Probably over 10,000 years ago, the Paleo Indians in the Moulton Valley looked south and saw a beautiful continuous ridge of virgin timber crossing their country. The Ridge Path, being a continuous link across most of the Southeastern United States, became a pathway and boundary for these prehistoric people.

After the Indians of long ago trod upon The Path, Europeans began exploiting the riches in the northern portions of Georgia, Alabama, and Mississippi via the Indian trail. The Cherokee, Chickasaw, and Creek traded skins and later their precious lands for the trinkets, tools, and guns of the white man.

As the European exploitation slowed, settlers begin moving into Indian country and marrying into the Indian tribes. These mixed-blood families moved along The Path opening up the new and beautiful frontier. Early communities and homesteads were established along the old Ridge Path. Much evidence still exists that indicate the Indians and later the early settlers to the High Town Path utilized the route not only in migration into Lawrence County and places further west, but also as a site to raise their families. Easy access by way of the High Town Path and seclusion within the mountainous forest was probably the reason for the Indians and the early mixed-blood Indian settlers living along the route in Lawrence County. Most of the old home sites and all of the Ridge Path's early schools are now gone with most of the area presently reverted to forest lands.

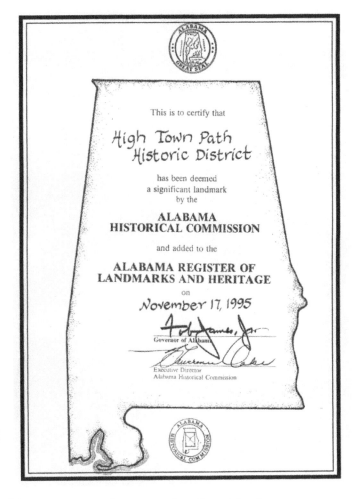

This is to certify that

High Town Path Historic District

has been deemed a significant landmark by the

ALABAMA HISTORICAL COMMISSION

and added to the

ALABAMA REGISTER OF LANDMARKS AND HERITAGE

on

November 17, 1995

Governor of Alabama

Executive Director
Alabama Historical Commission

Presently, most of the High Town Path route through the Lawrence County area is national forest lands and part of the William B. Bankhead National Forest.

Each historic and aboriginal site of Indians, mixed blood Indians, and early white settlers along this primitive Indian trail, as well as the remains of the old original High Town Path itself, needs protection under the National Historic Preservation Act. The route of the High Town Path should be placed on the <u>National Register of Historic Places</u>.

SECONDARY INDIAN TRAILS

Many ancient routes and trails meander across our ancestral landscapes of the Warrior Mountains of North Alabama. Many of our early settlers to this area were of Celtic-Indian mixed ancestry. These Indian mixed bloods migrated into the area of the Warrior Mountains for the isolation and protection from removal provided by the wilderness. The roots of our ancestors were of Cherokee, Creek or Chickasaw and of Irish, Scots, or Scots-Irish descent.

In the progression of events shaping the cultural heritage of this area, secondary Indian trails connected to major thoroughfares through the Warrior Mountains. Many times the trails were short by standards of the High Town Path but were vital routes for communities of forest dwellers. The following is a listing and description of a few secondary Indian trials.

Braziel Creek Trail

The Braziel Creek Trail was once trod upon by our Indian ancestors and parts of the trail are unspoiled by modern man. Portions of the trail represent the escape route of some Cherokees during removal as well as other Southern Indians and black slaves; it appears untouched by the white man. According to Jim Manasco, the trail was a secret route, which runs through Bankhead Forest's Sipsey Wilderness Area in Lawrence County, Alabama.

The trail of freedom to the south was used by some of our Southeastern Indian ancestors, and later a flight to the north for black slaves as part of the Underground Railroad. The trail was strategically located between the Byler Road to the west, and the Cheatham Road to the east. Both roads traverse north-south directions. Isolated from military movements and traffic along the two major Bankhead roads during the 1830s and passing through the forest on a north-south course, the trail offered protection from detection over its long course from the south to its junction with the High Town Path on the northern border of the forest near the Youngtown Mountain area.

In certain sections of the trail, the path appears to be untouched by wagons or other modern machinery of white men. In these sections, the path is some two feet wide and has been trod down some three to six inches deep. Along the trail is a marker tree estimated to have been bent some 150 years ago. The tree has two common names, yellow chestnut oak and chinquapin white oak. The tree marks a ninety degree turn in the trail direction and appears to have been deliberately selected by historical Indian people to mark trails and other important sites.

The goalpost-shaped marker tree in Indian Tomb Hollow is also a yellow chestnut oak or chinquapin white oak. The oak is an extremely slow growing tree which thrives where limestone outcroppings appear close to the topsoil level. They are, almost certainly, found in association with the eastern red cedar. However, in the case with both Indian marker trees these oaks are the only trees of their species within the immediate area of their location. This species isolation does not appear to be accidental and the chestnut or chinquapin oak marker trees are somewhat out of place. Additionally, in both cases, no eastern red cedars are found in close proximity.

Shortly after passing north of the trail marker tree, about one-half mile, a huge rock shelter is visible some 150 yards west of the trail. A quick examination revealed an abundance of flint chipping, three quartzite grinding stones, one perfect middle Woodland projectile point, and a small wire screen left behind by pot hunters. The shelter appeared to be extremely rich in artifacts with only one small area disturbed.

Continuing along the trail, enormous American beech trees, cucumber magnolias, yellow poplars, and other tree species represent climax vegetation with very limited numbers of understory trees. Another mile north of the shelter, adjacent to and touching the trail is a large beech tree bearing an inscribed snake similar to the copperhead. The horizontal snake symbol appeared to be extremely old and was located on the west side of the tree facing the trail. The snake's head was pointed south along the trail with its tail pointing north. According to folk lore and Indian legend passed through some 130 years of time, the snake was drawn by Indian people around the time of removal. According to Jim Manasco, his Indian ancestors passed through the area along the trail to the Rocky Plains.

The American beech is the oldest living hardwood tree in our area and can live in excess of eight hundred years. Because of the beech's extremely slow growth rate, it can retain carvings made into its bark over two hundred years. For these reasons Indian people, as well as early pioneers such as Davy Crockett, left their marks on the trees.

202

After traveling another mile along the route in a northwesterly direction, another rock shelter was examined. The shelter was also extensively used and had significant quantities of flint, pottery shards, and quartzite grinding stones. Since this bluff shelter lies close to the road, which is now closed under wilderness protection, the shelter showed evidence of extensive digging.

Approximately one hundred yards north of the shelters situated on a beautiful knoll, from which an enormous canyon to the north is visible, was another huge American beech with carvings. On the south side of the beech tree was another large inscribed snake, which appeared to be a rattlesnake. The snake symbol was in a vertical position facing the well- used rock shelter with its head pointing toward the ground. The snake's tail appeared to have rattles. Other shelters lay ahead to the north along the old worn Indian trail before it finally intersected the High Town Path on the northern edge of the Warrior Mountains of Bankhead National Forest. It is thought the Freedom Trail continued north through the Youngtown area of Lawrence County toward the Muscle Shoals of the Tennessee River.

Cahaba Valley Trail

The Cahaba Valley Trail was a south fork from High Town Path at Gadsden, Alabama. The trail traversed south toward Springville, Big Canoe Creek Valley near Asheville (site of a large Indian town called Cataula). The trail passed into the Cahaba River Valley and became known as Cahaba Valley Road and also the Old Ashville Road.

Cullman Motorway

This route will be referred to as the Cullman Motorway because the old road followed along an early Indian trail through the middle of the Warrior Mountains. This Indian trail started in Lawrence County near present-day Landersville. The route actually had two beginnings with one segment forking off the Old Chickasaw Trail at Landersville and the other forking off Doublehead's Trace near Hickory Grove.

The Landersville (east) fork traversed south from the Old Chickasaw Trail to Youngtown, where it meandered to the mountaintop to intersect the High Town Path. From the intersection with the High Town Path, the Indian trail traversed west one and one-half miles along the present-day Ridge Road toward the Gum Pond Road. At the Gum Pond Road, the east fork of the trail joined the fork coming from Hickory Grove. The west fork of the Indian trail left the Old Buffalo Trail or Doublehead's Trace at

Hickory Grove and traversed southeast toward Rocky Ridge. The Hickory Grove fork traversed up the east side of Rocky Ridge to the mountaintop where it also intersected the High Town Path near Goat's Bluff. From Goat's Bluff, the old Indian trail turns east along the Ridge Road for approximately a half mile to the Gum Pond Road intersection.

Near the route at Youngtown, extensive archaeological sites are found along the upper portion of Town Creek. These prehistoric Indian sites are multi-component from Paleo through Mississippian culture. A rock shelter near the Youngtown route contains several petroglyphs. From Doublehead's Trace at Hickory Grove to the High Town Path on the Ridge Road, numerous prehistoric archaeological sites are located along the trail on the upper drainage of Town Creek.

Many of the families in the area of Landersville, Hickory Grove, and Youngtown are descendants of the early Cherokee people who inhabited the area. Many children in the area are in Lawrence County Schools' Indian Education Program and are Indian descendants of the Riddle, Garrison, Borden, Blankenship, and other families who still live there. In historic times, these Indian families lived along the Cullman Motorway and eventually moved to the Youngtown-Hickory Grove area when the government bought land while establishing the national forest.

From the High Town Path, the old Indian trail traverses south along the Gum Pond Road and Braziel Creek Road passing Gum Pond Cemetery prior to entering the Sipsey Wilderness Area. From the Sipsey Wilderness road closure near Gum Pond, the trail traversed south along the Braziel Creek Road to an old segment of the Northwest Road. The trail followed southeast along the Northwest Road for about one-half mile before turning south along the now abandoned Bunyan Hill Road. From the Northwest Road, the Indian trail traveled south approximately one and one half miles along the Bunyan Hill Road before turning south along the Old Cullman Motorway just northwest of the headwaters of Fall Creek.

The Cullman Motorway ran south along a flat ridge toward Sipsey River. Just prior to reaching the river, the trail passed the Garrison family's old homeplace before meandering down a ridge to Saltpeter Well. This segment of the Cullman Motorway passes the beautiful flat glade of Saltpeter Well adjacent to Sipsey River. In this beautiful valley, the Old Cullman Motorway forded Sipsey River and ascended a ridge traversing toward the junction of the Caney Creek and the Cranal Road just east of Wolf Pen Cemetery. Near the Wolf Pen location lived the Indian family of John (Doc) Riddle (five eighths Cherokee) and his wife, Cordelia "Delie" Gray (Full Cherokee). You can read about the Indian families of Cullman Motorway in the book "*Warrior Mountains Folklore.*"

After crossing the Cranal Road, the Cullman Motorway followed along the present-day Caney Creek Road for approximately three-fourths of a mile before turning south to ford North Caney Creek in the southwest quarter of section 18 of Range 8 West and Township 9 South. From this creek crossing, the Cullman Motorway traversed westerly some two miles along present-day Jim Brown Road before turning south to ford South Caney Creek near the north edge of the northeast quarter of section 26 of Range 9 West and Township 9 South.

The Cullman Motorway followed the old Indian trail traversing east along the ridge between Sandy Creek and Sipsey River. The road crossed Sandy Creek in the southwest quarter of Section 11 of Range 8 West and Township 10 South. The Cullman Motorway continued east to ford Sipsey River near its junction with present-day Highway 278, and then traversed along the corridor of Highway 278 to Cullman, Alabama.

Cuttyatoy's Trail

In 1808, Captain Edmund Pendleton Gaines, just prior to reaching Spring Creek, noted an Indian trail running north and south. The trail led to a large island near the mouth of Spring Creek in the Tennessee River later known as Gilchrist Island. During the Creek Indian War in November 1813, the old Indian Chief Cuttyatoy lived on the island. Cuttyatoy's trail led south from the island crossing Gaines' Trace, then south past Swoope Pond where it intersected the Brown's Ferry Road.

During the late 1770s, Cuttyatoy was an aggressive Cherokee Warrior of the Chickamauga faction, fighting the whites to prevent settlement of the Big Bend of the Tennessee River and to protect Cherokee lands. After a keelboat raid in 1788, which led to the death of Joseph Brown's father along with two of his brothers, Cuttyatoy tried to kill Joseph Brown, who was fifteen years old at that time. During the raid, Cuttyatoy took the black slaves of the Brown family. It wasn't until the Battle of Talladega in November 1813, that Joseph Brown found out where his father's slaves were being held in present-day Lawrence County on Gilchrist Island across from the mouth of Elk River.

It was by Indian trails that Colonel Joseph Brown and his party of ten soldiers made their way to Cuttyatoy's home. The next day, Cuttyatoy and his people traveled the local Indian trails to Brown's Ferry where they crossed the Tennessee River and proceeded to Fort Hampton in Limestone County. By the time Cuttyatoy reached Fort Hampton, the slaves had already been sent to Huntsville. Colonel Joseph Brown, who became a preacher, spared the life of old Cuttyatoy and said he would let God take care of him. Joseph Brown became a large landowner in the Pulaski, Tennessee area. It is ironic that the slaves retaken by Joseph Brown wound up killing him. Some say they put poison or ground glass in his food.

Indian Creek Trail

Proceeding down the western slope of a ridge near the mouth of Indian Creek is an early pathway from Flint Creek Road to alluvial bottom land that was farmed by early mixed ancestry settlers of the area. The Indian Creek Road winds down the sloping ridge from the east and one fork fords Indian Creek where it meanders west up the ridge and joins the Blowing Springs Road on top of the mountain. The sandstone-walled banks of the eastern portion of this secondary trail wind like a snake to the bottomland. This unique roadbed, like many other old roads and trails through the Warrior Mountains, is part of the historical and ancestral landscape.

Another fork turns up Indian Creek and follows the creek drainage all the way to the Leola Road (High Town Path). This fork follows the east side of the creek and winds its way up a ridge to Smith Cemetery, which is located three-fourths of a mile north of the High Town Path near the Hickory Grove Road and Leola Road junction. This route probably led from Black Warriors' Path in Poplar Log Cove to the Moreland area of the Sipsie Trail.

Little Oakfuskee Chickasaw Path

This Indian trail was a trade route from the Tallapoosa River crossing at Little Oakfuskee located near Sawyers Ferry to Flat Rock in or near present-day Haleyville, Alabama. Traders coming from Georgia would use this route to transport goods to the Chickasaw towns on the upper Tombigbee River.

Old Houston Trail

Just one mile south of present-day Speake High School in eastern Lawrence County, the Black Warriors' Path split, with the Old Houston Trail forking off to the south. While the Black Warriors' Path traversed southeasterly, the Old Houston Trail turned south some three miles where the Blowing Springs Road forked to the southwest prior to Washspring Mountain. The Blowing Springs Road would eventually rejoin the Old Houston Trail at present-day Hickory Grove Cemetery in the northern portion of Winston County.

206

The Old Houston Trail crossed Washspring Mountain and followed along Sheats Branch, which is a small tributary of West Flint Creek. Near the Sheats Branch junction with the Old Houston Trail, the old roadbed is cut deep into the sloping hillside. Old trails and roads would eventually rut out and were constantly moved over leaving berms between the sections. The old trail continued adjacent to the branch along the present Flint Creek Road, and in the old days, crossed Flint Creek near present-day Chenault Bridge which was just west of the junction of Wiggins Creek and Flint Creek. Prior to reaching Chenault Bridge, the old trail intersected the Poplar Log Cove Road.

As the Old Houston Road meandered up the hillside of West Fork of Flint Creek, a deep rutted trail is clearly visible on the west side of the present road. The old trail continued to the mountaintop and intersected the High Town Path near the long gone Community of Templeton. The trail then followed the High Town Path westerly approximately one mile before turning south toward the Hickory Grove Cemetery where the Blowing Springs Road rejoined the old route. The Indian Creek Trail and the Old Houston Trail ran along the same ridge toward Hickory Grove Cemetery.

From Hickory Grove, the Old Houston Trail continued south toward Moreland. Prior to reaching the community of Moreland, the old trail passed the homesite of Buckner and Seleth Walker's descendants. My grandmother, Maudy Nevady Legg Walker, traveled with her husband Dan and sometimes her children to get medicines from the Buckner Walker family. My grandmother considered Mrs. Walker to be one of the best medicine people who lived in the Warrior Mountains. Their medicines were old Indian remedies. Buckner's family descendants still live on the ridge east of Moreland.

Buckner Walker and his family are found in the military and genealogical records of the famous beloved Cherokee woman Nancy Ward. The Walkers, as was I, are descendants of Nancy Ward. Our families were actually descendants of John Walker (half Cherokee) and Catherine Kingfisher (full-blooded Cherokee), who was the daughter of Nancy Ward and the Kingfisher. Nancy was married to the Cherokee Indian Kingfisher prior to being married to Bryan Ward, a white man. John and Catherine had a son William Walker around 1760. He is buried in Blount County. William fathered my great, great, great, granddaddy William A. Walker (1790 - 1900). He is buried in Cullman County at Old Emeus Cemetery near Logan (on the Black Warriors' Path) next to my great granddaddy Sidney Walker.

From Moreland, the Old Houston Trail follows the corridor of the old highway that traverses the dividing ridges to the Community of Old Houston. From Old Houston, the route traversed south toward Jasper and on toward Tuscaloosa where it joined other Indian trails leading south to Mobile. Tuscaloosa was the largest Mississippian Indian town on the Black Warrior River and today still contains some forty mounds at nearby Moundville. This made the area one of the largest prehistoric Indian trading areas in the southeastern United States.

Poplar Log Cove Trail

On a cold December morning before daylight, my grandpa Authur Wilburn left his old log house with his Uncle Hiram Johnson to check trap lines on Indian Creek. Grandpa and I had made a deal to work our trap lines during my Christmas vacation and split the money. I had been staying each night at my grandpa's house but mother made me stay home that night because grandpa's uncle was spending the night.

My grandpa's home was on the west side of Mull Johnson Mountain about five hundred yards downhill from the Hattie Hogan Spring. The east edge of their land was bordered by a 40-acre block of U.S. Forest Service Property. The south and west side of their land was bordered by the vast Alexander Plantation. To the north was Cedar Mountain, to the west was Brushy Mountain, and to the south was Sugar Camp Hollow. I was supposed to be at grandpa's house before daylight but my parents overslept. By the time I got to my grandparents' house, Grandpa and Uncle Hiram had been gone about one hour. I told my grandma, Ila Wilburn, that I could catch up with the men. Reluctantly, she allowed me to strike out by myself.

About 7:30 that morning, I caught up with grandpa and Uncle Hiram just south of the Mastengill Hole on the West Fork of Flint Creek. By the time I finally caught up with the trappers, I had gone about two miles on a heavily overcast and cold day. At that time, they were walking the Poplar Log Cove Trail that crossed the creek at the mouth of Thompson Creek on the Old Alexander Plantation which was always called the Walnut Ford. The ford was known as Walnut Ford because the bottomland along Thompson Creek was covered with gigantic walnut trees.

At the Walnut Ford was a large field known as the Cyclone New Ground. The field lay to the southwest of the ford and was cleared by a cyclone or tornado. When the cyclone came through, it blew the top off Jake Alexander's old plantation house. A hired hand, Ed Welborn, was upstairs in bed with the typhoid fever. The storm left Mr. Welborn in bed but removed the roof.

From Walnut Ford at the mouth of Thompson Creek, the Flint Creek Trail proceeded toward High House Hill passing between the Nichols Cemetery and the Gray Cemetery. The trail crossed Gillespie Branch and up High House Hill, and passed southwest along the ridge crossing the High Town Path and on toward Brushy Creek. The Poplar Log Cove Road preceded northwest from the mouth of Thompson Creek toward Moulton with the southeast portion we were walking going toward Poplar Log Cove Spring at the headwaters of West Flint Creek.

The old Poplar Log Cove Spring became the home site of Mr. Tom Poole and the beautiful valley was known by many people as Tom Poole Hollow. The road went right by the edge of Mr. Tom Poole's yard. The spring was just a few yards behind Mr. Poole's house and the branch ran beside his home site. In Mr. Poole's day, all travelers would stop at his house to get water before heading to Basham Gap and Cave. From Mr. Poole's, an old road continued southeasterly toward Piney Grove and was called the Black Warriors' Path.

The morning was extremely cold and I did not take enough time to dress as warmly as I should. I remember the cold just seeping through my clothes every time we stopped to check or re-set our traps. The only traps we checked while heading to our final destination at the upper end of Indian Creek were those which would be out of the way on our return home. The round trip was some twenty miles which ended approximately four hours after first darkness.

Butch Walker in Poplar Log Cove Road at Blizzard Branch

I had caught grandpa and Uncle Hiram just past the mouth of McVay Hollow. As we proceeded along the Old Poplar Log Cove Trail, I listened to the two men talk about the people who lived along the old road when they were young boys. Even though the trail was no longer an old horse and wagon road, Grandpa always tried to point out where everyone had a cabin. On the north side of the Pearson Field was a large log cabin near the mouth of Lindsey Hollow. At the upper end of the Six Acre Patch, which was the last southeasternmost field on the Alexander Place, was large log house with three chimneys and a hand dug rock-walled well forty feet from the house. Between the house and well was a dug out rectangular hole that may have been a root celler. In the mouth of McVay Hollow on the north side of the branch was a large log house with an old rock chimney. It was probably the home of a member of the McVay family. As I got to the old McVay Place, I was extremely happy to see my Grandpa and Uncle Hiram near the middle of the Six Acre Patch. I had already made up my mind to go back home if I had not caught up with them before the last field on the Alexander Place.

We proceeded south and east out of the Six Acre Patch, through the woods past the three old chimneys to the Matt Pearson Old Field. We continued past the mouth of Lindsey Hollow, across Blizzard Branch, crossed the Blowing Spring Road, up the hill just south of the Old Friendship Cemetery, past the old cave just south of the road on the hill, and back into the West Flint Creek bottom toward Indian Creek. At the mouth of Indian Creek, we sat down on the side of the old trail and ate our lunch. As always, Grandpa offered me some of his food. We never carried water because we knew the location of every spring and we would sometimes drink from the little feeder streams.

Butch, Grandpa Arthur, and Mike with our trapline catch in
February 1964 just a month before grandpa died

After finishing lunch, we went up Indian Creek to check the most distant traps.

On the east side of Indian Creek not far from its junction with Flint was the Old Indian Creek Trail that led south toward Hickory Grove. The trail serpentined its way down the hill from the east and turned south along the creek's eastern bank, then traversed up the valley to the High Town Path at the creek's headwaters. On Indian Creek, we had three raccoons within a short distance. I placed the coons in a tow sack which was swung across my back. The sack of animals helped keep me warm on the long trek back toward home. All three helped bear the burden of animals.

210

When we got back to the Pearson Field about 4:00 p.m. that afternoon, snow began falling so thick you could hardly see over twenty yards. By the time we got back to the Walnut Ford and hit the Flint Creek Trail, which led toward the Alexander Bridge and Cedar Mountain, the snow was three to four inches deep. I well remember looking into the sky, watching those big flakes of snow falling like a swarm of bees. By the time we reached the old wooden bridge, the snow was five to six inches deep and was well over my shoe tops. My feet felt like chunks of ice.

Uncle Hiram said he was walking home. He lived about two miles west from the bridge, past the old Alexander plantation home, and past the entrance of the Welborn-Alexander Cemetery. Grandpa and I wished Uncle Hiram well and thanked him for helping carry our day's catch. I remember well that Grandpa looked at me and said "Butch we have about a dozen traps left on the Old Suck Branch and into Beech Bottoms. Let's check those tonight because they will be snowed in for the next few days." I agreed with Grandpa even though I felt like I was freezing to death. We got to the Old Suck Branch and found a large boar mink in our first trap. We continued checking all the traps before crossing the south end of Brushy Mountain toward home. I was tickled to death to get to Grandpa's home by about 8:30 that night. It was a great feeling to stand next to the old wood stove and thaw out from a day that was extremely cold. Shortly after warming by the fire, I started skinning the day's catch. Grandpa never cleaned the animals. That job was left to me and my grandmother. Sometime around midnight, we had all the hides stretched and all coons and possums soaking in pans of water in the refrigerator. The foot of snow stayed on the ground for about a week.

The above true story was blazed into my mind as an unforgettable memory of the largest snowfall I had experienced in my lifetime of walking the Indian Trails of the Warrior Mountains. It represents only one day that I walked portions of the Flint Creek Trail and Poplar Log Cove Trail. Since that day in the early 1960s, I have walked these old trails many times, which were also walked by my Indian ancestors for hundreds of years.

Both the Flint Creek Trail and the Poplar Log Cove Trail were important Indian routes; however, in this section, I will focus on the Poplar Log Cove Trail. Poplar Log Cove was a site of Paleo Indian occupation based on the discovery of flint tools left by early Paleo people some twelve thousand years ago. Uniface scrapers and other Paleo artifacts have been found near the old Poplar Log Cove Spring, which is the source of the West Fork of Flint Creek. The spring is found in Township 8 South, Range 6 West, and Section 11 and was located near the junction of the Poplar Log Cove Trail and Black Warriors' Path. The Black Warriors' Path led southeasterly from the cove to

Elyton (Birmingham) and then into the Chattachoochee River Valley and north to Melton's Bluff and on to the French Lick (Nashville).

The Poplar Log Cove Trail traversed west to northwesterly from the old Poplar Log Cove Spring to Moulton, where it intersected the Coosa Path, Sipsie trail, and Old Chickasaw Path; therefore, the Poplar Log Cove Trail was basically a local Indian route from Moulton to Poplar Log Cove Spring. About the middle of the Poplar Log Cove Trail was an extensive Woodland Indian village site. The Indian town was located on the Old Alexander Plantation and is presently owned by Dallas Yeager. The ancient Indian town has been referred to as the Alexander Mound, since the Smithsonian excavated the site in 1924.

In the early historical records of Lawrence County, Alabama, the Poplar Log Cove Trail was upgraded to a public county road from Moulton to Poplar Log Cove; however, by the early 1900s, the road was used as a wagon route to various patches of cotton and corn from the Old Alexander Plantation eastward into Poplar Log Cove. By the early 1960s, the remains of the road were still visible, but the road was no longer in use by the general public.

During the 1930s, several people lived on the Poplar Log Cove Road between the Alexander Plantation and Elam Creek toward Moulton. After the Poplar Log Cove Road passed south of the Alexander House, it continued toward Gus Welborn's house where it curved toward the Welborn-Alexander Cemetery. The road actually passed between the Old Alexander Cemetery, which is now in woods, and the Welborn Cemetery which is next to the newer Alexander Cemetery to the east.

According to my Uncle Curtis Welborn, the old Poplar Log Cove Road passed between the old barn and silo (which still stand on Dallas Yeager's property) at the Jake Alexander home. The Gray Cemetery and the Gray Hill Graveyard Field was next to the old road. The cemetery had four marble tomb stones which were marked. Several of the graves just had sandstone head stones. Presently, the remains of the Gray Cemetery are in a bulldozer pile at that site.

The first house going northwest from Mr. Jake Alexander was the old Gus Welborn house which stood where the late G. H. Melson's home is located. The road actually went between the old dogtrot log house and the junction of the present gravel road that goes to the Welborn-Alexander Cemetery. After passing the cemetery, the next house was known as the Middle Quarter House. Continuing toward Moulton, the old road passed between the old Leer House and the Middle Quarter House. Mr. Jim Robbins bought the Middle Quarter House after World War I and lived there for a while. Also, the Kay McVay family lived in the house before they moved east of the Alexander Bridge which crossed Flint Creek. The next house was Mrs. Hill's, which had a small log store in her front yard. The old log store did not have any windows. The road then turned northwest by Mr. Floyd Hill's mother's store toward the next house on the Woodard Place. The road then passed the Frank Simpson family home, the Bob Barrett home, and the Mack Clemons Family lived in the next house. Prior to crossing present-day Highway 36 and Elam Creek, the road passed by the home of the late Mr. Paul Miller Johnson to the west of his house. The old road continued north, crossing the old wooden bridge on Elam Creek just northwest of present-day Tim Johnson's house. From Elam Creek, the road continued north to the present-day Pinhook Road where it entered Moulton on the present-day Sommerville Avenue. After crossing Elam Creek, the Poplar Log Cove Road became known as the Pin Hook Road and traversed toward Sommerville Avenue in Moulton, which was its junction with the Coosa Path.

A short trail known as the Sugar Camp Hollow Path connected the Flint Creek Trail to the Poplar Log Cove Trail east of their junction at Walnut Ford. Mr. Emory Hyde lived on the Sugar Camp Hollow Path which turned off the Flint Creek Trail on the east side of Sugar Camp Hollow. He made a china cabinet for my grandmother Ila Wilburn. She swapped three turkey hens and a turkey gobbler for the old china cabinet. She cracked the glass hauling the cabinet in her old mule drawn sled. Sandy Welborn was the one that actually broke the glass bringing it down the hill. Sandy Welborn lived in the old Mull-Johnson house.

Mr. Hyde lived on top of the mountain east of Sugar Camp. Two fields were located in the mouth of Sugar Camp Hollow. The field south of Flint Creek Trail was Sugar Camp Field and to the north was the Eight Acre Bottom where Sugar Camp Branch goes into Flint Creek. The Sugar Camp Hollow Road went by Mr. Emory's house, and crossed over the mountain to Mr. Lo Spears place. Later Mr. Terrapin Lowery moved into the Spears Home. The road then crossed Blizzard Branch to the old Poplar Log Cove Road.

Mr. Lo Spears had a red horse with blaze face and a brindle steer, which he worked together. Mr. Shirley Smith owned two brindle steers, Boss and Tony, which he worked. Both men plowed and broke land for Mr. Jake Alexander. As they were going from Blizzard Branch to the Alexander Place, they traveled the Poplar Log Cove Road. Mr. Lo Spears and Shirley Smith would break and plow the Lagoon Field and John Spivey Patch adjacent to Thompson Creek. Mr. John Spivey cleared the field; therefore, it was named after him.

According to my Uncle Curtis, when he was a small boy, he would ride the old mule-drawn cotton wagon along the old Poplar Log Cove Road to the old Moulton Cotton Gin. He remembers well that sometimes the old mule-drawn wagon would get stuck in the road. The cotton gin was located adjacent to the east side of the present-day Western Auto in Moulton. He also remembers when Dr. Price Irwin would ride a horse and buggy along the old road to his grandparents' house; their names were Pascal Sandy and Dora Johnson Welborn. He was told that Dr. Price stayed all night with the Welborns the evening that their son Willard Welborn was born.

Rat Poison Gap Trail and Devil's Well Road

The Rat Poison Gap Trail is a secondary trail which leads to alluvial bottomland along Montgomery and Borden Creeks. The trail is deeply worn as it traverses west before proceeding through a deep cut in the sandstone bluffs. The trail then winds gently down a long ridge, where it intersects Montgomery Creek. At the creek junction, the first settlers to the area built limestone abutments for a timbered bridge that provided passage over the creek. The trail then goes around the end of Oil Well Ridge to the lush Borden Creek Valley. Most of the bottom lands have returned to hardwood timber except for the Borden Cove portion originally settled by half-blood Cherokee David Borden. David married a full-blood and produced a large and prominent family, to which his descendants still proudly trace their Indian roots.

The road traverses west where it fords Borden Creek near the old home-site that is thought to be that of Christopher Borden. After passing the home site on a western knoll of the creek, the old road gently ascends a ridge to a saddle.

Butch Walker and Lamar Marshall at Rat Poison Gap

To the west of the saddle is a well known cave called the Devil's Well, which contains an underground waterfall approximately one hundred feet high.

Proceeding west past the cave, the Devil's Well Road begins a moderately steep climb up a short ridge to the mountaintop. A few yards north of the road near the edge of the canyon are the remains of another home place. The road gently rises toward the Mountain Springs Road and then turns north approximately one half mile to the High Town Path.

The Rat Poison Gap Trail connects the Sipsie Trail to the High Town Path and Old Buffalo Trail. The trail led to alluvial farmlands in the present-day Montgomery Creek and Borden Creek bottomlands. The rich creek bottoms were utilized for growing corn, potatoes, and other crops important to the survival of early Indian people and their families.

Uncle Dick Payne Trail

Recently, Dr. Charles Borden talked to me about an old Indian trail that went by the homeplace of a famous Bankhead resident that his granddad Doc Borden referred to as Uncle Dick Payne. Dr. Charles Borden, a member of the Echota Cherokee Tribe of Alabama and a life-long resident of the Bankhead, is a seventh generation descendent of Christopher Borden. Christopher, for whom Borden Creek is named, married a full blood Cherokee woman. Next in Charles' ancestry was Christopher's son David, a half-blood Cherokee who married a full blood Cherokee Indian. Dr. Charles' Cherokee grandparents include: Thomas Phillip Borden (half); Minnie England (half); William Rufus Adley Hooper (three quarters); Melvina McVay (three quarters); Uranis "Tirey" England (half); and Mary LouDusky Pearson (one quarter).

According to Dr. Borden, he, his granddad, the Hoopers, and the Englands regularly used the Dick Payne Trail for travel. Dr. Borden particularly remembers one story his granddad Doc told of himself and Johnny England, when they were very young, taking some corn to be milled at the Collier Creek Falls Gristmill. The mill was operated by Will Riddle, another local Cherokee descendent. They traveled in a two-wheeled cart pulled by two oxen along the trail by Uncle Dick Payne's place and took a side trail to the mill. The main trail traversed south toward Moreland.

On the way back from the mill the oxen spooked while coming down the steep trail west of the Beech Creek crossing and took them for a wild ride racing down the hill and crossing Beech Creek at a full run. Doc, his cousin Johnny and their cargo were bouncing wildly. They finally got the oxen under control and no one was hurt. The freshly ground cornmeal made it home. Doc said it was the wildest ride he ever took.

Dick Payne, who served under Confederate General Longstreet and coined the phrase "Free State of Winston," lived about one mile east of the Beech Creek crossing on this trail. His house was on top of a bluff near a stream and waterfall where he had a gristmill. A post office was also located very near the house. Dick even printed his own currency for a time.

The Uncle Dick Payne Indian Trail was used for hundreds if not thousands of years. It connected the High Town Path to Moreland and on south to Houston. The Uncle Dick Payne Trail branched off the High Town Path just west of Shiloh Church and followed the Wilson Ridge west along the present day Brushy Creek Road to the junction of the Miss Little Ridge, present day Shelton Road. Payne's Trail turned south along the Shelton Road for some two miles before turning west along a ridge to the Brushy Creek crossing in the northwest quarter of Section 33, T8S, and R7W. The trail continues west and intersects the Mt. Olive Road approximately one quarter mile southeast of the junction of the Brushy Creek Road with the Mt. Olive Road.

The Uncle Dick PayneTrail traversed one quarter mile south on Mt. Olive Road before turning southwest and crossing Beech Creek in the east half of Section 8, T9S, R7W. The trail continued west climbing a steep hill and again interesecting the Mt. Olive Road. The trail turned southeast immediately along Walston's Ridge crossing Collier Creek just west of where it empties into Brushy Creek in the southwest quarter of Section 16, T9S, and R7W. The trail then follows a gentle curve to the southwest to Moreland where it passes the homeplace of the Buckner Walker family. The trail continues along the west ridge of Brushy Creek and intersects Mile Creek about one half mile from its mouth on Brushy Creek. After crossing Mile Creek, the route intersects present-day Highway 278 and proceeds directly south to Houston.

West Flint Creek-High House Hill Trail

The West Flint Creek Trail began southwest at Oakville and led toward Indian Tomb Hollow. Near Oakville, the West Flint Creek Trail forked off the Black Warriors' Path. According to old residents of the area, the southern route to Black Warrior Town split at Oakville with the western fork running east of the creek and crossing present-day Highway 157 about one half mile from the bridge. The trail proceeds through a gap between Cedar Mountain and Mull-Johnson Mountain into Hickory Flats Hollow toward the forks of West Flint Creek and Thompson Creek. The West Flint Creek Path continued east past the creek junction up West Flint into Poplar Log Cove back to the Black Warriors' Path.

From the West Flint-Thompson Creek junction, the trail ran along the northeastern side of the creek until it intersected with Blizzard Branch on the Blowing Springs Road. The trail traversed east up a hill after crossing the Blowing Springs Road about three quarters of a mile north of the bridge and then back into the creek valley where it proceeded into Poplar Log Cove. In Poplar Log Cove, the Flint Creek Trail rejoined the Black Warriors' Path.

At Walnut Ford, located at the junctions of Thompson Creek and West Flint Creek, the High House Hill Trail forked to the southwest toward the High Town Path, then passed Nichols Cemetery, and then into the mouth of Indian Tomb Hollow. The trail proceeded up High House Hill within a few feet of High House Hill Spring. The trail ascends the mountain at the point of the ridge which separates the watersheds of Lee and Gillespie Creeks, and joined the High Town Path about two miles southwest along the ridge. The route southwest from Oakville shortened the route to the High Town Path from its junction with Black Warriors' Path by some twenty miles and also connected Oakville to the present-day Moreland area.

The High House Hill Trail proceeded southwest from the High Town Path to the point of Wilson Ridge where it crossed Brushy Creek. The trail proceeded from Brushy up the ridge to Pine Torch Road crossing about two miles southeast of present day Highway 33. At the Pine Torch Road the trail forked, with one route toward Pine Torch Church and the other fork to Beech Creek. Both routes eventually rejoined near the Collier Creek Falls at the old grist mill site. From Collier Creek Falls, the route proceeded south and rejoined the Cheatham Road near Moreland.

Conclusion

During some 14,000 years of aboriginal Indian prehistory, trails and paths were important to the settlement of this area and survival of our people. The original trails of our early Indian people were developed along old animal paths. These paths later became the early roads of the Warrior Mountains and North Alabama. Some of these early road or path corridors developed into the more modern roads of our area.

Today, we travel these roads in our vehicles never thinking of the thousands of years that our ancestors utilized them as paths; therefore, today we walk and ride where our forefathers and mothers once walked. We live in the towns and villages that have been inhabited for hundreds of generations. We survive off the same lands that nurtured our people over ten thousand years. Maybe, one day, we can learn to respect, protect, and love our ancestral landscapes that give life to every living creature.

References

American States Papers, *Indian Affairs*. 7th Congress 1st session. Number 95. pp. 656-657.

Belue, Ted Franklin, *The Long Hunt: Death of the Buffalo East of the Mississippi*, 1996.

Bierce, Lucius Verus, Journal-*Travels in the Southland* 1822-1823. Ohio State Press.

Buggey, L. JoAnne, and Others, *America! America*! Illinois: Scott, Foresman and Company, 1980.

Brannon, Peter, *By-Paths in Alabama*. The Paragon Press. Montgomery, 1929.

Cagle, Willa Jean, *Folklore of East Lauderdale County*. Journal of Muscle Shoals History. Volume I, 1977.

Cambron, James W. and David C. Hulse, *Handbook of Alabama Archaeology*. David L. DeJaruette, editor, Alabama Archaeological Society. Huntsville, Alabama, 1986.

Carter, Clarence Edwin, editor, *The Territorial Papers of the United States: Alabama 1817-1819.* Washington: United States Government Publishing Company, 1952.

Carter, Clarence Edwin, editor, *The Territorial Papers of the United States: Mississippi Volumes V and VI.* Washington: United States Government Publishing Company, 1938.

Chapman, Oscar L. and Arthur E. Demaray, *Natchez Trace Parkway*. United States Department of the Interior, 1951.

Clark, Thomas D. and John D. W. Guice, *The Old Southwest 1795-1830.* Frontiers in Conflict. University of Oklahoma Press Norman and London, 1989.

Cowart, Maragret Matthews, *Old Land Records of Lawrence County Alabama*. Huntsville, Alabama. 1991.

Cresap, Bernarr, editor, *History of Lauderdale County, Journal of Muscle Shoals History*. Tennessee Valley Historical Society, Vol. 5, 1977.

Dodd, Donald B., *Historical Atlas of Alabama*. Alabama: University of Alabama Press, 1974.

Dunnavant, Robert Jr., *Historic Limestone County*. Pea Ridge Press, 1993.

Editor, *Forty-Fourth Annual Report of the Bureau of American Ethnology* 1926-1927. United States Government Printing Office, Washington, D.C., 1928.

Elliot, Carl, *Winston: An Antebellum and Civil War History of a Hill Country of North Alabama*. Alabama: Oxmoor Press, 1972.

Foreman, Grant, *Indian Removal*. University of Oklahoma Press. Norman, 1932.

Fowke, Gerard, *Forty-Fourth Annual Report of the Bureau of American Ethanology*. United States Printing Office. Washington, D.C., 1928.

Gentry, Dorothy, *Life and Legend of Lawrence County, Alabama*. Tuscaloosa: Nottingham-SWS, Inc., 1962.

Gibson, Arrell, *The Chickasaws*. Norman: University of Oklahoma Press, 1971.

Govan, Gilbert E. and James W. Livingood, *The Chattanooga Country, 1540-1976*. From Tomahawks to TVA, The University of Tennessee Press, Knoxville, 1977.

Graves, William H., *"The Five Civilized Tribes and the Beginning of the Civil War,"* Journal of Cherokee Studies, X:209-211, 1985.

Hathern, Stacye and Robin Sabino, *Views and Vistas: Traveling Through the Choctaw, Chickasaw, and Cherokee Nations in 1803*. The Alabama Review. Volume 54 Number 3. The University of Alabama Press. July, 2001.

Harris, W. Stuart, *Dead Towns of Alabama*. University, Alabama: The University Press, 1977.

Hatley, Tom, *The Dividing Paths*. Cherokees and South Carolinians Through the Era of Revolution. Oxford University Press, New York, 1995.

Holstein, Harry O., Curtis E. Hill, and Keith J. Little, *"Archaeological Investigation of Stone Mounds on the Fort McClellan Military Reservation"*. Calhoun County, Alabama. United States Department of Defense. January, 1995.

Hood, Charlotte, *Jackson's White Plumes*. "Ten Islands of the Coosa River" Journal of Alabama Archaeology, Vol. 38, Number 2, 1992.

Hyatt, Rayford, *Last Indian and White Battle in Lawrence County. Melton's Bluff*. Old Lawrence Reminiscences, 1993.

Jacobs, Wilbur R., *The Appalachian Indian Frontier*. University of Nebraska Press, Lincoln, 1967.

Johnson, Gaylon D., *Before the German Settlement of 1873*: The Land and People that Became Cullman County, 1982.

Johnson, Kenneth, editor, *A History of Colbert County, Alabama*. The Journal of Muscle Shoals History. Vol. IV, 1976.

Jones, Margaret Jean, *Combing Cullman County*. Cullman, Alabama: Modernistic Printers, Inc., 1972.

Knox, John, *Were the Cherokees Red Welshmen? 800 Years of History Give Proof*. The Decatur Daily, August 19, 1964.

Leftwich, Nina, *Two Hundred Years at Muscle Shoals*. Northport, Alabama. The American Southern Publishing Company, 1935.

M.A.H., *Historical Traditions of Tennessee*. The Captivity of Jane Brown and Her Family. The American Whig Review, Vol. 15, Issue 87, Cornersville, TN, Dec. 25, 1851. Published at 120 Nassau Street, New York, 1852.

Malone, Henry T., *Cherokees of the Old South. A People in Transition*. The University of Georgia Press, Athens, 1956.

Manasco, Jim, *Indian Heritage Deep in Walker, Winston*. Daily Mountain Eagle, 1981.

McDonald, William Lindsey, *Lore of the River...The Shoals of Long Ago*, Heart of Dixie Publishing 1st ed. 1989, 2nd ed., 2001.

McDonald, William Lindsey, *The Journal of Muscle Shoals History*. Cultures of Early Peoples at the Muscle Shoals. Vol. VII, 1979.

Mooney, James, *Myths of the Cherokee and Sacred Formulas of the Cherokee*. Nashville, TN. Charles Elder, 1972.

Moore, Albert Burton, *History of Alabama*. Tuscaloosa, Alabama: Alabama Bookstore, 1951.

Owens, Marie Bankhead. *The Story of Alabama*. New York: Lewis Historical Publishing Company, Inc., 1949.

Pickett, Albert James, *History of Alabama*. 1851.

Perdue, Theda, *Slavery and the Evolution of Cherokee Society, 1540-1866*. The University of Tennessee Press, Knoxville, TN. 1981.

Ponder, Odalene, *Lawrence County Census 1820, 1830, 1840, and 1850*. Gregarth Company, 1983

Royall, Anne, *Letters from Alabama 1817-1822*. University of Alabama Press, 1969.

Rozeman, Vicki, *Footsteps of the Cherokees*. A Guide to the Eastern Homelands of the Cherokee Nation, John F. Blair, Publisher, Winston-Salem, N.C., 1995.

Saunders, James Edmund, *Early Settlers of Alabama*. Southern Historical Press, 1977. Reprint of 1899 edition.

Stone, James H., *Surveying the Gaines Trace*, 1807-1808. Alabama Historical Quarterly, Summer 1971.

Summersell, Charles Grayson, *Alabama History for Schools*. Montgomery: Viewpoint Publications, 1981.

Swanton, John R., *Final Report of the United States DeSoto Expedition Commission*. Washington, D.C., Smithsonian Institution Press, 1985.
————-*The Indians of the Southeastern United States*. Smithsonian Institution Press. Washington, D.C., 1987

Thompson, Wesley S., *The Free State of Winston*. Winfield, Alabama: Pareil Press, 1968.

Waco, *Letter From Texas*. Waco, Texas, May 9th, 1882. The Moulton Advertiser, May 25, 1882.

Walker, Rickey Butch, *A Cultural Heritage Outline of Indian History in Lawrence County and North Alabama*. Lawrence County Schools' Indian Education Program, 1988.

————-*High Town Path*. Lawrence County Schools' Indian Education Program, 1992.

————-*Indians of the Warrior Mountains*. Lawrence County Schools' Indian Education Program, 1997.

————-*Warrior Mountains Folklore*. Lawrence County Schools' Indian Education Program, 1995.

Watts, C. Wilder, *Indians at the Muscle Shoals*. The Journal of Muscle Shoals History. Vol. 1, 1973.

W.H.G. and Spencer Waters, *"Ittaloknah or The Battle of Indian Tomb Hollow - A Story of North Alabama."* The Moulton Democrat 1856 and researched by Waters, *1967.*

Webb, William S., *An Archaeological Survey of Wheeler Basin on the Tennessee River in Northern Alabama*. Smithsonian Institute Bureau of American Ethnology, Bulletin No. 122, 1939.

Wright, Ronald, *Stolen Continents*. Boston: Houghton and Mifflin Company, 1992.

Index

Big Lick, 31, 98, 99
Big Muscle Shoals, 29, 83, 105, 119, 125, 127, 150
Big Spring, 103, 110, 113, 119, 120, 121, 122, 134
Big Stone, 178
Big Wills Creek, 50, 66, 68, 70, 71, 76
BigBee Settlements, 113
Bingham, Marion S., 179
Bird Tail, 18
Black Dutch, 9, 188
Black Fox, 13, 14, 15, 19, 40, 41, 53, 94, 98, 99
Black Fox Trail, 99
Black Irish, 9, 188
Black Warrior, 98, 105, 108, 109, 110, 111, 112, 125, 128, 176, 178, 182, 183, 184, 189, 208, 216
Black Warrior Road, 48, 75, 106, 111, 176
Black Warrior Town, 48, 75, 106, 109, 112, 176, 189, 216
Black Warriors' Path, 14, 27, 36, 37, 40, 43, 77, 98, 99, 105, 106, 107, 108, 109, 110, 111, 121, 122, 141, 143, 149, 154, 157, 176, 189, 206, 207, 209, 211, 216, 217
Black Warriors' Road, 106
Blankenship, 204
Bledsoe's Fort, 103
Blizzard Branch, 210, 213, 217
Bloody Fellow, 72
Blount County, 124, 144, 176, 207
Blount, Gov., 182
Blount, William, 71
Blountsville, 141
Blowing Spring Road, 210
Blue Water, 17, 28, 41, 43, 126, 150
Blue Water Creek, 25, 26, 29, 41, 125, 126, 127, 150
Bluewater, 17, 127
Boiling Pot, 104
Boiling-pot, 94
Bonnefoy, Antoine, 102

Boone Creek, 144
Bootsville, 20, 65, 66, 67, 68
Borden, 187, 197, 204, 214, 215
Borden, Charles, 197, 215
Borden, Christopher, 118, 214, 215
Borden, David, 214
Borden, Doc, 215
Boudinot, Elais, 93
Bowle, 38, 47
Bowle, The, 38
Brainerd, 15, 49, 64
Braziel Creek, 187, 204
Breed Camp, 102, 165
Breed Town, 101, 102, 169
Bridgewater, 37, 99, 105, 107
Brindley Mountain, 51
British, 22
Brooks, Aunt Jenny, 117
Broom Town, 20, 67, 68, 69, 79
Brown Creek, 49, 191
Brown Springs, 144
Brown, Captain John, 43, 48, 49, 59, 60, 118
Brown, Catherine, 49, 124
Brown, David, 60
Brown, James, 128
Brown, Jennie, 46
Brown, John, 124, 176, 191
Brown, Joseph, 33, 78, 113, 114, 205, 206
Brown, Patsy, 48, 59
Brown, Richard, 48, 59, 60, 62, 66, 176
Brown, Robert, 46
Brown's Ferry, 16, 17, 33, 36, 40, 41, 42, 43, 44, 59, 86, 88, 92, 103, 105, 112, 113, 114, 133, 149, 154, 205
Brown's Ferry Road, 40, 43, 114, 133, 149
Brown's Island, 86
Brown's Village, 19, 122, 172, 175, 176
Browns Ferry, 14, 40, 59, 77, 78, 112, 113, 114
Browns Ferry Road, 40, 114
Brown's Ferry Road, 205
Browns Village, 48, 59

236

Bluewater Publications is a multi-faceted publishing company capable of meeting all of your reading and publishing needs. Our two-fold aim is to:

1) Provide the market with educationally enlightening and inspiring research and reading materials.

2) Make the opportunity of being published available to any author and or researcher who desire to be published.

We are passionate about preserving history; whether through the re-publishing of an out-of-print classic, or by publishing the research of historians and genealogists. Bluewater Publications is the *Peoples' Choice Publisher*.

For company information or information about how you can be published through Bluewater Publications, please visit:

www.BluewaterPublications.com

Also check Amazon.com to purchase any of the books that we publish.

Confidently Preserving Our Past,

Bluewater Publications.com

CPSIA information can be obtained at www.ICGtesting.com
Printed in the USA
LVOW03s0257110314

376696LV00001B/1/P